TIMES LEARN

STAN
MALAY
MADE SIMPLE

Dr Liaw Yock Fang

TIMES BOOKS INTERNATIONAL
Singapore • Kuala Lumpur

By the same author:

Speak Standard Malay: A Beginner's Guide
Standard Indonesian Made Simple
Speak Standard Indonesian: A Beginner's Guide
Indonesian In 3 Weeks
Easy Indonesian Vocabulary: 1001 Essential Words
Indonesian Grammar Made Easy

First published 1988
Reprinted 1989, 1991, 1992, 1995, 1996

Published by Times Books International
an imprint of Times Editions Pte Ltd

Times Centre, 1 New Industrial Road
Singapore 536196
Fax: (65) 285 4871   Tel: (65) 284 8844
e-mail: te@corp.tpl.com.sg

Times Subang
Lot 46, Subang Hi-Tech Industrial Park
Batu Tiga, 40000 Shah Alam
Selangor Darul Ehsan, Malaysia
Fax & Tel: (603) 736 3517

Printed by JBW Printers & Binders Pte Ltd

ISBN 981 204 212 1

CONTENTS

PART II

PREFACE

Standard Malay Made Simple is a Malay language course intended to help the adult learners to gain a mastery of the language. I use the word to help and not to teach, because language mastery is not possible through teaching alone. It must be learnt, the hard way.

There are several varieties of Malay. The form of Malay presented in Malaysia and Singapore is the standard form taught in school and used in formal and semi-formal occasions by everyone in daily life. This is also the type of Malay very similar to that used by educated Indonesians. In other words, learners of this course who have mastered the materials will be able also with some adjustment to understand the standard form of Bahasa Indonesia, both in its written and spoken forms.

This course is divided into two parts. Part I consists of 20 lessons. Each lesson consists of four sections:

(a) Conversation
(b) Sentence Patterns
(c) Grammar
(d) Word Formation and Word Study

(a) Conversation

The conversation is meant for memorization. After memorizing the conversation, learners should be able to carry on a conversation in Malay, in social gatherings or in an examination hall. This is the easiest part of the course. If a learner has difficulty in following the lessons in the order presented here, he should learn this section very well first before tackling the others.

(b) Sentence Patterns

Sentence pattern is the most important part of the course. In every lesson there is one, sometimes more than one, sentence pattern. These sentence patterns are taught through the usual substitution drills as well as question-answer excercises. The question-answer exercises will strengthen the learner's communication skills. It is best to learn them orally before putting them down in writing.

(c) **Grammar**

This section aims to give learners a knowledge of the intricacy of Malay grammar. Explanation, however, is kept to the minimum. Learners who wish to learn more about Malay language should refer to the author's *Nahu Melayu Modern* (Modern Malay Grammar) published in 1985 or its English version which is being prepared.

(d) **Word Formation and Word Study**

This section consists of two parts: word formation and word study. Word formation discusses the various affixes used to form the various parts of speech in Malay. Word study discusses a number of commonly used words with all its possible combinations of affixes.

All the exercises in *(b), (c)* and *(d)* are provided with an English translation for reference purposes. Learners should try to ignore the English translation of the exercises and refer to them only when they have difficulty in doing the exercises.

Part II consists ten comprehension passages, an article on the relationship between Malay and Bahasa Indonesia contributed by Dr. Leo Suryadinata and an English-Indonesia-Malay vocabulary in the appendix. All the comprehension passages are taken from the author's *Kursus Bahasa Nasional I – IV*, a series of four 'Malay As A Second Language' texts for secondary schools in Singapore.

To facilitate learning, the first four passages have been re-written in simple sentences with an English rendering. Learners who have gone through this course are strongly recommended to continue with *Kursus Bahasa Nasional I – IV*. They will be surprised to find that they can pursue this series of secondary school textbooks without much difficulty. It also means that they have reached a standard comparable to that of 'O' level students. They should by now be able to read anything written in Malay with or without the help of a Malay dictionary.

Dr. Leo Suryadinata's article is meant to put the relationship between Malay and Bahasa Indonesia in proper perspective, and to help learners to switch from Malay to Bahasa Indonesia. With the aid of the English–Indonesia–Malay vocabulary, I am sure learners of this book will also be able to understand standard Bahasa Indonesia. With some adjustment, they may be able to speak Bahasa Indonesia too.

Though this course is meant mainly for adult learners with no knowledge of Malay, it will be useful to students taking 'O' or 'AO' level Malay in the **Singapore G.C.E. Examination**. Students preparing for Bahasa Malaysia paper in the **Sijil Rendah Pelajaran**, and or even the **Sijil Pelajaran Malaysia** Examination may find this book useful. It may even benefit Malay-speaking students wishing to brush up their English.

Finally it remains for me to thank various people who have helped to make the publication of this book possible. First and foremost, I would like to thank Dr. Tan Cheng Lim for going through the manuscript and making many valuable suggestions. Thank is also due to Dr. Edmund Anderson, for going through part of the manuscript and Dr. Leo Suryadinata for contributing the chapter on the relationship between Malay and Bahasa Indonesia. If there are still shortcomings and weaknesses in this book, the responsibilities are entirely the author's.

January 1988

Dr. Liaw Yock Fang
Department of Malay Studies
National University of Singapore
Singapore

NOTES ON PRONUNCIATION

Vowels

There are five vowels in Malay. Each vowel, except **e**, represents one sound.

a	sounds like	*a* in 'ask', e.g. *atas*
e	sounds like	*a* in 'sofa', e.g. *kera*
	(when stressed) sounds like	*e* in 'bed', e.g. *meja*
i	sounds like	*i* in 'fit', e.g. *kita*
o	sounds like	*o* in 'go', e.g. *kota*
u	sounds like	*u* in 'put', e.g. *buku*

Diphthongs

ai	sounds like	*i* in 'I', e.g. *pandai*
au	sounds like	*o* in 'now', e.g. *pulau*
oi	sounds like	*oi* in 'boy', e.g. *sepoi*

Consonants

Malay consonants can be pronounced just like English consonants except that initiated consonants are not aspirated and **p**, **t** and **k** are not explosive.

Please note that though vowels in Bahasa Indonesia are pronounced almost like Malay, its alphabets are pronounced differently. Below is the pronunciation of alphabets in Bahasa Indonesia.

A (al), B (be), C (ce), D (de), E (e), F (ef), G (ge), H (ha), I (i), J (je), K (ka), L (el), M (em), N (en), O (o), P (pe), Q (ki), R (er), S (es), T (te), U (u), V (fe), W (we), X (eks), Y (ye), Z (zet).

PART I

LESSON 1

1A. Conversation

Diri Sendiri
(About Oneself)

Ahmad: *Selamat pagi. Siapa nama encik?*
(Good morning. What is your name?)

Tan: *Selamat pagi. Nama saya Tan Ah Lek.*
(Good morning. My name is Tan Ah Lek.)

Ahmad: *Bila Encik Tan dilahirkan?*
(When were you born?)

Tan: *Saya dilahirkan pada 20hb. Ogos 1940. [20hb. = dua puluh haribulan Ogos sembilan belas empat puluh.]*
(I was born on 20th August 1940.)

Ahmad: *Encik Tan dilahirkan di mana?*
(Where were you born?)

Tan: *Saya dilahirkan di Singapura. Saya orang Singapura. Encik Ahmad juga orang Singapurakah?*
(I was born in Singapore. I am a Singaporean. Are you also a Singaporean, Mr. Ahmad?)

Ahmad: *Bukan, saya orang Malaysia. Saya datang dari Johor.*
(No, I am a Malaysian. I come from Johore.)

Tan: *Saya senang sekali berkenalan dengan Encik Ahmad. Selamat tinggal.*
(I am glad to make your acquaintance. Good-bye.)

Ahmad: *Selamat jalan.*
(Good-bye.)

1B. Structure

Read the following sentences.

SUBJECT	PREDICATE
Saya I	*guru.* (am a) teacher.
Awak You	*murid.* (are a) pupil.
Dia He/She	*pelajar.* (is a) student.
Encik Ali Mr. Ali	*saudagar.* (is a) businessman.
Kita We	*wartawan.* (are) journalists.
Mereka They	*pegawai.* (are) officers.

Notes: There is no copula verb "to be" in Malay. To say: 'He is a teacher', you just say: *'Dia guru'*. Thus *'Dia guru'* is literally translated: 'He teacher'.

Exercise 1. Substitute the noun in the model sentence with the one given.

e.g.	*Orang laki-laki itu* ***guru.*** (The man is a teacher.)
kerani (clerk)	*Orang laki-laki itu* ***kerani.*** (The man is a clerk.).
peguam (lawyer)	*Orang laki-laki itu* ***peguam.*** (The man is a lawyer.)

hakim (judge)	*Orang laki-laki itu* ***hakim.*** (The man is a judge.)
pensyarah (lecturer)	*Orang laki-laki itu* ***pensyarah.*** (The man is a lecturer.)
pekerja (worker)	*Orang laki-laki itu* ***pekerja.*** (The man is a worker.)

1. *askar* (soldier)
2. *kelasi* (sailor)
3. *mata-mata* (policeman)
4. *ustaz* (Islamic religious teacher)
5. *mahasiswa* (undergraduate)
6. *siswazah* (graduate)
7. *majikan* (employer)
8. *peragawan* (fashion model)
9. *pramugara* (steward)
10. *sarjana* (scholar)

Exercise 2. Expand the following sentences by inserting ***'seorang'*** into them.

e.g.

Before Expansion	*Expanded Form*
Encik Ali jurubahasa. (Mr. Ali [is an] interpreter.)	*Encik Ali* ***seorang*** *jurubahasa.* (Mr. Ali [is] an interpreter.)
Abang saya guru bahasa. (My elder brother [is a] language teacher.)	*Abang saya* ***seorang*** *guru bahasa.* (My elder brother [is] a language teacher.)
Kassim tukang kayu. (Kassim [is a] carpenter.)	*Kassim* ***seorang*** *tukang kayu.* (Kassim [is] a carpenter.)

Kakak saya tukang masak.
(My elder sister [is a] cook.)

Kakak saya **seorang** *tukang masak.*
(My elder sister [is] a cook.)

Notes: Please note that although there is no copula verb in Malay and that nouns in the Malay can be preceded by words called classifiers; in this case *seorang* (a person) which is simply rendered as 'a/an'.

1. *Encik Atan jurucakap.*
   (Mr. Atan [is a] spokeman.)
2. *Dia juruhebah.*
   (He/She [is an] announcer.)
3. *Dia jurutera.*
   (He/She [is an] engineer.)
4. *Puan Fatimah jurutaip.*
   (Miss Fatimah [is a] typist.)
5. *Dia jurutrengkas.*
   (He/She [is a] stenographer.)
6. *Osman tukang kebun.*
   (Osman [is a] gardener.)
7. *Dia tukang jahit.*
   (He/She [is a] tailor.)
8. *Puan Khadijah pemegang wang tunai/kasir.*
   (Miss Khadijah [is a] cashier.)
9. *Dia tukang cetak.*
   (He/She [is a] printer.)
10. *Ah Lam tukang emas.*
    (Ah Lam [is a] goldsmith.)

Exercise 3. Give affirmative answers to the following questions.

e.g.

Question	*Answer*
Dia seorang senimankah? (Is he/she an artist?)	***Ya**, dia seorang seniman.* (Yes, he/she is an artist.)
Dia seorang guru sekolahkah? (Is he/she a school teacher?)	***Ya**, dia seorang guru sekolah.* (Yes, he/she is a school teacher.)
Abang Ahmad seorang merinyukah? (Is Ahmad's elder brother an inspector?)	***Ya**, Abang Ahmad seorang merinyu* (Yes, Ahmad's elder brother is an inspector.)
Ayah Ahmad seorang hartawankah? (Is Ahmad's father a millionaire?)	***Ya**, ayah Ahmad seorang hartawan.* (Yes, Ahmad's father is a millionaire.)

Notes: The word *'dia'* means 'he/she'. However, for the sake of simplicity, we shall use 'he' in translating *'dia'* in the rest of the book; except where *'dia'* refers to 'she', not 'he'.

1. *Dia seorang tukang kasutkah?*
   (Is he a shoemaker?)
2. *Dia seorang buruhkah?*
   (Is he a labourer?)
3. *Dia seorang penjajakah?*
   (Is he a hawker?)
4. *Dia seorang nelayankah?*
   (Is he a fisherman?)
5. *Dia seorang nakhodakah?*
   (Is he a sea captain?)

6. *Dia seorang pegawai bahasakah?*
(Is he a language officer?)

7. *Dia seorang pegawai kerajaankah?*
(Is he a government officer?)

8. *Dia seorang pegawai tinggikah?*
(Is he a senior officer?)

9. *Dia seorang pelakonkah?*
(Is he an actor?)

10. *Dia seorang pemandukah?*
(Is he a driver?)

Exercise 4. Give negative answers to the following questions.

e.g.

Question	*Answer*
Dia seorang ahli bahasakah? (Is he a linguist?)	***Bukan,*** *dia* ***bukan*** *seorang ahli bahasa.* (No, he is not a linguist.)
Dia seorang ahlikah? (Is he a member?)	***Bukan,*** *dia* ***bukan*** *seorang ahli..* (No, he is not a member.)
Dia seorang ahli sukankah? (Is he a sportsman?)	***Bukan,*** *dia* ***bukan*** *seorang ahli sukan.* (No, he is not a sportsman.)
Dia seorang ahli ekonomikah? (Is he an economist?)	***Bukan,*** *dia* ***bukan*** *seorang ahli ekonomi.* (No, he is not an economist.)

1. *Dia seorang ahli biasakah?*
   (Is he an ordinary member?)
2. *Yusuf seorang ahli bersekutukah?*
   (Is Yusuf an associate member?)
3. *Datuk Tan seorang ahli kehormatkah?*
   (Is Datuk Tan an honorary member?)
4. *Dia seorang ahli tetapkah?*
   (Is he a permanent member?)
5. *Ahmad seorang ahli sejarahkah?*
   (Is Ahmad a historian?)
6. *Dia seorang ahli bedahkah?*
   (Is he a surgeon?)
7. *Talib seorang ahli ubatkah?*
   (Is Talib a pharmacist?)
8. *Dia seorang ahli jiwakah?*
   (Is he a psychologist?)
9. *Encik Lim seorang ahli negarakah?*
   (Is Mr. Lim a statesman?)
10. *Samy seorang ahli sainskah?*
    (Is Samy a scientist?)

1C. Grammar

There are eight parts of speech in Malay, namely, noun, pronoun, adjective, verb, adverb, preposition, conjunction and interjection.

Nouns

Nouns are naming words. A noun names person, place, thing or idea. Nouns have several characteristics. They are followed by determiners like *ini* (this/the) and *itu* (that/the), and can be preceded by numerals like *satu* (one), *semua* (all), *banyak* (a lot of), *sedikit* (few), etc.

Note: The word 'the' may sometimes be used to translate *ini* and *itu*, depending on the context.

e.g. *(a)* followed by determiners:

Pisau ***ini*** *tumpul.*
(This knife is blunt.)

Bas ***itu*** *sudah berhenti.*
(That bus has stopped.)

Hari ***ini*** *panas.*
(Today is hot.)

Air ***itu*** *keruh.*
(That water is muddy.)

(b) preceded by numerals:

Dia makan ***dua*** *biji telur pagi ini.*
(He ate two eggs this morning.)

Semua *orang tahu hal itu.*
(All the people know about that matter.)

Orang laki-laki itu menyimpan ***banyak*** *wang di dalam bank.*
(The man has a lot of money in the bank.)

Ramai *orang Singapura tahu bercakap bahasa Inggeris.*
(Many Singaporeans can speak English.)

Exercise 5. Fill in the blanks with suitable nouns.

1. *Pemuda itu ialah* _________ *saya.*
   (The young man is my __________.)
2. __________ *yang nakal itu dimarah oleh gurunya.*
   (The naughty __________ was scolded by his teacher.)

3. __________ *ini buatan Jepun.*
   (This __________ was made in Japan.)

4. *Simpanlah* __________ *itu di dalam laci.*
   (Please keep that __________ in the drawer.)

5. *Buku itu seratus* __________ *harganya.*
   (That book costs one hundred __________.)

6. *Ramai* __________ *berkelah ke Pantai Cantik.*
   (Many __________ are picnicking at Pantai Cantik.)

7. *Berilah saya sedikit* __________.
   (Please give me some __________.)

8. *Separuh daripada* __________ *itu dibahagikan kepada anak lelakinya.*
   (One half of the __________ is (divided and) given to his son.)

9. *Para* __________ *di sekolah itu rajin-rajin belaka.*
   (The __________ in that school are hardworking.)

10. *Beberapa orang* __________ *tidak hadir hari ini.*
    (A few __________ are not present today.)

Note: Many nouns can fill in the above blanks. Some of these nouns are:-

teman (friend)	*murid* (pupil)	*budak* (child)
anak (child)	*barang* (thing)	*kerusi* (chair)
meja (table)	*air* (water)	*pensel* (pencil)
suratkhabar (newspaper)	*rokok* (cigarettes)	*dolar* (dollars)
ringgit (ringgit)	*harga* (price)	*nilai* (value)

orang (people)	*wira* (hero)	*pelayan* (waiter)
pelakon (actor)	*wang* (money)	*roti* (bread)
buah-buahan (fruits)	*ikan* (fish)	*harta* (property)
daging (meat)	*telur* (egg)	*duit* (money)
guru bahasa (language teacher)	*pegawai* (officer)	*pegawai polis* (police officer)

Exercise 6. Pick out the nouns in the following sentences.

1. *Pada suatu pagi, kami pergi berkelah ke Pantai Cantik.*
   (One morning, we went picnicking at Pantai Cantik.)

2. *Di sana ramai orang sedang mandi.*
   (Many people are bathing there.)

3. *Mereka memakai baju yang berwarna-warni.*
   (They wear colourful clothes.)

4. *Adik saya takut akan ombak.*
   (My younger brother is afraid of waves.)

5. *Saya membawa adik bermain pasir di pantai.*
   (I brought my younger brother to play with the sand on the beach.)

6. *Saya nampak seorang laki-laki terbaring di atas pasir.*
   (I saw a man lying on the sand.)

7. *Orang itu telah dipagut oleh ular.*
   (The man had been bitten by a snake.)

8. *Orang itu dibawa ke rumah sakit.*
   The man was taken to hospital.)

1D. Word Formation

Nouns

Nouns can often be formed by using affixes. Two of the most common noun-forming affixes are the prefix ***pe-*** and the suffix ***-an.***

(a) The prefix ***pe-*** has three important functions:-

(i) indicating the person doing the action; doer, e.g.

pembaca (reader)	-	*orang yang membaca (baca)* [one who reads]
pengarang (writer)	-	*orang yang mengarang (karang)* [one who writes]
pengirim (sender)	-	*orang yang mengirim (kirim)* [one who sends things]

(ii) indicating the instrument used in the action, e.g.

penggali (digger)	-	*alat untuk menggali (gali)* [a thing used for digging]
pemotong (cutter)	-	*alat untuk memotong (potong)* [a thing used for cutting]
penyapu (sweeper)	-	*alat untuk menyapu (sapu)* [a thing used for sweeping]

(iii) indicating a person who has the characteristic indicated by the root word, e.g.

pemalas	-	*orang yang malas* [a lazy person]
pemarah	-	*orang yang selalu marah* [a quick-tempered person]
peramah	-	*orang yang ramah* [a sociable person]

Please note that words in group (ii) above may also refer to the person performing the action. Hence, *'penggali'* may refer to the person doing the digging as well.

pe-, when added to the root word, may become ***pem-***, ***pen-***, ***peng-*** and ***peny-***, depending on the first letter or syllable of the root word. The changes are parallel to ***me-***, which will be discussed in Lesson 4D.

(b) The suffix *-**an*** has three functions:-

(i) indicating the result of the action, e.g.

ucapan	-	from *ucap* (to say); *hasil mengucap* (the result of saying something, speech)
harapan	-	from *harap* (to hope); *hasil mengharap* (the result of hoping, hope)

(ii) indicating the thing or product of an action, e.g.

makanan	-	from *makan* (to eat); the thing that is eaten (food)
pakaian	-	from *pakai* (to wear); the thing that is worn (clothes)

(iii) indicating the instrument used in an action, e.g.

tapisan	-	from *tapis* (to filter); *alat untuk menapis* (an instrument for filtering, a filter)
kukusan	-	from *kukus* (to steam); *alat untuk mengukus* (an instrument for steaming foods, a steamer)

(iv) indicating a thing having the characteristic indicated by the root word, e.g.

manisan	-	from *manis* (sweet); *makanan yang manis* (food which is sweet, sweets)

lapang	-	from *lapang (*spacious); *tempat yang lapang* (a spacious place, open space)
harian	-	from *hari* (day); *setiap hari* (daily)
mingguan	-	from *minggu* (week); *setiap minggu* (weekly)

Exercise 7. Replace phrases in bold with single words formed by the prefix ***pe-***.

1. ***Orang yang menumpang*** *kapal terbang sudah tiba.*
   (People who are riding (= passengers) the airplane have arrived.)

2. ***Orang yang berniaga*** *itu kawan bapa saya.*
   (The person who is trading is my father's friend.)

3. *Ahmad hendak menjadi* ***orang yang menjual barang.***
   (Ahmad wishes to become a man who sells goods.)

4. ***Gadis yang menari*** *itu kakak kawan saya.*
   (The girl who is dancing is my friend's elder sister.)

5. *Suami perempuan itu* **lekas marah.**
   (The woman's husband is a quick-tempered man.)

6. *Tidak ada lagi* ***orang yang bertani*** *di Singapura.*
   (There are no more people who work on farms in Singapore.)

7. *Emak baru sahaja membeli sebatang* **alat untuk menyapu.**
   (Mother has just bought a broom.)

8. *Pekedai itu menimbang gula* **dengan alat menimbang.**
   (The shopkeeper weighs sugar with a pair of scales.)

9. *Dia menggunakan* **alat menggaris** *untuk membuat garis.*
   (He uses a ruler to draw lines.)

10. *Guru kita* ***orang yang bengis.***
(Our teacher is a stern person.)

Exercise 8. Form a noun by adding the suffix ***-an*** to the root word in bold.

1. *Guru kita suka memberi* ***ucap.***
(Our teacher likes to give speeches.)

2. *Sudah tidak ada* ***harap*** *untuk saya.*
(There is no more hope for me.)

3. *Saya suka* ***makan*** *pedas.*
(I like spicy food.)

4. ***Pakai*** *budak itu basah.*
(The child's clothes are wet.)

5. *Dia suka* ***minum*** *sejuk.*
(He likes cold drinks.)

6. *Ibu menapis beras dengan* ***tapis.***
(Mother filters the rice with a filter.)

7. *Semut mati kerana* ***manis.***
(Ants die because of sweets.)

8. *Tidak ada* ***lapang*** *untuk olahraga di sini.*
(There is no open space for sports here.)

9. ***Hari*** *'Utusan Melayu' mempunyai banyak pembaca.*
(The daily 'Utusan Melayu' has many readers.)

10. ***Minggu*** *kesukaan saya ialah 'Era'*
(My favourite weekly is 'Era'.)

LESSON 2

2A. Conversation

Keluarga
(Family)

Tan: *Selamat petang, Encik Yusuf.*
(Good afternoon, Mr. Yusuf.)

Yusuf: *Selamat petang, Encik Tan. Apa khabar?*
(Good afternoon, Mr. Tan. How are you?)

Tan: *Khabar baik. Terima kasih. Encik Yusuf, bolehkah saya tumpang tanya?*
(Fine. Thank you. Mr. Yusuf, may I ask you some questions?)

Yusuf: *Tanyalah. Apa salahnya.*
(Just ask. I don't mind.)

Tan: *Di manakah Encik Yusuf tinggal?*
(Where do you live?)

Yusuf: *Saya tinggal di nombor 20, Jalan Seaview, Singapura.*
(I live at 20, Seaview Road, Singapore.)

Tan: *Encik Yusuf sudah kahwinkah?*
(Mr. Yusuf, are you married?)

Yusuf: *Sudah. Anak-anak saya sudah masuk sekolah.*
(Yes. My children are already in school.)

Tan: *Berapakah anak Encik Yusuf?*
(How many children have you?)

Yusuf: *Dua orang, seorang anak laki-laki dan seorang anak perempuan.*
(Two, one boy and one girl.)

Tan: *Itu sahaja. Terima kasih.*
(That is all. Thank you.)

Yusuf: *Sama-sama.*
(The same to you.)

2B. Structure

Read the following sentences.

SUBJECT	PREDICATE
Ini This	*buku.* (is a) book.
Ini This	*kamus.* (is a) dictionary.
Ini This	*majalah.* (is a) magazine.
Itu That	*laci.* (is a) drawer.
Itu That	*loceng.* (is a) bell.

Exercise 1. Give affirmative answers to the following questions.

e.g

Question	*Answer*
Ini pintukah? (Is this a door?)	***Ya,** ini pintu.* (Yes, this is a door.)

Ini lampukah?
(Is this a lamp?)

Ya, *ini lampu.*
(Yes, this is a lamp.)

Itu tingkapkah?
(Is that a window?)

Ya, *itu tingkap.*
(Yes, that is a window.)

Itu almarikah?
(Is that a cupboard?)

Ya, *itu almari.*
(Yes, that is a cupboard.)

1. *Ini kuncikah?*
   (Is this a key?)
2. *Itu kerusikah?*
   (Is that a chair?)
3. *Ini mejakah?*
   (Is this a table?)
4. *Itu bangkukah?*
   (Is that a stool?)
5. *Ini kipaskah?*
   (Is this a fan?)
6. *Itu kertaskah?*
   (Is that [a piece of] paper?)
7. *Ini pembariskah?*
   (Is this a ruler?)
8. *Itu papan hitamkah?*
   (Is that a blackboard?)
9. *Ini pemadamkah?*
   (Is this a duster?)
10. *Itu dakwatkah?*
    (Is that ink?)

Exercise 2. Give negative answers to the following questions.

e.g.

Question	*Answer*
Ini bakulkah? (Is this a basket?)	***Bukan,*** *ini* ***bukan*** *bakul.* (No, this is not a basket.)
Ini gambarkah? (Is this a picture?)	***Bukan,*** *ini* ***bukan*** *gambar.* (No, this is not a picture.)
Itu suratkah? (Is that a letter?)	***Bukan,*** *itu* ***bukan*** *surat.* (No, that is not a letter.)
Itu sampul suratkah? (Is that an envelope?)	***Bukan,*** *itu* ***bukan*** *sampul surat.* (No, that is not an envelope.)

1. *Ini piringkah?*
   (Is this a plate?)
2. *Itu dapurkah?*
   (Is that a kitchen?)
3 *Ini cangkirkah?*
   (Is this a cup?)
4. *Itu jam tangankah?*
   (Is that a watch?)
5. *Ini cerminkah?*
   (Is this a mirror?)
6. *Itu sikatkah?*
   (Is that a comb?)
7. *Ini pisaukah?*
   (Is this a knife?)
8. *Itu suratkhabarkah?*
   (Is that a newspaper?)

9. *Ini perpustakaankah?*
   (Is this a library?)

10. *Itu asramakah?*
    (Is that a hostel?)

Exercise 3. Give affirmative answers, using ***adalah*** or ***ialah***, to the following questions.

e.g.

Question	*Answer*
Dia teman kamukah? (Is he your friend?)	*Ya, dia* ***adalah*** *teman saya.* (Yes, he is my friend.)
Ayah kamu seorang saudagarkah? (Is your father a businessman?)	*Ya, ayah saya* ***adalah*** *seorang saudagar.* (Yes, my father is a businessman.)
Ahmad orang Melayukah? (Is Ahmad a Malay?)	*Ya, Ahmad* ***adalah*** *orang Melayu.* (Yes, Ahmad is a Malay.)
Fatimah isteri Alikah? (Is Fatimah Ali's wife?)	*Ya, Fatimah* ***adalah*** *isteri Ali.* (Yes, Fatimah is Ali's wife.)

1. *Orang laki-laki itu sahabat kamukah?*
   (Is that man your friend?)

2. *Perempuan itu ibu kamukah?*
   (Is that woman your mother?)

3. *Gadis itu adik perempuan kamukah?*
   (Is that girl your younger sister?)

4. *Wanita itu seorang doktorkah?*
   (Is that woman a doctor?)

5. *Orang laki-laki tua itu datuk kamukah?*
(Is that old man your grandfather?)

6. *Perempuan tua itu nenek kamukah?*
(Is that old woman your grandmother?)

7. *Pemuda itu seorang juruterakah?*
(Is that young man an engineer?)

8. *Perempuan muda itu seorang jururawatkah?*
(Is that young woman a nurse?)

9. *Orang itu jiran kamukah*
(Is that person your neighbour?)

10. *Rumah itu rumah kamukah?*
(Is that house yours?)

Exercise 4. Change the following statements into questions.

e.g.

Statement	*Question*
Encik Ali sasterawan. (Mr. Ali is a literary man.)	*Encik Ali sasterawan**kah?*** (Is Mr. Ali a literary man?)
Encik Lim seorang pedagang. (Mr. Lim is a trader.)	*Encik Lim seorang pedagang**kah?*** (Is Mr. Lim a trader?)
Usman seorang penulis. (Usman is a writer.)	*Usman seorang penulis**kah?*** (Is Usman a writer?)
Ah Kow seorang pekedai. (Ah Kow is a shopkeeper.)	*Ah Kow seorang pekedai**kah?*** (Is Ah Kow a shopkeeper?)

1. *Ahmad peserta.*
   (Ahmad is a participant.)
2. *John seorang pelancong.*
   (John is a tourist.)
3. *Cik Fatimah setiausaha.*
   (Miss Fatimah is a secretary.)
4. *Cik Timah seorang jurusolek.*
   (Miss Timah is a beautician.)
5. *Tuan Talib seorang tabib.*
   (Mr. Talib is a physician.)
6. *Encik Tan doktor gigi.*
   (Mr. Tan is a dentist.)
7. *Ahmad ahli bomba.*
   (Ahmad is a fireman.)
8. *Dr. Lee seorang menteri.*
   (Dr. Lee is a minister.)
9. *Dr. Yusuf duta besar.*
   (Dr. Yusuf is an ambassador.)
10. *Abdullah ketua kampung.*
    (Abdullah is a village chief.)

2C. Grammar

Noun Modifier

A noun can be modified by a pronoun, an adjective or another noun to form a noun phrase. It can also be followed by a phrase preceded by *yang* (who/that/which). Although *yang* is translated as 'who/ that/which', this is not done when translating some of the following sentences in order to avoid awkward sentence construction in English.

e.g. *(a)* modified by pronoun/adjective/noun:

Abang ***saya*** *guru.*
(My elder brother is a teacher.)

Budak ***kecil*** *itu menangis.*
(The small boy/girl is crying.)

Guru ***sekolah*** *itu pandai.*
(The school teacher is clever.)

Rumah ***Ahmad*** *jauh sekali.*
(Ahmad's house is far away.)

(b) followed by phrase preceded by *'yang'*:

Abang saya ***yang tinggal di bandar itu*** *guru.*
(My elder brother who stays in that town is a teacher.)

Budak ***yang kecil*** *itu menangis.*
(The boy/girl who is small is crying.)

Guru ***yang mengajar di sekolah*** *itu pandai.*
(The teacher who is teaching in that school is clever.)

Rumah ***yang dibeli Ahmad itu*** *jauh sekali.*
(The house which was bought by Ahmad is very far away.)

Exercise 5. Fill in the blanks with suitable noun modifiers.

1. *Bahasa* __________ *penting.*
   (__________ language is important.)
2. *Tingkatan pelajaran* __________ *itu tinggi.*
   (The standard of the __________ lessons is high.)
3. *Lelaki* __________ *itu kedekut.*
   (That __________ man is stingy.)

4. *Tin* __________ *berbunyi kuat.*
   (An __________ tin makes the loud noise.)

5. *Kasut* __________ *mahal.*
   (__________ shoes are expensive.)

6. *Budak* __________ *itu rajin.*
   (The __________ child is diligent.)

7. *Sekolah* __________ *itu sudah dibuka.*
   (The __________ school has opened.)

8. *Baju* __________ *saya kotor.*
   (My __________ dress is dirty.)

9. *Budak* __________ *itu sakit.*
   (The __________ child is sick.)

10. *Anjing* __________ *itu menyalak.*
    (The __________ dog is barking.)

Note: Many modifiers can fill in the blanks. Some of them are:-

Melayu (Malay)	*Inggeris* (English)	*sekolah* (school)
madrasah (Islamic religious school)	*kaya* (rich)	*malang* (unlucky)
kosong (empty)	*penuh* (full)	*kulit* (leather)
kayu (wood)	*miskin* (poor)	*kasar* (rough)
baru (new)	*lama* (old)	*perempuan* (female)
laki-laki (male)	*hitam* (black)	*putih* (white)

Exercise 6. Omit all phrases preceded by ***yang*** from the following sentences.

e.g.

Before Omission	*After Omission*
Budak laki-laki ***yang kecil*** *itu menangis.* (The boy who is small is crying.)	*Budak laki-laki itu menangis.* (The boy is crying.)
Guru yang ***mengajar di sekolah*** *itu pandai.* (The teacher who is teaching in that school is clever.)	*Guru itu pandai.* (The teacher is clever.)

1. *Orang laki-laki yang sedang membaca buku itu ialah bapa saudara saya.*
   (The man who is reading a book is my uncle.)
2. *Anjing yang garang itu menggigit seorang budak lelaki.*
   (The dog which is fierce bites a boy.)
3. *Penulis yang masyhur itu guru kita.*
   (The writer who is famous is our teacher.)
4. *Hujan yang lebat telah reda.*
   (The rain which is heavy has subsided.)
5. *Budak lelaki yang lapar itu sentiasa menangis.*
   (The boy who is hungry was always crying.)
6. *Ikan yang di dalam air itu bermain-main.*
   (The fish which in the water is playing.)
7. *Buku yang terletak di atas meja itu buku saya.*
   (The book which is on the table is my book.)
8. *Ali yang baru berumur dua belas tahun itu pandai.*
   (Ali who is just twelve years' old is clever.)

9. *Pemandu yang baik hati itu abang saya.*
(The driver who kind-hearted is my elder brother.)

10. *Orang yang menggunakan jalan raya itu hendaklah berhati-hati.*
(People who use the road should be careful.)

2D. Word Formation

Nouns (continuation)

Besides ***pe-*** and -***an; pe-an, per-an*** and ***ke-an*** are also widely used to form nouns.

(a) ***Pe-an*** has many meanings, the most important being:

(i) indicating the process of an activity, e.g.

Penulisan *buku teks sekolah sukar sekali.*
(The writing of school text books is very difficult.)

Pengambilan *terlalu banyak pekerja asing tidak baik.*
(The employing (literally 'taking') of too many foreign workers is not good.)

(ii) indicating the result of an activity, e.g.

Saya menerima ***pemberian*** *itu dengan senang hati.*
(I accept the gift (what is being given) gladly.)

Saya belum mendengar ***pengumuman*** *itu.*
(I have not heard the announcement (what is being announced).)

Please note that ***pe-an*** will become ***pem-an, pen-an, peng-an*** and ***peny-an*** according to the initial letter of the verb it joins.*** The changes are in accordance with that of the verb ***me-,*** which is discussed later in Lesson 4D.

(b) ***per-an*** has three important functions:

(i) indicating an activity, e.g.

Perkelahian *sudah terjadi.*
(A fight broke up.)

Perniagaan *lelaki itu maju.*
(The man's business is prospering.)

(ii) indicating a place where an activity take place, e.g.

Mereka menanti di ***perhentian*** *bas.*
(They are waiting at the bus stop.)

Itu ***perkuburan*** *orang Cina.*
(That is a Chinese cemetery.)

(iii) indicating instrument used in an activity, e.g.

Permainan *budak lelaki itu banyak sekali.*
(The boy's toys are many.)

Pendengaran *lelaki tua itu masih baik.*
(The old man's hearing (referred to as a faculty) is still good.)

The meanings of ***pe-an*** and ***per-an*** are very close and are rather difficult to differentiate. Suffice if we can remember that ***pe-an*** is always derived from verbs using prefix ***me-,*** where ***per-an*** tends to be derived from verbs using prefix ***ber-.***

(c) ***ke-an*** has many meanings, the most important being:

(i) indicating the fact that something is being done, e.g.

Kedatangan *abang sedang ditunggu.*
(Elder brother's arrival is awaited.)

Kemajuan *budak lelaki itu cepat sekali.*
(The boy's advancement is very fast.)

(ii) indicating a place, e.g.

***Kementerian** Pelajaran terletak di Kay Siang Road.*
(The Ministry of Education is situated at Kay Siang Road)

*Rumah itu tempat **kediaman** orang kaya.*
(The house is a rich man's dwelling place.)

Exercise 7. Add ***pe-an*** to the words in bold to form nouns.

1. *Buku itu **beri** ibu saya.*
   (The book is a gift from my mother.)
2. ***Dengar** datuk saya masih baik.*
   (My grandfather's hearing is still good.)
3. ***Aku** itu dibuat di depan seorang hakim.*
   (The confession is made in front of a judge.)
4. ***Bahagi** harta akan diumumkan esok.*
   (The dividing of property will be announced tomorrow.)
5. ***Bangun** rumah-rumah pangsa berjalan dengan pesat.*
   (The building of flats is going on speedily.)
6. ***Bayar** mesti dibuat pada akhir bulan.*
   (Payment must be made at the end of the month.)
7. ***Betul** akan dibuat tidak lama lagi.*
   (Correction will be made soon.)
8. ***Besar** rumah mahal.*
   (Enlarging [The enlargement of] the house is expensive.)
9. ***Dapat** ayahnya seribu sebulan.*
   (His father 's income is one thousand a month.)
10. *Tidak ada **beza** gaji antara laki-laki dan perempuan di sini.*
    (There is no difference between men's and women's salaries here.)

Exercise 8. Add ***per-an*** to the words in bold to form nouns.

1. ***Buat*** *budak lelaki itu baik.*
   (The boy's action is good.)
2. ***Kerja*** *Ali baik.*
   (Ali's work is good.)
3. ***Tahan*** *Singapura sedang dibincangkan.*
   (Singapore's defence is being discussed.)
4. ***Tanding*** *bola sepak menarik.*
   (A football match is interesting.)
5. ***Saing*** *adalah suatu hal yang baik.*
   (Competition is a good thing.)
6. ***Jalan*** *itu memakan lima jam.*
   (The journey takes five hours.)
7. ***Ubah*** *itu besar sekali.*
   (The change is great.)
8. ***Tanya*** *masih belum dijawab.*
   (The question has not been answered.)
9. ***Bual*** *itu tidak menarik.*
   (The chit-chit is not interesting.)
10. *Hari* ***kahwin*** *sudah ditentukan.*
    (The date of marriage has been fixed.)

Exercise 9. Add ***ke-an*** to the words in bold to form nouns.

1. *Saya akan ingat* ***baik*** *hati kamu.*
   (I will remember your kindness.)
2. *Kita mesti menjaga* ***sihat*** *kita.*
   (We must look after our health.)

3. *Lelaki itu hanya menjaga* ***penting*** *diri.*
(The man is only looking after his own interest.)

4. ***Daulat*** *raja-raja Melayu diakui oleh Perlembagaan.*
(The Malay rulers' sovereignty is recognised by the Constitution.)

5. *Guru memuji* ***rajin*** *muridnya.*
(The teacher praised his pupil's diligence.)

6. *Kita mesti menjaga* ***makmur*** *kita.*
(We must defend our prosperity.)

7. *Saya masih menunggu* ***benar*** *dari ketua saya.*
(I am still waiting for my chief's permission.)

8. *Kita tidak boleh menyalahgunakan* ***bebas*** *kita.*
(We must not misuse our freedom.)

9. ***Duduk*** *Singapura mustahak.*
(Singapore's position is important.)

10. ***Hidup*** *lelaki itu susah.*
(The man's life is difficult.)

***

	ROOT WORD	*-pe* FORM
(1)	l m ng ny r w	Unchanged
(2)	a, e, i, o, u, h, g, (k)	Add ***-ng***
(3)	b, (p)	Add ***-m***
(4)	z (t)	Add ***-n***
(5)	(s)	Add ***-ny***
(6)	root word consists of only one syllable, e.g. *bom, cat,* etc.	Add ***-nge***

Letters in brackets will be dropped when given prefixes.

LESSON 3

3A. Conversation

Pekerjaan
(Occupation)

Amin:	*Selamat pagi, saudara. Bolehkah saya bertanya sedikit tentang diri saudara?* (Good morning, sir. May I ask something about yourself?)
Suparman:	*Tanyalah, apa salahnya.* (Just ask, I don't mind.)
Amin:	*Apa pekerjaan saudara?* (What is your profession?)
Suparman:	*Saya seorang pegawai bank.* (I am a bank officer.)
Amin:	*Di manakah letaknya bank tempat saudara bekerja?* (Where is the location of the bank where you work?)
Suparman:	*Bank tempat saya bekerja itu letaknya di Jurong.* (The bank where I work is situated in Jurong.)
Amin:	*Bagaimana saudara pergi bekerja?* (How do you go to work?)
Suparman:	*Saya pergi bekerja dengan kereta saya sendiri.* (I go to work in my own car.)
Amin:	*Maafkan saya, apakah kelulusan saudara?* (Excuse me, what are your qualifications?)

Suparman: *Saya ada ijazah Sarjana Muda Perakaunan dari sebuah universiti di Amerika Syarikat.*
(I have a B.Acc. degree from a university in the United States.)

Amin: *Patutlah saudara boleh menjadi pegawai bank.*
(No wonder you can become a bank officer.)

3B. Structure

Read the following sentences.

SUBJECT	PREDICATE
Saudagar itu The businessman	*kaya.* (is) rich.
Penuntut itu The student	*rajin.* (is) diligent.
Wanita itu The woman	*cantik.* (is) beautiful.
Kereta itu The car	*baru.* (is) new.
Buku itu The book	*tebal.* (is) thick.

Exercise 1. Substitute the adjectives in the model sentence with the one given.

e.g. *Pemuda itu* ***berani.***
(The young man is brave.)

pandai (clever)	*Pemuda itu* ***pandai.*** (The young man is clever.)
kacak (handsome)	*Pemuda itu* ***kacak.*** (The young man is handsome.)
malas (lazy)	*Pemuda itu* ***malas.*** (The young man is lazy.)
gemuk (fat)	*Pemuda itu* ***gemuk***. (The young man is fat.)
kuat (strong)	*Pemuda itu* ***kuat.*** (The young man is strong.)
pendek (short)	*Pemuda itu* ***pendek***. (The young man is short.)

1. *nakal* (naughty)
2. *sedih* (sad)
3. *gembira* (happy)
4. *cerdas* (intelligent)
5. *degil* (stubborn)
6. *lokek* (stingy)
7. *jujur* (honest)
8. *sihat* (healthy)
9. *sibuk* (busy)
10. *sombong* (proud)

Exercise 2. Join the words given below to produce five sentences.

e.g.

Word(s)	*Sentence*
Hassan *lapar* = hungry	*Hassan lapar.* (Hassan is hungry.)
gadis itu = the girl *jelita* = beautiful	*Gadis itu jelita.* (The girl is beautiful.)

1. *pakaian itu* (the clothes)
2. *murah* (cheap)

3. *kemeja itu* (the shirt)
4. *mahal* (expensive)

5. *seluar itu* (the trousers)
6. *panjang* (long)

7. *jalan itu* (the road)
8. *lebar* (wide)

9. *lorong itu* (lane)
10. *sempit* (narrow)

Exercise 3. Give affirmative answers to the following questions.

e.g.

Question	*Answer*
Air itu bersihkah? (Is the water clean?)	*Ya, air itu bersih.* (Yes, the water is clean.)
Makanan itu sedapkah? (Is the food delicious?)	*Ya, makanan itu sedap.* (Yes, the food is delicious.)
Pelajaran itu sukarkah? (Is the lesson difficult?)	*Ya, pelajaran itu sukar.* (Yes, the lesson is difficult.)
Anak itu lucukah? (Is the child funny?)	*Ya, anak itu lucu.* (Yes, the child is funny.)

1. *Bangunan itu tinggikah?*
   (Is the building tall?)

2. *Rumah ini rendahkah?*
   (Is this house low?)

3. *Air itu jernihkah?*
   (Is the water clear?)

4. *Lampu itu terangkah?*
(Is the lamp bright?)
5. *Murid itu tekunkah?*
(Is the student hardworking?)
6. *Sungai itu dalamkah?*
(Is the river deep?)
7. *Taman itu indahkah*?
(Is the garden beautiful?)
8. *Bunga itu wangikah?*
(Is the flower fragrant?)
9. *Tempat itu gelapkah?*
(Is the place dark?)
10. *Meja itu beratkah?*
(Is the table heavy?)

Exercise 4. Change the following statements into questions.

e.g.

Statement	*Question*
Peguam itu bijak. (The lawyer is sagacious.)	*Peguam itu bijakkah?* (Is the lawyer sagacious?)
Hakim itu adil. (The judge is fair.)	*Hakim itu adilkah*? (Is the judge fair?)
Penuntut itu penat. (The student is tired.)	*Penuntut itu penatkah?* (Is the student tired?)
Masakan itu tawar. (The food is tasteless.)	*Masakan itu tawarkah?* (Is the food tasteless?)

1. *Pekerja itu cekap.*
(The worker is competent.)

2. *Ketua itu bengis.*
   (The chief is stern.)

3. *Perempuan itu hodoh.*
   (The woman is ugly.)

4. *Tasik itu tohor.*
   (The lake is shallow.)

5. *Orang itu kejam.*
   (The man is cruel.)

6. *Tukang itu pandai.*
   (The craftsman is clever.)

7. *Emak Yusuf bimbang.*
   (Yusuf's mother is anxious.)

8. *Pekerja asing itu malang.*
   (The foreign worker is unlucky.)

9. *Masakan itu pedas.*
   (The food is spicy.)

10. *Minuman itu panas.*
    (The drink is hot.)

3C. Grammar

Adjective

An adjective is a word used to describe a noun or a pronoun and is always placed behind the noun or pronoun it describes.

e.g.

bilik besar (big room)	*orang muda* (young person)	*gambar cantik* (beautiful picture)
budak gemuk (fat child)	*pelajar rajin* (diligent student)	

When an adjective is used in a sentence, it can be preceded by words signifying very such as *amat*, *sungguh* and *sangat*; or words meaning really, truly and indeed such as *sekali*, *betul* and *benar*. It can of course be preceded by *agak* (rather) too.

e.g. *Bilik itu* ***amat*** *besar.*
(The room is very big.)

Lelaki itu ***sangat*** *muda.*
(The man is very young.)

Gambar itu cantik ***sekali.***
(The picture is really beautiful.)

Budak lelaki itu gemuk ***benar***.
(The boy is really fat.)

Lelaki itu ***agak*** *tinggi.*
(The man is rather tall.)

An adjective has three degrees of comparison. The comparison is expressed by the use of *sama ... seperti* (as ... as) for positive degree, *lebih ... daripada* (more ... than) or *kurang ... daripada* (less ... than) for comparative degree, and *paling* (most) for superlative degree.

e.g.

Saya tinggi.
(I am tall.)

Samad ***sama tinggi seperti*** *saya.*
(Samad is as tall as I am.)

Ali ***lebih tinggi daripada*** *saya.*
(Ali is taller than I am.)

Atan ***kurang tinggi daripada*** *saya.*
(Atan is less tall than I am.)

Yaming ***paling*** *tinggi.*
(Yaming is the tallest.)

Bapa saya kaya. (My father is rich.)	*Bapa Samad* ***sama kaya seperti*** *bapa saya.* (Samad's father is as rich as my father.) *Bapa Ali* ***lebih kaya daripada*** *bapa saya.* (Ali's father is richer than my father.) *Bapa Atan* ***kurang kaya daripada*** *bapa saya.* (Atan's father is less rich than my father.) *Bapa Yaming* ***paling kaya.*** (Yaming's father is the richest.)

Exercise 5. Fill in the blanks with suitable adjectives.

1. *Rumah itu* __________.
   (The house is __________.)
2. *Rumah* __________ *itu ialah rumah Encik Yahya.*
   (That __________ house is Mr. Yahya's house.)
3. *Budak itu* __________.
   (The child is __________.)
4. *Budak* __________ *itu kuat makan.*
   (The __________ child eats a lot.)
5. *Rumah saya rumah* __________.
   (My house is an/a __________ house.)
6. *Rumah* __________ *saya masih kuat.*
   (My __________ house is still strong.)
7. *Meja itu* __________.
   (The table is __________.)

8. *Meja* __________ *bukan meja tulis.*
(The __________ table is not a writing table.)

9. *Lelaki itu sangat* __________.
(The man is very __________.)

10. *Orang* __________ *boleh menolong orang lemah.*
(A __________ person can help weak a person.)

Note: Many adjectives can fill in the blanks. Some of them are:-

baru (new)	*gemuk* (fat)	*jahat* (bad)
sihat (healthy)	*lama* (old)	*lucu* (funny)
malang (unlucky)	*garang* (fierce)	*berat* (heavy)
ringan (light)	*penting* (important)	*sukar* (difficult)
kuat (strong)	*cekap* (capable)	*sulit* (secret)
lemah (weak)	*sopan* (polite)	*sombong* (proud)
bongkak (arrogant)	*rendah* (low)	

Exercise 6. Pick out the adjectives from the following sentences.

1. *Saudagar itu sangat kedekut.*
(The businessman is very stingy.)

2. *Peguam itu amat bijak.*
(The lawyer is very clever.)

3. *Perempuan itu gelisah betul.*
(The woman is really worried.)

4. *Pelajar itu sopan sekali.*
   (The student is very polite.)
5. *Pekerja itu kasar benar.*
   (The worker is really rude.)
6. *Kerja ini lebih penting.*
   (This job is more important.)
7. *Kari ini kurang pedas.*
   (This curry is less spicy.)
8. *Bahasa Melayu lebih mudah daripada bahasa Inggeris.*
   (Malay is easier than English.)
9. *Bahasa Inggeris sama sukar seperti bahasa Cina.*
   (The English language is as difficult as Chinese.)
10. *Bahasa Arab paling sukar.*
    (Arabic is the most difficult.)

3D. Word Formation

Adjectives

Se- and ***ter-*** are two affixes often used to form adjectives.

e.g. *Rumah Ali tidak* ***sebesar*** *rumah saya.*
(Ali's house is not as big as my house.)

Bapa saya ***setua*** *bapa Ahmad.*
(My father is as old as Ahmad's father.)

Yaming adalah murid yang ***terpandai.***
(Yaming is the cleverest student.)

Bapanya orang yang ***terkaya****.*
(His father is the richest man.)

Besides ***se-*** and ***ter-***, some words with the affixes ***pe-*** and ***ber-*** are also classified as adjectives because they can be preceded by words of comparison like *sangat* and *amat* which mean very.

e.g. *Orang laki-laki itu* ***sangat peramah.***
(The man is very polite.)

Perempuan itu ***sangat penyayang***.
(The woman is very compassionate.)

Ibu saya ***sangat berhemat***.
(My mother is very thrifty.)

Sup itu ***sangat berminyak***.
(The soup is very oily.)

Buku itu ***sangat menarik***.
(The book is very interesting.)

Exercise 7. Replace phrases in bold with single words using the affix ***se-*** or ***ter-***.
e.g.

Saya tidak ***sama pandai seperti*** *Atan.* (I am not as clever as Atan.)	*Saya tidak* ***sepandai*** *Atan.* (I am not as clever as Atan.)
Bapanya ***sama kaya*** *seperti bapa saya.* (His father is as rich as my father.)	*Bapanya* ***sekaya*** *bapa saya.* (His father is as rich as my father.)
Rumah Suyin ***paling*** *besar.* (Suyin's house is the biggest.)	*Rumah Suyin* ***terbesar***. (Suyin's house is the biggest.)
Wangnya ***paling sedikit***. (His money is the least.)	*Wangnya* ***tersedikit***. (His money is the least.)

1. *Gadis itu* ***sama cantik seperti*** *bidadari.*
   (The girl is as beautiful as a nymph.)
2. *Ali tidak* ***sama kuat seperti*** *abangnya.*
   (Ali is not as strong as his elder brother.)
3. *Hassan* ***sama tinggi seperti*** *abangnya.*
   (Hassan is as tall as his elder brother.)
4. *Lelaki itu* ***sama bodoh seperti*** *keldai.*
   (The man is as stupid as a donkey.)
5. *Pensel kamu tidak* ***sama baik seperti*** *pensel saya.*
   (Your pencil is not as good as mine.)
6. *Sekolah itu* ***paling dekat*** *dengan rumah saya.*
   (The school is nearest to my house.)
7. *Dia orang yang* ***paling istimewa.***
   (He is the most unusual person.)
8. *Hang Tuah pahlawan Melayu yang* ***paling dikenal orang***.
   (Hang Tuah is the most famous of Malay heroes.)
9. *Fatimah anak yang* ***paling disayangi***.
   (Fatimah is the most loved child.)
10. *Dia dilahirkan di sebuah kampung yang* ***paling pencil***.
    (He was born in the most isolated village.)

Exercise 8. Pick out the adjectives from the following sentences.

1. *Perempuan itu sangat pemalu.*
   (The woman is very shy.)
2. *Bapa saya seorang yang agak pendiam.*
   (My father is a rather quiet person.)
3. *Dia seorang perempuan yang sangat pengasih.*
   (She is a very affectionate woman.)

4. *Tuan Basir itu sangat peramah.*
(Mr. Basir is very friendly.)
5. *Lelaki itu sangat berbahaya.*
(The man is very dangerous.)
6. *Kamus sangat berguna.*
(A dictionary is very useful.)
7. *Saya sangat bergembira.*
(I am very happy.)
8. *Abang saya sangat berterima kasih.*
(My elder brother is very thankful.)
9. *Lelaki itu sangat bersemangat.*
(The man is very lively.)
10. *Pegawai itu sangat bertimbang rasa.*
(The officer is very considerate.)

LESSON 4

4A. Conversation

Salam
(Greetings)

Lim: *Selamat pagi, Encik Ali.*
(Good morning, Mr. Ali.)

Ali: *Selamat pagi, Encik Lim.*
(Good morning, Mr. Lim.)

Lim: *Apa khabar Encik Ali?*
(How are you, Mr. Ali?)

Ali: *Khabar baik, terima kasih. Bagaimana dengan Encik Lim?*
(Fine, thank you. How are you, Mr. Lim?)

Lim: *Saya pun baik juga, terima kasih. Apa khabar keluarga Encik Ali?*
(I am also fine, thank you. How is your family, Mr. Ali?)

Ali: *Keluarga saya baik-baik sahaja. Isteri saya masih bekerja. Anak-anak saya sudah masuk sekolah.*
(My family is fine. My wife is still working. My children have started school.)

Lim: *Maafkan, Encik Ali. Encik Ali bercakap bahasa apa di rumah?*
(Excuse me, Mr. Ali. What languages do you speak at home?)

Ali: *Kami bercakap bahasa Melayu dan Inggeris di rumah.*
(We speak Malay and English at home.)

Lim: *Anak-anak Encik Ali pasti fasih dalam bahasa Melayu dan Inggeris.*
(Your children will certainly be fluent in Malay and English.)

Ali: *Mudah-mudahan begitu.*
(I hope so.)

4B. Structure

Read the following sentences.

SUBJECT	PREDICATE
Saya I	*akan balik.* will return (home).
Dia He	*hendak pergi.* wants to go.
Dia He	*hilang.* disappears.
Matahari Sun	*belum terbit.* has not risen yet.
Air The water	*surut.* is subsiding.

Notes: The verb in Malay does not indicate present or past tenses. *Dia datang* may mean 'He comes/came.' However auxiliary verbs like *akan* (will/would/shall/should), *sedang* (is/are/was/were ...ing) and *sudah/telah* (has/have/had) are used in Malay as in English. Observe that even in the use of these auxiliary verbs, there is no differentiation between present and past.

Exercise 1. Complete the following sentence by adding verb phrases given.

e.g.	*Dia ....*
akan balik (will return [home])	*Dia* ***akan pulang.*** (He will return [home].)
akan kembali (will return)	*Dia* ***akan kembali.*** (He will return.)
akan keluar (will go out)	*Dia* ***akan keluar***. (He will go out.)
sudah keluar (has gone out)	*Dia* ***sudah keluar***. (He has gone out.)
sudah tidur (has slept)	*Dia* ***sudah tidur.*** (He has slept.)

1. *sudah lari* (has run away/has run)
2. *sudah masuk* (has entered)
3. *akan sampai* (will arrive)
4. *akan pergi* (will go)
5. *telah pindah* (has removed)
6. *sedang makan* (is eating)
7. *sudah kahwin* (has married)
8. *bangun* (get up)
9. *sedang ketawa* (is laughing)
10. *mandi* (to bathe)

Exercise 2. Give affirmative answers to the following questions.

e.g.

Question	*Answer*
Dia jatuhkah? (Did he fall?)	*Ya, dia jatuh.* (Yes, he fell.)
Dia tinggal di bandarkah? (Does he live in town?)	*Ya, dia tinggal di bandar.* (Yes, he lives in town.)
Dia hendak pergikah? (Does he want to go?)	*Ya, dia hendak pergi.* (Yes, he wants to go.)
Dia sudah makankah? (Has he eaten?)	*Ya, dia sudah makan.* (Yes, he has eaten.)

1. *Dia gagalkah?*
   (Did he fail?)
2. *Lelaki itu menangkah?*
   (Did the man win?)
3. *Dia belum sembuhkah?*
   (Hasn't he recovered (from illness) yet?)
4. *Pencuri itu telah lepaskah?*
   (Did the thief get free/away?)
5. *Dia lupakah?*
   (Did he forget?)
6. *Dia kalahkah?*
   (Was he defeated?)
7. *Pelajar itu sudah tamatkah?*
   (Has the student graduated?)
8. *Dia masih belum siapkah?*
   (Is he still not ready?)
9. *Harga beras sudah turunkah?*
   (Is the price of rice falling?)

10. *Harga rumah sudah naikkah*?
(Is the price of houses increasing?)

Note: *Belum* is translated as 'has/have/had not' or 'is/are/was/were not'. (Refer to questions 3 and 8 above.)

Exercise 3. Change the following statements into questions.

e.g.

Statement	*Question*
Matahari masih belum terbit. (The sun has not risen yet.)	*Matahari masih belum terbitkah?* (Hasn't the sun risen yet?)
Kapal itu tenggelam. (The ship sank.)	*Kapal itu tenggelamkah?* (Did the ship sink?)
Pensel itu patah. (The pencil was broken.)	*Pensel itu patahkah?* (Was the pencil broken?)
Pohon itu tumbang. (The tree is falling.)	*Pohon itu tumbangkah?* (Is the tree falling?)

1. *Kedai itu masih belum tutup.*
(The shop was not closed yet.)
2. *Burung terbang.*
(Birds fly.)
3. *Rantai itu sudah putus.*
(The chain has broken.)
4. *Cawan itu sudah pecah.*
(The cup has broken.)
5. *Pokok itu sudah tumbuh.*
(The tree has grown.)

6. *Daun gugur.*
   (Leaves are droping.)
7. *Bangunan itu roboh.*
   (The building is collapsing.)
8. *Gigi nenek tanggal.*
   (Grandmother's teeth are falling out.)
9. *Harga barang-barang naik.*
   (Prices of things are going up.)
10. *Perniagaan mundur.*
    (Business is declining.)

Exercise 4. Answer the following questions by using the words provided.

e.g.

Question	*Answer*
Bila dia hendak datang? - *besok* (When does he want to come? - tomorrow)	*Dia hendak datang besok.* (He wants to come tomorrow.)
Bila dia pergi? - semalam (When did he go? - yesterday)	*Dia pergi semalam.* (He went yesterday.)
Bila dia jaga? - *semalaman suntuk* (When was he awake? - the whole night)	*Dia jaga semalaman suntuk.* (He was awake the whole night.)

Bila air surut?
- pagi tadi
(When did the water subside?)
- this morning

Air surut pagi tadi.
(The water subsided this morning)

1. *Bila dia kerja? - hari ini*
   (When does he work? - today)
2. *Bila dia sakit? - kelmarin*
   (When was he sick? - yesterday)
3. *Bila dia akan sembuh? - lusa*
   (When will he recover? - day after tomorrow)
4. *Bila dia jatuh? - minggu lepas*
   (When did he fall? - last week)
5. *Bila dia akan pulang? - minggu depan*
   (When will he return? - next week)
6. *Bila dia akan terbang ke Jakarta? - esok*
   (When will he fly to Jakarta? - tomorrow)
7. *Bila dia singgah di rumah kamu? - malam tadi*
   (When did he stop by your house? - last night)
8. *Bila anak kamu lahir? - setahun kemudian*
   (When was your child born? - one year later)
9. *Bila kamu lalu di depan kedai itu? - tiap-tiap hari*
   (When do you pass by the shop? - every day)
10. *Bila lampu padam? - jam enam.*
    (When did the light go off? - six o'clock)

4C. Grammar

Pronoun

A pronoun is a word used in place of a noun or nouns, e.g.

Fatimah berkata bahawa Fatimah akan datang esok. (Fatimah said that Fatimah would come tomorrow.)	*Fatimah berkata bahawa dia akan datang esok.* (Fatimah said that she would come tomorrow.)
Ahmad dan saya pergi menonton wayang gambar. Ahmad dan saya sangat suka hati. (Ahmad and I went to see a show. Ahmad and I were very happy.)	*Ahmad dan saya pergi menonton wayang gambar. Kami sangat suka hati.* (Ahmad and I went to see a show. We were very happy.)
Murid-murid sedang menyanyi. Murid-murid sedang menyanyikan lagu kebangsaan. (The students are singing. The students are singing national anthem.)	*Murid-murid sedang menyanyi. Mereka sedang menyanyikan lagu kebangsaan.* (The students are singing. They are singing the national anthem.)

Kinds of Pronouns

(a) Personal Pronouns

There are three classes of personal pronouns: first person, second person and third person. First person pronouns indicate the person who is speaking. Second person pronouns indicate the person spoken to. And third person pronouns indicate the person spoken of. Below is a list of personal pronouns in Malay.

CLASS	SINGULAR	PLURAL
First person	*Saya* (I, me, my) *aku* (I, me, my)	*kita* (we, us, our) *kami* (we, us, our)
Second person	*awak* (you, your) *engkau* (you, your) *kamu* (you, your)	*awak sekalian* (all of you) *engkau sekalian* (all of you) *kamu sekalian* (all of you)
Third person	*ia* (he/she, him/her) *dia* (he/she, him/her) *beliau* (he/she, him/her)	*mereka* (they,them,their)

Personal pronouns should be used carefully, lest we offend the person we speak to. Please note that there is no difference between *saya* and *aku*, both mean 'I' and 'me', but *saya* can be used when speaking to anyone whereas *aku* is used when speaking to intimate friends only. There is also a difference between *kami* and *kita*, e.g.

Kami bersahabat baik sejak kecil.
(We have been good friends since young.) - excluding the person spoken to

Marilah kita pergi ke perpustakaan.
(Let us go to the library.) - including the person spoken to

The use of second person pronouns is even more difficult. *Awak*, engkau and *kamu* can only be used when speaking to friends or to a younger person. When speaking to a stranger, an older person or one of higher social standing, *tuan* or *encik* (for man) and *puan* or *cik* (for woman) are often used.

Under the influence of Bahasa Indonesia, *saudara* (for males) and *saudari* (for female) are increasingly being used for addressing one's equal or juniors. When addressing one's seniors or persons holding high position, *pak* (*bapak*, literally 'father') and *bu* (*ibu*, literally 'mother') are used. About twenty years ago, a new pronoun, *anda*, was coined in Indonesia. It is used as a general form of address, irrespective of social position, age and sex. This pronoun is being increasingly used in Malay.

There is practically no difference between *dia* and *ia*. Usually *ia* is used in the written Malay. *Ia* can also be translated as 'it' even though some prefer *ianya*. *Beliau* is adopted in addressing persons of high social standing. *Dia* and *beliau* are often written as *-nya* when joined to a noun. This seldom applies to *ia*, e.g.

Bapa ***dia*** *guru sukan.*
(His father is a sports teacher.)

Bapanya *guru sukan.*
(His father is a sport teacher.)

Ibu ***beliau*** *guru bahasa.*
(His mother is a language teacher.)

Ibunya *guru bahasa.*
(His mother is a language teacher.)

There is no possessive pronoun in the Malay language, except for the suffix ***-nya***. The words stated in the table above are also used as possessive pronouns, e.g.

Beg itu beg saya.
(That bag is mine [my bag].)

Dia meletakkan begnya di atas meja.
(He places his bag on the table.)

Exercise 5. Fill in the blanks with suitable pronouns.

e.g.

Fatimah *seorang pelajar.* __________ *belajar di sekolah rendah.* (**Fatimah** is a pupil. _________ is studying in a primary school.)

Fatimah seorang pelajar. ***Dia*** *belajar di sekolah rendah.* (Fatimah is a pupil. **She** is studying in a primary school.)

Husin dan Ali *pemandu.* _________ *memandu kereta.* (**Husin and Ali** are drivers. __________ drive cars.)

Husin dan Ali pemandu. ***Mereka*** *memandu kereta.* (Husin and Ali are drivers. **They** drive cars.)

1. ***Ali*** *seorang penjahat.* __________ *selalu mencuri wang.*
   (**Ali** is a criminal. __________ always steals money.)
2. ***Razak dan Ali*** *pekedai.* __________ *menjual berbagai barang di kedai mereka.*
   (**Razak and Ali** are shopkeepers. __________ sell various things in their shops.)
3. ***Saya dan Ramli*** *pekerja.* __________ *bekerja di bandar.*
   (**Ramli and I** are workers. __________ work in the town.)
4. ***Fauziah dan Laila*** *perempuan.* __________ *tinggal di rumah.*
   (**Fauziah and Laila** are women. __________ stay at home.)
5. ***Halimah*** *jurutaip.* __________ *sedang menaip.*
   (**Halimah** is a typist. __________ is typing.)
6. ***Ahmad*** *nakal.* __________ *suka mengusik teman-temannya.*
   (**Ahmad** is naughty. __________ like to tease his friends.)
7. ***Murid*** *itu rajin.* __________ *seorang murid yang rajin.*
   (**The student** is hard-working. __________ is a hard-working student.)

8. ***Fauziah dan Laila*** *cantik. __________ suka berpakaian cantik.*
(**Fauziah and Laila** are beautiful. __________ like to dress elegantly.)

9. ***Ahmad dan abangnya*** *mahasiswa. __________ belajar di Universiti Nasional Singapura.*
(**Ahmad and his brother** are undergraduates. __________ study at the National University of Singapore.)

10. ***Fatimah dan kakaknya*** *sombong. __________ sangat kaya.*
(**Fatimah and her sister** are arrogant. __________ are very wealthy.)

Exercise 6. Fill in the blanks with suitable pronouns.

e.g.

'__________ datang dari mana ?' pegawai itu bertanya. ('Where do __________ come from?' the officer asked.)	*'**Tuan** datang dari mana?' pegawai itu bertanya.* ('Where do **you** come from?' the officer asked.)
'__________ datang dari Kelantan ,' Rusli menjawab. ('__________ come from Kelantan,' Rusli answered.)	*'**Saya** datang dari Kelantan,' Rusli menjawab.* ('**I** come from Kelantan,' Rusli answered.)

Note: The officer may use *saudara, encik* and even *awak*. However *tuan* is more courteous.

1. *' __________ orang apa?' pegawai itu bertanya.*
('Where are __________ from?' ['What kind of people are you?'] the officer asked.)

2. *'__________ orang Singapura,' Yaming menjawab.*
('__________ am a Singaporean,' Yaming answered.)

3. *'Siapa nama __________?' Ali bertanya kepada gadis itu.*
('What is __________ name?' Ali asked the girl.)

4. *'Nama __________ Siti,' gadis itu menjawab.*
('__________ name is Siti,' the girl answered.)

5. *__________ kenalkah orang itu?'*
('Do __________ know that person?')

6. *'Tidak, __________ belum pernah berjumpa dia.'*
('No, __________ have never met him.')

7. *'Apa khabar, __________ Suparman?' Maslan bertanya kepada seorang pelancong dari Jakarta.*
('How are you, __________ Suparman?' Maslan asked a tourist from Jakarta.)

8. *'Petang ini, __________ berehat sahaja,' kata Ahmad kepada kawan- kawannya.*
('This afternoon, let __________ just rest,' Ahmad said to his friends.)

9. *'Jangan ganggu __________. Saya sedang bekerja,' kata Mahmud kepada adiknya.*
('Do not disturb __________. I am working,' Mahmud told his younger brother.)

10. *Ahmad bertanya kepada lelaki itu, '__________ mencari apa?'*
(Ahmad asked the man, 'What are __________ looking for?')

4D. Word Formation

Verbs

The prefix ***me-*** is a very important verb-forming affix. Indeed, some linguists argue that all transitive verbs must use the prefix ***me-***. But the general opinion is that though the use of ***me-*** is preferred in formal communication, ***me***- is often dropped in informal communication and newspaper headings. Students learning Malay for examination purposes are strongly advised to use ***me***- where its use is applicable. Lesson 5 explains further the application of ***me***-.

Please note that prefix ***me***- may become ***men***-, ***mem***-, ***meng***-, and ***meny***-, depending on the initial letter of the root word. Below are some rules for guidance:

(a) ***me***- is used when the root word begins with ***l***, ***m***, ***n***, ***ng***, ***ny***, or ***r***. e.g.

Ali sedang ***melukis*** *gambar.* (Ali is painting a picture.)	(*lukis* - to paint)
Kucing itu ***memakan*** *seekor tikus.* (The cat eats a rat.)	(*makan* - to eat)
Budak-budak itu sedang ***menanti*** *bas.* (The children are waiting for buses.)	(*nanti* - to wait)
Budak lelaki itu suka ***menganga***. (The boy likes to open his mouth widely.)	(*nganga* - to open one's mouth widely)
Fatimah sedang ***menyanyi.*** (Fatimah is singing.)	(*nyanyi* - to sing)
Perompak telah ***merompak*** *lelaki itu.* (A robber has robbed the man.)	(*rompak* - to rob)

(b) ***mem***- is used when the root word begins with ***b*** or ***p***. (***p*** is dropped.) e.g.

Tiap-tiap hari kami ***membaca*** *buku.* (Every day we read books.)	(*baca* - to read)
Pemandu teksi itu ***memandu*** *teksinya dengan cepat.* (The taxi driver drives his taxi fast.)	(*pandu* - to drive)

(c) ***men-*** is used when the root word begins with ***c***, ***d***, ***j***, ***z***, ***sy*** and ***t***. (***t*** is dropped.) e.g.

Yaming sedang ***mendengar*** *radio.* (*dengar* - to listen)
(Yaming is listening to the radio.)

Kucing itu ***mencuri*** *seekor ikan.* (*curi* - to steal)
(The cat steals a fish.)

Emak Yusuf ***menjual*** *nasi.* (*jual* - to sell)
(Yusuf's mother sells rice.)

Dia ***menziarahi*** *kubur datuknya.* (*ziarah* - to visit)
(He visits his grandfather's grave.)

Kami ***menonton*** *wayang gambar.* (*tonton* - to watch)
(We watch a picture.)

Dia ***mensyaratkan*** *kelulusan bahasa kedua.* (*syarat* - condition)
(He makes a pass in a second language as condition.)

(d) ***meng-*** is used when the root word begins with vowels ***a***, ***e***, ***i***, ***o***, ***u***, and the letters ***g***, ***h*** and ***k***. (***k*** is dropped.) e.g.

Dewi ***mengajak*** *saya ke rumahnya.* (*ajak* - to invite)
(Dewi invited me to her house.)

Saya tidak dapat ***mengeja*** *perkataan itu.* (*eja* - to spell)
(I cannot spell the word.)

Adik saya ***mengikut*** *ibu ke pasar.* (*ikut* - to follow)
(My younger brother follows mother to the market.)

Marilah kita ***mengorak*** *langkah.* (*orak* - to start)
(Let us start walking.)

Juruukur ***mengukur*** *jalan itu.* (*ukur* - to measure)
(The surveyor measures the road.)

Adik saya ***menggosok*** *giginya tiap-tiap pagi.* (*gosok* - to brush)
(My younger brother brushes his teeth every day.)

(e) ***menge-*** is used when the root word consists of only one syllable, such as ***bom***, ***cat*** etc. e.g.

Tentera musuh ***mengebom*** *daerah kita.* (*bom* - to bomb)
(The enemy army bombs our area.)

Ayah saya ***mengecat*** *rumah.* (*cat* - to paint)
(My father paints the house.)

(f) ***meny-*** is used when the root word begins with *s*. (***s*** is dropped.) e.g.

Abang saya ***menyuruh*** *saya membuat kerja itu.* (*suruh* - to ask)
(My elder brother asked me to do the work.)

Pelayan ***menyapu*** *sampah.* (*sapu* - to sweep)
(The waiter swept away the rubbish.)

Exercise 7. Add the prefix ***me-***, ***mem-***, or ***men-*** to the verbs in bold.

1. *Dia sudah* ***lamar*** *pekerjaan itu.*
   (He applied for the job.)
2. *Kakak* ***masak*** *di dapur.*
   (Elder sister is cooking in the kitchen.)
3. *Ali* ***niaga*** *rempah ke seluruh negara.*
   (Ali sells spices throughout the country.)

4. *Orang tua itu sudah **nyanyuk**.*
   (The old man has become senile.)

5. *Orang buta itu **raba**.*
   (The blind man is groping.)

6. *Ali telah **bahas** pendapat temannya.*
   (Ali criticised his friend's opinion.)

7. *Saya **pekik** sekuat-kuatnya.*
   (I screamed out loudly.) (as loud as I could.)

8. *Dia sudah **dapat** khabar itu.*
   (He has received the news.)

9. *Kita tidak boleh **cabar** keputusan mahkamah.*
   (We cannot challenge the court's decision.)

10. *Dia **tampal** tembok.*
    (He plastered the wall.)

Exercise 8. Add prefix ***meng***-, ***menge***-, or ***meny***- to the words in bold.

1. *Pemuda itu sedang **anggur.***
   (The young man is at the moment unemployed.)

2. *Dia tidak **erti** makna perkataan itu.*
   (He does not understand the meaning of that word.)

3. *Dia cuba **ingat** segala pesan ibunya.*
   (He tries to remember all his mother's advice.)

4. *Saya boleh **orak** ikatan itu.*
   (I can untie the bundle.)

5. *Seorang isteri harus tahu **urus** rumah.*
   (A wife should know (how to) look after the house.)

6. *Anjing itu tidak* ***gigit*** *orang.*
   (That dog does not bite people.)

7. *Dia tidak* ***kirim*** *surat kepada orang tuanya.*
   (He did not send letter to his parents.)

8. *Dia* ***syor*** *supaya rancangan itu dibatalkan.*
   (He suggested that the programme be cancelled.)

9. *Dia* ***samar*** *sebagai seorang polis.*
   (He disguised himself as a policeman.)

10. *Dia pandai* ***sajak.***
    (He is adept at composing poems.)

LESSON 5

5A. Conversation

Mengenal Seseorang dengan Lebih Dekat
(Getting to Know a Person Better)

Muthu: *Selamat pagi, Saudara Kassim.*
(Good morning, Mr. Kassim.)

Kassim: *Selamat pagi, Saudara Muthu.*
(Good morning, Mr. Muthu.)

Muthu: *Saudara Kassim, bolehkah saya tumpang tanya?*
(Mr. Kassim, may I ask you something?)

Kassim: *Tentu saja boleh.*
(Certainly.)

Muthu: *Berapa orang adik-beradik saudara?*
(How many brothers and sisters have you?)

Kassim: *Kami berempat. Saya ada seorang abang, seorang kakak dan seorang adik perempuan.*
(There are four of us. I have one elder brother, one elder sister and one younger sister.)

Muthu: *Berapa umur adik perempuan kamu?*
(How old is your younger sister?)

Kassim: *Umurnya lima belas tahun. Dia masih di sekolah menengah. Mengapa kamu bertanya tentang dia?*
(She is fifteen years old. She is still in secondary school. Why do you ask about her?)

Muthu: *Tidak apa-apa. Saya ingin tahu sahaja.*
(For no reason. I am just keen to know.)

5B. Structure

Read the following sentences.

SUBJECT	PREDICATE	OBJECT
Saya I	*sudah bayar* have paid	*lelaki itu.* the man.
Kau You	*belum bantu* have not helped	*lelaki itu.* the man.
Dia He	*akan sokong* will support	*lelaki itu.* the man.
Kita We	*hendak pilih* intend to choose	*lelaki itu.* that man.
Mereka They	*mahu cabar* wish to challenge	*lelaki itu.* the man.

Exercise 1. Substitute the verb in the model sentence with the one given.

e.g	*Saudara boleh* ***maki*** *orang itu.* (You can scold the man.)
panggil (to call)	*Saudara boleh* ***panggil*** *orang itu.* (You can call the man.)
tolong (to help)	*Saudara boleh* ***tolong*** *orang itu.* (You can help the man.)
tanya (to ask)	*Saudara boleh* ***tanya*** *orang itu.* (You can ask the man.)
lantik (to appoint)	*Saudara boleh* ***lantik*** *orang itu.* (You can appoint the man.)

tangkap (to arrest)	*Saudara boleh* ***tangkap*** *orang itu.* (You can arrest the man.)

1. *bantu* (to assist)
2. *turut* (to follow)
3. *tuduh* (to accuse)
4. *bawa* (to bring along)
5. *laung* (to detain)
6. *tentang* (to challenge)
7. *tampung* (to give job to)
8. *tegur* (to greet)
9. *periksa* (to examine)
10. *tanggung* (to be responsible for)

Exercise 2. Give affirmative answers to the following questions.

e.g.

Dia ejek budak lelaki itukah? (Did he tease the boy?)	*Ya, dia ejek budak lelaki itu.* (Yes, he teased the boy.)
Dia ganggu gadis itukah? (Did he disturb the girl?)	*Ya, dia ganggu gadis itu.* (Yes, he disturbed the girl.)
Dia halau peminta sedekah itukah? (Did he chase the beggar away?)	*Ya, dia halau peminta sedekah itu.* (Yes, he chased the beggar away.)
Dia herdik pelajar itukah? (Did he scold the student?)	*Ya, dia herdik pelajar itu.* (Yes, he scolded the student.)

1. *Dia hukum orang jahat itukah?*
(Did he punish the criminal?)
2. *Dia jemput guru itukah?*
(Did he invite the teacher?)

3. *Dia tumbuk orang laki-laki itukah?*
   (Did he strike the man?)
4. *Dia sebat orang salah itukah?*
   (Did he cane the criminal/offender?)
5. *Dia puji budak laki-laki itukah?*
   (Did he praise the boy?)
6. *Dia sindir sahabat kitakah?*
   (Did he hint at our friend?)
7. *Polis kejar lelaki itukah?*
   (Did the policeman chase after the man?)
8. *Polis kenal lelaki itukah?*
   (Did the policeman identify the man?)
9. *Polis tembak orang jahat itukah?*
   (Did the policeman shoot the criminal?)
10. *Dia larang semua parti politikkah?*
    (Did he ban all political parties?)

Exercise 3. Give negative answers to the following questions.

e.g.

Question	*Negative Answer*
Dia jabat tangan orang itukah? (Did he grasp the man's hand?)	*Dia tidak jabat tangan orang itu.* (No, he did not grasp the man's hand.)
Dia sewa rumah itukah? (Did he rent the house?)	*Tidak, dia tidak sewa rumah itu.* (No, he did not rent the house.)

Guru kita pesan buku itukah? (Did our teacher order the book?)	*Tidak, guru kita tidak pesan buku itu.* (No, our teacher did not order the book.)
Budak lelaki itu cakap bohongkah? (Did the boy lie?)	*Tidak, budak lelaki itu tidak cakap bohong.* (No, the boy did not lie.)

1. *Kawan kita minta buku itukah?*
   (Did our friend ask for the book?)
2. *Anak itu berus gigikah?*
   (Does the child brush his teeth?)
3. *Anak itu cuci mukakah?*
   (Does the child wash his face?)
4. *Anak itu sisir rambutkah?*
   (Does the child comb his hair?)
5. *Perempuan itu basuh pakaiankah?*
   (Does the woman wash clothes?)
6. *Pekerja itu simpan wangkah?*
   (Does the worker save money?)
7. *Dia sudah pegang jawatan itukah?*
   (Has he held that position?)
8. *Dia sudah pasang lampukah?*
   (Has he lit the lamp?)
9. *Salimah sudah tukar bajukah?*
   (Has Salimah changed her dress?)
10. *Ayah minum kopikah?*
    (Does father drink coffee?)

Exercise 4. Change the following statements into questions.

e.g.

Statement	*Question*
Dia tulis surat itu. (He wrote the letter.)	*Dia tulis surat itukah?* (Did he write the letter?)
Dia baca buku itu. (He read the book.)	*Dia baca buku itukah?* (Did he read the book?)
Dia kaji perkara itu. (He studies the matter.)	*Dia kaji perkara itukah?* (Does he study the matter?)
Dia curi wang itu. (He stole the money.)	*Dia curi wang itukah?* (Did he steal the money?)

1. *Ibu sedang atur bunga.*
   (Mother is arranging flowers.)
2. *Tukang kayu sedang bakar kayu.*
   (The carpenter is burning wood.)
3. *Perempuan itu sedang cuci pakaian.*
   (The woman is washing clothes.)
4. *Penjaja itu buang sampah.*
   (The hawker is throwing the rubbish away.)
5. *Ibu sudah buka peti itu.*
   (Mother has opened the box.)
6. *Kakak belum bungkus nasi.*
   (Elder sister has not wrapped the rice.)
7. *Abang sedang cari dompetnya.*
   (Elder brother is looking for his wallet.)
8. *Ayah usir anjing itu.*
   (Father chases the dog away.)
9. *Lelaki miskin itu sudah gadai rumahnya.*
   (The poor man has mortgaged his house.)

10. *Lelaki kaya itu sudah beli rumah baru.*
(The rich man has bought a new house.)

5C. Grammar

Kinds of Pronoun (continuation)

(b) Demonstrative Pronouns

A demonstrative pronoun indicates the noun replaced or referred to. There are two demonstrative pronouns in Malay, namely ***ini*** (this) and ***itu*** (that).

e.g.

Ini *buku.*
(**This** is a book.)

Buku ***ini*** *buku saya.*
(**This** book is mine [literally 'my book'].)

Itu *kereta.*
(**That** is a car.)

Itu *kereta Encik Lim.*
(**That** is Mr. Lim's car.)

A demonstrative pronoun, when referring to a noun or qualifiying, always comes after the noun.

(c) Interrogative Pronouns

Interrogative pronouns are used in questions. There are four interrogative pronouns in Malay: *siapa* (who/whom) - applied to persons, *apa* (what) - applied to things, *yang mana* (which) and *berapa* (how many/much/etc.).

e.g. ***Siapa*** *datang?*
(**Who** comes?)

Saudara mencari ***siapa****?*
(**Whom** are you looking for?)

Apa *dia buat?*
(**What** did he do?)

Dia sedang buat ***apa****?*
(**What** is he doing?)

Yang mana *buku saudara?*
(**Which** is your book?)

Berapa *harga buku itu?*
(**How much** does the book cost?)

Note: The last sentence can also be translated as 'What is the price of the book?' However, *berapa* is always used in relation to degree of measurement.

(d) Relative Pronouns

There is just one relative pronoun in Malay, i.e. *yang* (which/who/whom/that). It is used to join two sentences. This pronoun will be further discussed in the section on expansion of simple sentences in Lesson 17C.

Exercise 5. Fill in the blanks with ***siapa*** or ***apa***.

e.g.

__________ *guru saudara?* (__________ is your teacher?)	***Siapa*** *guru saudara?* (**Who** is your teacher?)
Dia membuat __________*?* (__________ is he doing?)	*Dia membuat* ***apa****?* (**What** is he doing?)

1. *Itu buku* __________*? Itu buku Ali.*
   (__________ book is that? That is Ali's book.)
2. *Itu lagu* __________*? Itu lagu Melayu.*
   (__________ song is that? That is a Malay song.)

3. *Buku* __________ *itu? Itu buku saya.*
(__________ book is that? That is my book.)

4. *Buku* __________ *itu? Itu buku pelajaran.*
(__________ kind of book is that? That is a text book.)

5. __________ *nama orang itu?*
(__________ is the name of that person?)

6. __________ *nama buku itu?*
(__________ is the name of the book?)

7. *Kucing memakan* __________?
(__________ do cats eat?)

8. __________ *memakan ikan?*
(__________ eats fish?)

9. *Doktor merawat* __________?
(__________ is the doctor treating?)

10. __________ *merawat adik saya?*
(__________ is treating my younger brother?)

Exercise 6. Fill in the blanks with ***berapa*** or ***yang mana***?

e.g.

________ *orang datang?* (________ people came?)	*Berapa orang datang?* (How many people came?)
__________ *guru saudara?* (__________ is your teacher?)	*Yang mana guru saudara?* (Which is your teacher?)

1. __________ *tahun umur budak lelaki itu?*
(__________ old is the boy?)

2. __________ *kereta bapa saudara?*
(__________ is your father's car?)

3. __________ *budak lelaki yang nakal itu?*
(__________ is the naughty boy?)

4. __________ *orang yang akan hadir?*
(__________ people will be present?)

5. __________ *orang adik-beradik saudara?*
(__________ many brothers and sisters have you?)

6. __________ *baju kamu suka?*
(__________ dress do you like?)

7. __________ *kawan saudara?*
(__________ is your friend?)

8. __________ *adik Amin?*
(__________ is Amin's brother?)

9. __________ *orang kawan saudara?*
(__________ people are your friends?)

10. __________ *umur saudara?*
(__________ old are you?)

5D. Word Formation

Verb (Prefix *me-*)

The prefix ***me-*** can be added to verbs, nouns and adjectives to form a verb. The prefix ***me-*** is often used to form transitive verbs in formal communication, but in casual conversation and newspaper headlines it is often dropped. In brief, it is advisable to use the prefix ***me-*** in formal communication, except for the word *tinggal* (to stay) which, if a prefix ***me-*** is added to it, will become *meninggal*, meaning to pass away, to die.

The prefix ***me-***, when added to nouns, has two important meanings:

(a) to do something by using the noun as an instrument, e.g.

Dia sudah ***mengunci pintu****.* *- kunci*	=	*Dia sudah* ***menutup*** *pintu* ***dengan kunci****.* (He has closed the door with a key.)
Lelaki itu sudah ***menggunting*** *rambutnya.* *- gunting*	=	*Lelaki itu sudah* ***memotong*** *rambutnya* ***dengan gunting****.* (The man has cut his hair with a pair of scissors.)

(b) to do something relating to the noun or to go to a place mentioned by the noun, e.g.

Emak ***menggulai*** *hari ini.* *- gulai*	=	*Emak* ***membuat gulai*** *hari ini.* (Mother is making curry to day.)
Besok aku akan ***merantau****.* *- rantau*	=	*Besok aku akan* ***pergi ke rantau****.* (Tomorrow I will go to a foreign land.)

However, when ***me-*** is added to adjectives, it

(c) acquires the meaning to become like (*menjadi*) or take on the characteristic of the root, e.g.

Rambut bapa saya ***memutih.***	=	*Rambut bapa saya* ***menjadi putih****.* (My father's hair becomes white.)
Hawa mulai ***mendingin.***	=	*Hawa mulai* ***menjadi dingin****.* (The climate becomes cold.)

And when it is added to verbs, it means an activity indicated by the root word as shown in 4D a - d.

Notes: The sign = shows that both sentences carry the same meaning.

Exercise 7. Replace the word in bold in the model sentence or phrase by a verb using the prefix ***me-***.

e.g.

Kakak sedang ***menggosok*** *baju dengan seterika.*
- *seterika*
Elder sister was ironing the (clothes with an iron.
- *an iron)*

Kakak sedang ***menyeterika*** *baju.*
(Elder sister was ironing the clothes.)

Perempuan itu ***menyebat*** *anak lelakinya* ***dengan rotan****.*
- *rotan*
(The woman beats her son with a cane.)
- *a cane*

Perempuan itu ***merotan*** *anak lelakinya.*
(The women canes her son.)

1. *Dia* ***menetak*** *kayu itu* ***dengan parang****. - parang*
   (He chops the wood with a chopper. - chopper)
2. *Nelayan itu* ***menangkap*** *ikan* ***dengan jaring****. - jaring*
   (The fisherman caught fish with a net. - net)
3. *Adik* ***membersihkan*** *giginya* ***dengan berus****. - berus*
   (Younger brother is cleaning his teeth with a brush. - brush)
4. *Gadis itu* ***menutup*** *mukanya* ***dengan tudung****. - tudung*
   (The girl covers her face with a veil. - veil)

5. *Abang suka* **menangkap** *ikan* **dengan pancing**. *- pancing*
(Elder brother likes to catch fish with rod. - rod)

6. *Makcik saya sedang* **memasak sayur**. *- sayur*
(My auntie is cooking vegetables. - vegetables)

7. *Lelaki tua itu suka* **menghisap rokok**. *- rokok*
(The old man likes to smoke cigarettes. - cigarette)

8. *Kami* **pergi ke tepi**. *- tepi*
(We go to the side. - side)

9. *Kami* **pergi ke seberang** *jalan itu. - seberang*
(We go to the other side of the road. - the other side)

10. *Salmiah* **sedang melukis gambar** *di bawah pohon. - gambar*
(Salmiah is painting a picture under a tree. - picture)

Exercise 8. Replace phrases in bold in the model sentence with a verb using the prefix ***me-***.

e.g.

Darahnya **menjadi beku**.
- beku
(His blood becomes coagulated.
- coagulate)

Darahnya **membeku**.
(His blood coagulates.)

Kakinya **menjadi bengkak**.
- bengkak
(His foot becomes swollen.
- swell)

Kakinya **membengkak.**
(His foot swells.)

1. *Padi* **menjadi kuning**. *- kuning*
(The paddy becomes yellow. - yellow)

2. *Asap* **menjadi tebal**. *- tebal*
(The smoke becomes thick. - thick)

3. *Harapannya* ***menjadi tipis***. - *tipis*
   (His hope becomes slim. - slim)

4. *Luka itu* ***menjadi dalam***. - *dalam*
   (The wound becomes deep. - deep)

5. *Bulan sudah* ***menjadi rendah***. - *rendah*
   (The moon has become low. - low)

6. *Perbincangan* ***menjadi hangat***. - *hangat*
   (The discussion is warming up. - warm)

7. *Lembaga itu* ***menjadi besar***. - *besar*
   (The silhouette becomes large. - large)

8. *Pokok itu* ***menjadi tinggi*** *dari sehari ke sehari*. - *tinggi*
   (The tree becomes taller from day to day. - tall)

9. *Perhubungan kita* ***menjadi renggang***. - *renggang*
   (Our relationship becomes distant. - distant)

10. *Kedua pihak* ***menjadi rapat***. - *rapat*
    (The two parties become intimate. - intimate)

LESSON 6

6A. Conversation

Melawat Kawan
(Visiting Friends)

Ah Chong: *Selamat pagi.*
(Good morning.)

Muthu: *Selamat pagi.*
(Good morning.)

Ah Chong: *Nama saya Ah Chong. Siapa nama saudara?*
(My name is Ah Chong. What is your name?)

Muthu: *Nama saya Muthu. Saya bekerja di sini. Saudara bekerja di sinikah?*
(My name is Muthu. I am working here. Are you working here?)

Ah Chong: *Oh, tidak. Saya datang berjumpa kawan saya.*
(Oh, no. I have come to meet my friend.)

Muthu: *Siapa nama kawan saudara?*
(What is the name of your friend?)

Ah Chong: *Namanya Tan Kok Beng.*
(His name is Tan Kok Beng.)

Muthu: *Oh, itu kerani kita. Mari ikut saya. Saya tunjukkan biliknya.*
(Oh, that is our clerk. Come, follow me. I will show you his room.)

Ah Chong: *Terima kasih.*
(Thank you.)

6B. Structure

Read the following sentences.

SUBJECT	PREPOSITIONAL PHRASE
Dia He	*ke Jakarta.* goes to Jakarta.
Abangnya His elder brother	*di rumah.* is at home.
Orang gaji saya My servant	*dari Filipina.* is from the Philippines.
Surat ini This letter	*daripada ayah.* is from father.
Hadiah ini This gift	*untuk kamu.* is for you.

Exercise 1. Substitute the phrase in the model sentence with the one given.

e.g. *Saya di sekolah kelmarin.*
(I was at school yesterday.)

di perpustakaan (at the library) — *Saya* ***di perpustakaan*** *kelmarin.* (I was at the library yesterday.)

di maktab (at the college) — *Saya* ***di maktab*** *kelmarin.* (I was at the college yesterday.)

hari ini (today) — *Saya di sekolah* ***hari ini****.* (I will be at school today.)

1. *di masjid*
   (at the mosque)

2. *di gereja*
(at the church)

3. *di kedutaan*
(at the embassy)

4. *pagi ini*
(this morning)

5. *di madrasah*
(at the Islamic religious school)

6. *di makmal*
(at the laboratory)

7. *di makmal bahasa*
(at the language laboratory)

8. *malam tadi*
(last night)

9. *di panggung wayang*
(at the cinema)

10. *di pusat bahasa*
(at the language centre)

Exercise 2. Give affirmative answers to the following questions.

e.g.

Question	*Answer*
Buku-buku itu di dalam almarikah? (Are the books in the cupboard.)	*Ya, buku-buku itu di dalam almari.* (Yes, the books are in the cupboard.)
Pelajar itu di perpustakaankah? (Is the pupil in the library?)	*Ya, pelajar itu di perpustakaan.* (Yes, the pupil is in the library.)

Surat itu daripada ayahkah?
(Is the letter from father?)

Ya, surat itu daripada ayah.
(Yes, the letter is from father.)

Lelaki itu dari Johorkah?
(Is the man from Johore?)

Ya, lelaki itu dari Johor.
(Yes, the man is from Johore.)

1. *Cikgu Ali ke sekolahkah?*
(Is Teacher Ali going to school?)
2. *Kakak ke pasarkah?*
(Is elder sister going to the market?)
3. *Buah-buahan itu di dalam keranjangkah?*
(Are the fruits in the basket?)
4. *Surat itu di dalam lacikah?*
(Is the letter in the drawer?)
5. *Surat itu daripada abangkah?*
(Is the letter from elder brother?)
6. *Pelancong itu dari Indonesiakah?*
(Is the tourist from Indonesia?)
7. *Kamus Melayu itu di atas mejakah?*
(Is the Malay dictionary on the table?)
8. *Pejabat Pos Besar itu di hadapan rumah kamukah?*
(Is the General Post Office in front of your house?)
9. *Balai polis itu di belakang rumah kamukah?*
(Is the police station at the back of your house?)
10. *Ibu pejabat syarikat itu di sebelah rumah kamukah?*
(Is the company's headquarters by the side of your house?)

Exercise 3. Change the following statements into questions.

e.g.

Statement	*Question*
Ibu masih di pasar. (Mother is still at the market.)	*Ibu masih di pasarkah?* (Is mother still at the market?)
Pensyarah itu dari Kuala Lumpur. (The lecturer is from Kuala Lumpur.)	*Pensyarah itu dari Kuala Lumpurkah?* (Is the lecturer from Kuala Lumpur?)
Guru itu masih di dalam bilik darjah. (The teacher is still in the classroom.)	*Guru itu masih di dalam bilik darjahkah?* (Is the teacher still in the classroom?)
Surat itu di dalam sampul surat. (The letter is in the envelope.)	*Surat itu di dalam sampul-suratkah?* (Is the letter in the envelope?)

1. *Nelayan itu masih di laut.*
   (The fisherman is still at sea.)
2. *Sarjana itu dari negeri Belanda.*
   (The scholar is from Holland.)
3. *Pesakit itu tidak ke pejabatnya.*
   (The patient did not go to his office.)
4. *Bungkusan ini untuk kamu.*
   (The packet is for you.)
5. *Para tamu masih di lapangan terbang.*
   (The guests are still at the airport.)
6. *Kertas itu di atas meja.*
   (The paper is on the table.)

7. *Gambar ayah di dinding.*
(Father's picture is on the wall.)

8. *Cawan di dapur.*
(The cups are in the kitchen.)

9. *Bunga di kebun.*
(Flowers are in the garden.)

10. *Kasut di dalam bilik tidur.*
(The shoes are in the bedroom.)

Exercise 4. Answer the following questions by using the words supplied.

e.g.

Di mana bilik tidur saya? *- di belakang* (Where is my bedroom? - at the back)	*Bilik tidur kamu **di belakang**.* (Your bedroom is at the back.)
Di mana kolam renang? *- di sana* (Where is the swimming pool? - there)	*Kolam renang **di sana**.* (The swimming pool is there.)
Ke mana kamu semalam? *- bandar* (Where did you go last night? - town)	*Saya ke **bandar** semalam.* (I went to the town last night.)
Penceramah itu dari mana? *- Jakarta* (Where is the speaker from? - Jakarta)	*Penceramah itu dari **Jakarta**.* (The speaker is from Jakarta.)

1. *Di mana Perpustakaan Kebangsaan? - di Stamford Road*
(Where is the National Library? - on Stamford Road)

2. *Di mana Kebun Bunga? - di sana*
(Where is the Botanical Garden? - there)

3. *Di mana kawan-kawan Ali? - di sini*
(Where are Ali's friends? - here)

4. *Di mana Rumah Sakit Universiti Nasional? - di Kent Ridge*
(Where is the National University Hospital? - at Kent Ridge)

5. *Ke mana lelaki itu? - ke kota*
(Where did the man go? - to the town)

6. *Dari mana wartawan-wartawan itu? - dari Bangkok*
(Where are the journalists from? - from Bangkok)

7. *Di mana pensel saya? - di atas meja*
(Where is my pencil? - on the table)

8. *Ke mana kawan kamu semalam? - panggung wayang*
(Where did your friend go last night? - the cinema)

9. *Dari mana tamu itu? - London*
(Where is the guest from? - London)

10. *Danau Toba di mana? - di Sumatera*
(Where is Lake Toba? - in Sumatera)

6C. Grammar

Auxiliary Verbs

Verbs in Malay do not have tenses. *Saya pergi* (I go) may also mean 'I went.' However, auxiliary verbs are used in the Malay language. There are two forms of auxiliary verbs: aspect and modal auxiliary verbs. Below is a list of common auxiliary verbs:-

(a) Aspect Auxiliaries

(i) indicating completed action: ***telah, sudah*** (has/have/had)

(ii) indicating action which is: ***sedang, tengah, masih***
or was being carried out (is/are/was/were ...ing)

(iii) indicating action which is: ***akan***
or was to be carried out (shall/should/will/would)

e.g. *Saya* ***sudah*** *membaca buku itu.*
(I have/had read the book.)

Emak ***telah*** *menjahit baju itu semalam.*
(Mother had sewn the dress yesterday.)

Burung itu ***sedang*** *membuat sarang.*
(The bird is/was making a nest.)

Kakak ***tengah*** *memasak nasi.*
(Elder sister is/was cooking rice.)

Adik ***masih*** *tidur.*
(Younger brother is/was still sleeping.)

Saya ***akan*** *pergi besok.*
(I shall go tomorrow.)

Though the tense is not indicated by the verb, other indications such as time may be stated in the sentence. The sentence *'Emak telah menjahit baju itu semalam'* contains indication as to when the action has taken place i.e. yesterday. It follows that the verb should be in the past tense. Hence, it is acceptable to translate the sentence thus:'Mother sewed the dress yesterday'. (Note that the verb 'had sewn' is changed to 'sewed'.) This translation is equally applicable to the sentence *'Emak jahit baju itu semalam.'* However, the auxiliary verb *telah* or *sudah* means 'has/have/had'.

(b) Modal Auxiliaries

(i) expressing ability : ***boleh, dapat***
(can/could)

(ii) expressing possibility or permission : ***boleh, mungkin*** (may/might)

(iii) expressing volition or necessity : ***patut, mesti, harus*** (should/must/ought to/has(have/had) to)

(iv) expressing wish : ***hendak, mahu, ingin*** (wish(wishes/wished)/want(wants/wanted))

e.g. *Dia* ***boleh*** *bercakap bahasa Arab.*
(He can speak Arabic.)

Saya ***dapat*** *menyudahkan kerja itu.*
(I can complete the job.)

Saudara ***boleh*** *pergi sekarang.*
(You may go now.)

Kita ***patut*** *menolong lelaki itu.*
(We should help the man.)

Kita ***mesti*** *menjaga kesihatan diri.*
(We must look after our health.)

Saudara ***harus*** *menghukum budak nakal itu.*
(You ought to punish that naughty child.)

Auxiliary verbs always come before the verbs.

Another word commonly used with verbs is *dengan* (with/by/...ly/to). All verbs in Malay can be followed by *dengan*:

e.g. *Dewi makan nasi* ***dengan*** *kari.*
(Dewi eats rice with curry.)

Dia berjalan ***dengan*** *cepat.*
(He walks swiftly.)

Ali menerima berita itu ***dengan*** *sedih.*
(Ali receives the news sadly.)

Emak memasak nasi untuk ayah ***dengan*** *segera.*
(Mother cooks rice for father immediately.)

Ali bercakap ***dengan*** *Ahmad.*
(Ali speaks to Ahmad.)

Exercise 5. Fill in the blanks with suitable auxiliary verbs.

e.g.

Amin __________ sampai pada pukul lima pagi.
(Amin __________ arrived at five a.m.)

Amin ***sudah*** *sampai pada pukul lima pagi.*
(Amin has arrived at five a.m.)

Dia tentu __________ mencapai cita-citanya.
(He certainly __________ achieve his ambition.)

Dia tentu ***dapat*** *mencapai cita-citanya.*
(He certainly can achieve his ambition.)

1. *Rumah itu __________ siap dua hari lagi.*
   (The house __________ be ready in two days' time.)
2. *Saya __________ menulis surat itu malam tadi.*
   (I __________ wrote the letter last night.)
3. *Dia __________ melihat rumah itu semalam.*
   (He __________ seen/saw the house yesterday.)
4. *Dia __________ menjadi seorang pengarang.*
   (He __________ to be a writer.)
5. *Dia __________ belajar dengan tekun.*
   (He __________ is studying diligently.)
6. *Sekejap lagi abang __________ balik dari kerja.*
   (Soon elder brother __________ return from work.)

7. *Kapal itu* __________ *belayar malam ini.*
   (The ship __________ sail to-night.)

8. *Dia* __________ *pergi ke Johor besok.*
   (He __________ go to Johore tomorrow.)

9. *Kita pasti* __________ *berjaya.*
   (We __________ certainly be successful.)

10. *Emaknya* __________ *datang hari ini.*
    (Her mother __________ come today.)

Exercise 6. Fill in the blanks with suitable verbs.

e.g.

Budak itu __________ *dengan cepat.* (The boy __________ quickly.)	*Budak itu* ***berjalan*** *dengan cepat.* (The boy walks quickly.) *Budak itu* ***berlari*** *dengan cepat.* (The boy runs quickly.)

1. *Dia* __________ *dengan keras.*
   (He __________ hard.)

2. *Dia* __________ *surat itu dengan sedih.*
   (He __________ the letter sadly.)

3. *Dia* __________ *masalah itu dengan saksama.*
   (He __________ the problem justly.)

4. *Saya* __________ *wayang gambar dengan adik saya.*
   (I __________ a movie with my younger brother.)

5. *Dia* __________ *dengan sekuat hati.*
   (He __________ loudly.)

6. *Encik Lim* __________ *masalah itu dengan tenang.*
   (Mr. Lim __________ the problem calmly.)

7. *Suyin sedang __________ dengan kawan-kawannya.*
   (Suyin is __________ with her friends.)

8. *Polis __________ lelaki itu dengan teliti.*
   (The policeman __________ the man carefully.)

9. *Dia __________ dengan tiba-tiba.*
   (He __________ suddenly.)

10. *Angin laut __________ dengan kencang.*
    (The sea wind __________ strongly.)

Note: Many verbs can fill the above blanks. Some of them are:

bertiup (to blow)	*berhembus* (to blow)	*datang* (to come)
memeriksa (to examine)	*menyoal* (to ask)	*berbincang* (to discuss)
berbual (to chat)	*meninjau* (to look at)	*memerhatikan* (to watch)
menjerit (to shout)	*memekik* (to shout)	*menonton* (to watch)
melihat (to see)	*membaca* (to read)	*menerima* (to receive)
berjalan (to walk)	*berlari* (to run)	

6D. Word Formation

Prefix *ber-*

Ber- is a very important prefix used to form verb. Prefix ***ber-*** becomes ***be-*** when the root word begins with ***r*** or its first syllable ends with ***r***, e.g.

ber + rambut = *berambut* (to have hair)

ber + rehat = *berehat* (to rest)

ber + kerja = *bekerja* (to work)

The prefix ***ber-*** can be added to nouns and verbs. When added to nouns, it has three important functions:

(i) to possess or to use the things indicated by the noun, e.g.

Ahmad seorang yang ***berharta****. - ada harta*
(Ahmad is a person who possesses property. - to possess property)

Mereka ***berpayung*** *ke sekolah. - menggunakan payung*
(They use an umbrella to go to school. - to use an umbrella)

(ii) to produce the thing indicated by the noun, e.g.

Pokok itu sedang ***bertunas****. - menghasilkan tunas*
(The tree is sprouting. - to produce sprouts)

Budak lelaki itu sedang ***bersiul****. - menghasilkan siul*
(The boy is whistling. - to produce a whistle)

(iii) to do the work indicated by the noun or to work in a place indicated by the noun, e.g.

Ramai orang kampung ***berkuli*** *di kota.*
- bekerja sebagai kuli
(Many villagers **worked as coolies** in town.
- to work as a coolie)

Hampir semua orang kampung ***bersawah****.*
- bekerja di sawah
(Nearly all the villagers worked in rice field.
- to work in rice field)

Exercise 7. Replace phrases in bold, in the model sentence with verb using the prefix ***ber-***.

e.g.

Ahmad seorang yang ***mempunyai harta.***	*Ahmad seorang yang* ***berharta.***

(Ahmad is a man who possesses property.)

Kita masih ***ada peluang****.* *Kita masih* ***berpeluang.***
(We still have opportunities.)

1. *Kain itu* ***mempunyai warna*** *biru.*
   (The piece of cloth has blue colour.)
2. *Buku bacaan itu* ***mempunyai gambar****.*
   (The reader has pictures.)
3. *Rumah itu tidak* ***mempunyai lampu****.*
   (The house has no lamps.)
4. *Guru itu* ***mempunyai ilmu.***
   (The teacher has knowledge.)
5. *Budak lelaki itu tidak* ***mempunyai akal****.*
   (The boy has no intelligence.)
6. *Negeri itu tiada* ***mempunyai raja.***
   (The country does not have a ruler.)
7. *Lukisan itu tidak* ***mempunyai mutu****.*
   (The painting has no quality.)
8. *Ayah saya tidak* ***mempunyai wang****.*
   (My father does not have money.)
9. *Surat itu tidak* ***mempunyai alamat****.*
   (The letter does not have an address.)
10. *Lelaki itu* ***mempunyai duit.***
    (The man has money.)

Exercise 8. Replace phrases in bold, in the model sentence with a verb using the prefix ***ber-***.

e.g.

Budak lelaki itu *Budak lelaki itu*

***menggunakan basikal** ke sekolah* (The boy cycles to school.)	***berbasikal** ke sekolah.*
*Ramai orang Melayu bekerja **di kedai-kedai** di bandar.* (Many Malays work in shops in town.)	*Ramai orang Melayu **berkedai** di bandar*

1. *Budak lelaki itu tidak **memakai kasut** ke sekolah.*
   (The boy does not wear shoes to school.)

2. *Almari itu tidak **mempunyai cermin.***
   (The cupboard has no mirror.)

3. *Lelaki itu suka **memberi pidato**.*
   (The man likes to give speeches.)

4. *Kakak saya suka **memakai baju** cantik.*
   (My elder sister likes to wear beautiful dresses.)

5. *Kami **memakai kereta** ke Kuala Lumpur.*
   (We drive to Kuala Lumpur.)

6. *Lelaki itu **memakai cermin mata** hitam.*
   (The man wears black spectacles.)

7. *Sarjana itu suka **memberi ceramah.***
   (The scholar likes to give lectures.)

8. *Abang sedia **bekerja sebagai kuli.***
   (Elder brother is ready to work as a coolie.)

9. *Musim hujan ramai nelayan **bekerja di ladang.***
   (During the rainy season many fishermen work on the farms.)

10. *Sudah dua tahun dia **bekerja di kedai.***
    (For two years, he has been working in a shop.)

LESSON 7

7A. Conversation

Berkenalan
(Acquiantance)

Tan: *Maaf, siapa nama saudara?*
(Excuse me, what is your name?)

Hadi: *Nama saya Hadi. Siapa nama saudara?*
(My name is Hadi. What is yours?)

Tan: *Nama saya Tan. Apa pekerjaan saudara?*
(My name is Tan. What is your occupation?)

Hadi: *Saya pelajar.*
(I am a student.)

Tan: *Oh, saudara masih belajar? Di mana saudara belajar?*
(Oh, you are still studying? Where do you study?)

Hadi: *Saya belajar di Sekolah Menengah Serangoon.*
(I study at Serangoon Secondary School.)

Tan: *Saudara orang Singapurakah?*
(Are you a Singaporean?)

Hadi: *Bukan. Saya bukan orang Singapura. Saya orang Indonesia.*
(No. I am not a Singaporean. I am an Indonesian.)

Tan: *Patutlah saudara pandai bercakap bahasa Melayu. Mengapa saudara tidak belajar di Indonesia?*
(No wonder you can speak Malay very well. Why didn't you study in Indonesia?)

Hadi: *Bapa saya menghantar saya belajar di Singapura. Dia mahu saya pandai bercakap bahasa Inggeris.*

(My father sent me to study in Singapore. He wants me to be able to speak good English.)

Tan: *Sudahkah saudara pandai bercakap bahasa Inggeris?*
(Can you speak English fluently?)

Hadi: *Bolehlah, sedikit-sedikit.*
(Yes, a bit.)

7B. Structure

Read the following sentences carefully.

SUBJECT	PREDICATE
Ali Ali	*berbohong.* is lying.
Ahmad Ahmad	*sedang berenang.* is swimming.
Mereka They	*sedang berceloteh.* are chatting. (ceaselessly)
Mereka They	*akan bersatu.* will be united.
Dia He	*sudah bersara.* has retired.

Exercise 1. Substitute the verb in the model sentence with the one given.

e.g. *Saya tahu saudara* ***bekerja*** *dengan orang laki-laki itu.*

	(I know that you are working with the man.)
berkawan (to befriend)	*Saya tahu saudara* ***berkawan*** *dengan orang laki-laki itu.* (I know that you are friendly with the man.)
berbalah (to quarrel)	*Saya tahu saudara* ***berbalah*** *dengan orang laki-laki itu.* (I know that you quarrel with the man.)
bercampur (to mix with)	*Saya tahu saudara* ***bercampur*** *dengan orang laki-laki itu.* (I know that you keep company with the man.)
bercakap (to talk to)	*Saya tahu saudara* ***bercakap*** *dengan orang laki-laki itu.* (I know that you talk to the man.)

1. *bertengkar* (to argue)
2. *bergaul* (to associate)
3. *berbaik* (to be friendly terms with)
4. *berjumpa* (to meet)
5. *bertanding* (to compete)
6. *bermusuh* (to antagonize)
7. *bersahabat* (to befriend)
8. *bersalam* (to shake hands)
9. *berbincang* (to discuss)
10. *bertumbuk* (to punch each other)

Exercise 2. Change the following statements into questions.

e.g.

Statement	*Question*
Mereka sedang berbicara. (They are talking.)	*Mereka sedang berbicarakah?*

(Are they talking?)

Dia sedang berehat.
(He is resting.)

Dia sedang berehatkah?
(Is he resting?)

Mereka sudah berpisah.
(They have separated.)

Mereka sudah berpisahkah?
(Have they separated?)

Perempuan itu berbangsa Cina.
(The woman is of Chinese origin.)

Perempuan itu berbangsa Cinakah?
(Is the woman of Chinese origin?)

1. *Adik sedang berkhayal.*
   (Young brother is day-dreaming.)
2. *Orang itu sudah berkuasa.*
   (That person has power.)
3. *Orang itu sedang bermimpi.*
   (That person is dreaming.)
4. *Perempuan itu sedang bernyanyi.*
   (The woman is singing.)
5. *Budak lelaki itu belum berpuasa.*
   (The boy has not fasted yet.)
6. *Mereka belum bergerak.*
   (They have not moved.)
7. *Mereka masih berunding.*
   (They are still negotiating.)
8. *Mereka bersalah.*
   (They are guilty.)
9. *Mereka akan berpesta.*
   (They will celebrate.)
10. *Orang itu beragama Islam.*
    (The man is a Muslim.) (of the Islamic religion)

Exercise 3. Give affirmative answers to the following questions.

e.g.

Question	*Answer*
Saudara bertugas di sinikah? (Are you on duty here?)	*Ya, saya bertugas di sini.* (Yes, I am on duty here.)
Dia sedang berkhidmat dalam tenterakah? (Is he serving in the army?)	*Ya, dia sedang berkhidmat dalam tentera.* (Yes, he is serving in the army.)
Amin sudah bertukar ke Kuala Lumpurkah? (Has Amin been transferred to Kuala Lumpur?)	*Ya, Amin sudah bertukar ke Kuala Lumpur.* (Yes, Amin has been transferred to Kuala Lumpur.)
Mereka sedang beristirahat di rumahkah? (Are they resting at home?)	*Ya, mereka sedang beristirahat di rumah.* (Yes, they are resting at home.)

1. *Mereka sedang berkumpul di padang sekolahkah?*
   (Are they assembling at the school field?)
2. *Mereka sedang bermuafakat di pejabatkah?*
   (Are they holding a meeting in the office?)
3. *Mereka berniaga di Johorkah?*
   (Are they doing business in Johore?)
4. *Saudara berehat di rumahkah?*
   (Are you resting at home?)
5. *Saudara bersembahyang di masjidkah?*
   (Do you pray in a mosque?)
6. *Dia berada di Ipohkah?*
   (Is he hiding in Ipoh?)

7. *Perempuan itu bersolek di dalam bilikkah?*
(Is the woman making up in the room?)

8. *Rombongan itu akan berangkat ke Kuantankah?*
(Is the group leaving for Kuantan?)

9. *Orang itu sedang bercukur di bilikkah?*
(Is that person shaving in the room?)

10. *Perajurit sedang bertahan di kubukah?*
(Are the soldiers holding out at the fort?)

Exercise 4. Answer the following questions by using the phrases supplied.

e.g.

Bapa sedang berbaring di mana? - *di dalam bilik tidur*. (Where is father lying? - in the bedroom)	*Bapa sedang berbaring di dalam bilik tidur*. (Father is lying in the bedroom.)
Ibu berbelanja di mana? - *di kedai runcit* (Where does mother shop?) - in a provision shop)	*Ibu berbelanja di kedai runcit*. (Mother shops in a provision shop.)
Lelaki itu sedang berceramah di mana? - *di sekolah* (Where is the man giving a talk? - at a school)	*Lelaki itu sedang berceramah di sekolah*. (The man is giving a talk at a school.)
Guru kita sedang bercuti di mana? - *di tepi pantai* (Where is our teacher holidaying?	*Guru kita sedang bercuti di tepi pantai*. (Our teacher is holidaying near the seaside.)

- near a seaside)

1. *Guru itu berdiri di mana? - di depan darjah*
(Where does the teacher stand? - in front of the class)

2. *Bas itu berhenti di mana? - di depan perpustakaan*
(Where did the bus stop? - in front of the library)

3. *Murid-murid berhimpun di mana? - di padang sekolah*
(Where do the pupils assemble? - in the school field)

4. *Tamu kita bermalam di mana? - di hotel*
(Where did our guest spend the night? - in a hotel)

5. *Kereta itu berlalu di mana? - di belakang rumah saya*
(Where did the car pass by? - at the back of my house)

6. *Perahu itu belayar ke mana? - ke Sumatera*
(Where did the boat sail to? - to Sumatera)

7. *Mereka berkelah di mana? - di Port Dickson*
(Where did they picnic? - at Port Dickson)

8. *Peristiwa itu berlaku di mana - di hadapan mata kita*
(Where did the incident happen? - in front of our eyes)

9. *Ali bersembunyi di mana? - di balik pokok*
(Where did Ali hide? - behind a tree)

10. *Amin berlatih di mana? - di Jepun*
(Where did Amin undergo his training? - in Japan)

7C. Grammar

Active Voice and Passive Voice

There are two types of verbs in Malay: transitive verbs and intransitive verbs. A transitive verb is one that is followed by an object. The verbs illustrated in the *Structure*, section of Lessons 5, 9, and 10 are transitive verbs. On the other hand an intransitive verb denotes an action that is not performed on an object. The verbs discussed in section B of this lesson and Lessons 4 and 8 are intransitive verbs.

Transitive verbs have voices. A verb is said to be in the active voice when the subject of the verb is performing the action indicated by the verb.

e.g. *Ali membaca buku itu.*
(Ali reads the book.)

Anjing mengejar orang itu.
(A dog chases the man.)

Dia sudah mendengar berita itu.
(He has heard the news.)

Encik Yusuf sudah ***membeli*** *rumah itu.*
(Mr. Yusuf has bought the house.)

A verb is in the passive voice when it expresses an action performed on its subject. When a verb appears in the passive voice, the prefix ***me-*** is replaced by ***di-*** and the performer of the action appears at the end of the sentence. Sometimes, the performer is omitted.

e.g. *Buku itu* ***dibaca*** *oleh Ali.*
(The book is read by Ali.)

Lelaki itu ***dikejar*** *oleh anjing.*
(The man is chased by a dog.)

Berita itu sudah ***didengar*** *oleh dia.*
(The news has been heard by him.)

Rumah itu sudah ***dibeli*** *oleh Encik Yusuf.*
(The house has been bought by Mr. Yusuf.)

Please note that *didengar oleh dia* is always written *didengarnya*. The third sentence above could therefore read: *Berita itu sudah didengarnya*.

Some linguists argue that the passive voice rule above applies only if the subject is in the third person. If the subject is in the first or second person, it is not applicable. Hence, the following sentences are not acceptable to them

Pensel itu ***diambil oleh saya.***
(The pencil was taken by me.)

Buku itu ***diambil oleh kamu.***
(The book was taken by you.)

The above sentences have been derived from the following:

Saya ***mengambil*** *pensel itu.*
(I took the pencil.)

Kamu ***mengambil*** *buku itu.*
(You took the book.)

The verbs of these two sentences are in active voice. In order to convert them into passive voice, the sentences should be written thus:

Pensel itu ***saya ambil.***
(The pencil I took.)

Buku itu ***kamu ambil.***
(The book you took.)

Readers, especially students sitting for examinations, are strongly advised to learn both rules. Below are more examples on the application of the second rule:

ACTIVE	PASSIVE
Saya ***menendang*** *bola itu.* I kicked the ball.	*Bola itu* ***saya tendang***. The ball I kicked.
Kamu ***menendang*** *bola itu.* You kicked the ball.	*Bola itu* ***kamu tendang***. The ball you kicked.
Aku ***menendang*** *bola itu.* I kicked the ball.	*Bola itu* ***kutendang***. The ball I kicked.
Engkau ***menendang*** *bola itu.* You kicked the ball.	*Bola itu* ***kautendang***. The ball you kicked.

Please note that *ku* and *kau* are clitic forms of *aku* and *engkau*; and are normally used in passive voice.

Exercise 5. Change the following into passive sentences.

e.g.

Kucing ***makan*** *ikan.*
(Cats eat fish.)

Ikan ***dimakan*** *kucing.*
(Fish is eaten by cat.)

Dia ***menulis*** *surat itu.*
(He wrote the letter.)

Surat itu ***ditulisnya***.
(The letter was written by him.)

1. *Saleh sudah* ***menulis*** *surat itu.*
   (Saleh has written the letter).)
2. *Guru selalu* ***memuji*** *Fatimah.*
   (The teacher always praises Fatimah.)
3. *Laila sedang* ***memegang*** *pensel itu.*
   (Laila was holding the pencil.)
4. *Pencuri sudah* ***mencuri*** *wangnya.*
   (The thief has stolen his money.)

5. *Siti Salina* ***membasuh*** *pakaian.*
   (Siti Salina washed clothes.)
6. *Halimah sedang* ***menyapu*** *bilik darjah.*
   (Halimah is sweeping the classroom.)
7. *Cikgu Ali belum* ***membaca*** *suratkhabar.*
   (Teacher Ali has not read the paper.)
8. *Ali sedang* ***menanti*** *temannya.*
   (Ali is waiting for his friend.)
9. *Ibu sedang* ***menjahit*** *baju.*
   (Mother is sewing a dress.)
10. *Ahmad* ***menolong*** *orang itu.*
   (Ahmad helped the person.)

Exercise 6. Change the following into active sentences.

e.g.

Buku itu sedang ***saya baca****.* (The book I am reading.)	*Saya sedang membaca buku itu.* (I am reading the book.)
Anjing itu ***kamu pukul.*** (The dog you beat.)	*Kamu memukul anjing itu.* (You beat the dog.)

1. *Pokok kelapa itu* ***saya panjat.***
   (The coconut tree I climb.)
2. *Berita itu sudah* ***saya dengar****.*
   (The news I have heard.)
3. *Nasi itu sudah* ***saya makan.***
   (The rice I have eaten.)
4. *Karangan itu sudah* ***kutulis.***
   (The essay I have written.)
5. *Surat iut sudah* ***kamu terima.***
   (The letter you have received.)

6. *Kamus itu sudah* ***kaubawa.***
   (The dictionary you have brought.)

7. *Penselmu sudah* ***saya pinjam.***
   (Your pencil I have borrowed.)

8. *Budak itu* ***kaupukul.***
   (The boy you hit.)

9. *Kopi itu sudah* ***kuminum.***
   (The coffee I have drunk.)

10. *Ayam itu sudah* ***kamu tangkap.***
    (The chicken you have caught.)

7D. Word Formation

Prefix *ber-* (continuation)

The prefix ***ber-*** can also be added to verbs. When added to verbs, it has three important functions:

(i) reflexive, indicating an action being done on oneself.

e.g. *Orang itu* ***berbaring*** *di tempat tidurnya.*
- *membaringkan diri*
(The man is lying on his bed.
- to put himself in a lying position)

Gadis itu suka ***berhias.***
- *menghiaskan diri*
(The girl likes to make up.
- to apply make up on herself)

(ii) reciprocal, indicating an action being done between two persons.

e.g. *Ahmad* ***berkelahi*** *dengan kawannya.*
- *saling berkelahi*

(Ahmad is fighting with his friend.
- fight with each other)

Zain dan Mazlan sedang berbual.
- saling berbual
(Zain and Mazlan are talking.
- talk to each other)

(iii) passive, indicating an action being done to the subject.

e.g. *Kain itu belum* ***berjahit.***
- dijahit
(The cloth has not been sewn.
- to be sewn)

Soalan itu tidak ***berjawab.***
- dijawab
(The question was not answered.
- to be answered)

In addition, some verbs with prefix ***ber-*** have meaning different from their root words. These words can only be memorised.

e.g.	*salin* (to change)	*Isterinya sudah* ***bersalin.*** *- melahirkan anak* (His wife has given birth. - to give birth)
	angkat (to carry)	*Mereka sudah* ***berangkat*** *ke Mekah.* *- pergi* (They have left for Mecca. - to leave for)
	tolak (to push)	*Dia akan* ***bertolak*** *petang ini* *- pergi* He will depart this afternoon. - to depart)

pulang (to return)	*Bapanya sudah berpulang tahun lepas. - mati* (His father died last year. - to die)

Exercise 7. Add prefix ***ber-*** to the words in bold.

e.g.

*Budak lelaki itu **lari** ke sekolah.* (The boy runs to school.)	*Budak lelaki itu **berlari** ke sekolah.*
*Ahmad **cerai** dengan kawannya.* (Ahmad has parted with his friend.)	*Ahmad **bercerai** dengan kawannya.*

1. *Aminah **lindung** di belakang tabir.*
   (Aminah is hiding behind the curtain.)
2. *Bapa **cerita** tiap malam.*
   (Father tells stories every night.)
3. *Orang laki-laki itu **taubat.***
   (The man has repented.)
4. *Gadis itu suka **dandan.***
   (The girl likes to dress up.)
5. *Bumi kita **pusing.***
   (Our world is rotating.)
6. *Dia tidak berani **suara.***
   (He dares not speak up.)
7. *Manusia tidak boleh **nafas** di dalam air.*
   (Man cannot breathe in water.)
8. *Pemuda tidak mahu **ganjak** ke tepi.*
   (The young man refuses to move to the side.)

9. *Budak-budak sudah* ***atur*** *di padang.*
   (Children have queued up in the field.)

10. *Kami akan* ***kunjung*** *ke Singapura.*
    (We will visit Singapore.)

Exercise 8. Fill in the blanks with suitable words.

e.g.

Cintanya tidak __________ (His love was not __________ .)	*Cintanya tidak* ***berbalas.*** (His love was not reciprocated.)
Pejabat itu sudah __________ (The office has __________ .)	*Pejabat itu sudah* ***berpindah.*** (The office has moved.)

1. *Cuti sekolah sudah* __________ .
   (The school holiday has __________ .)

2. *Tayar basikal itu tiada* __________ .
   (The tyre of the bicycle has __________ .)

3. *Bangkai itu* __________ .
   (The carcas __________ .)

4. *Pokok itu* __________ .
   (The plant __________ .)

5. *Pendapat mereka* __________ .
   (Their opinion __________ .)

6. *Langit tiada* __________ .
   (The sky has no __________ .)

7. *Rambutan* __________ .
   (Rambutans __________ .)

8. *Pinjaman itu tidak* __________ .
   (The loan has not __________ .)

9. *Buku itu* _________ .
   (The book _________ .)

10. *Surat itu tiada* _________ .
    (The letter has not _________ .)

The blanks may be filled by the following words:

berdaftar (to be registered)	*bergambar* (to have illustrations)
berguna (to be useful)	*berbuah* (to produce fruit)
berbintang (to have stars)	*berbeza* (to be different)
berambut (to have hair/ fine filaments)	*berbau* (smelly)
berangin (to have air)	*berakar* (to grow roots)
beralih (to shift)	*berbukti* (to have proof)
berbulu (to have hair)	*berakhir* (to end)
beralamat (to have an address)	*berbunga* (to pay interest)

LESSON 8

8A. Conversation

Di Majlis
(At a Gathering)

Rama: *Saudara Lim, siapakah gadis yang duduk di situ?*
(Mr. Lim, who is the girl sitting there?)

Lim: *Oh, itu jurutaip kami. Ada apa?*
(Oh, that is our typist. Is there anything?)

Rama: *Saudara kenalkah dia?*
(Do you know her?)

Lim: *Tentu saja. Kami bekerja di bahagian yang sama.*
(Certainly. We work in the same section.)

Rama: *Bolehkah saudara kenalkan saya kepada dia?*
(Can you introduce me to her?)

Lim: *Tentu saja. Marilah kita pergi sekarang.*
(Certainly. Let us go now.)

[*Mereka pergi ke arah gadis itu.*]
(They walked towards the girl.)

Lim: *Saudari Chan, ini ada kawan hendak berkenalan dengan saudari.*
(Miss Chan, here is a friend who would like to make your acquaintance.)

Rama: *Nama saya Rama, Saudari Chan. Saya senang hati dapat berkenalan dengan saudari.*
(My name is Rama, Miss Chan. I am happy to make your acquaintance.)

Chan: *Saya pun suka berkenalan dengan saudara.*
(I am also glad to meet you.)

8B. Structure

Read the following sentences carefully.

SUBJECT	PREDICATE	ADVERBIAL
Bayi itu The baby	*sedang merangkak* is crawling	*ke dalam bilik.* into the room.
Anak itu The child	*tidak menangis* did not cry	*malam tadi.* last night.
Dia He	*suka menyanyi* likes to sing	*di dalam bilik mandi.* in the bathroom.
Mereka They	*suka merantau* like to travel	*ke Jawa.* to Java.
Pak Sudin Pak Sudin	*meninggal* passed away	*tahun lalu.* last year.

Exercise 1. Substitute the verb in the model sentence with the one given.

e.g. *Saya menginap di rumah sahabat malam tadi.*
(I stayed at a friend's house last night.)

menari (to dance) — *Saya* ***menari*** *di rumah sabahat malam tadi.*
(I danced at a friend's house last night.)

merokok (to smoke) — *Saya* ***merokok*** *di rumah sahabat malam tadi.*
(I smoked at a friend's house last night.)

menjerit (to scream)	*Saya **menjerit** di rumah sahabat malam tadi.* (I screamed at a friend's house last night.)
mengelamun (to engage in day-dreaming)	*Saya **mengelamun** di rumah sahabat malam tadi.* (I was day-dreaming at a friend's house last night.)

1. *mengantuk* (to be sleepy)
2. *memekik* (to shout)
3. *membohong* (to lie)
4. *membisu* (to remain speechless)
5. *mengeluh* (to moan)
6. *menangis* (to cry)
7. *mengarut* (to talk nonsense)
8. *merungut* (to grumble)
9. *menguap* (to yawn)
10. *menyanyi* (to sing)

Exercise 2. Give affirmative answers to the following questions.

e.g.

Question	*Answer*
Belanja hidup sudah meningkatkah? (Has the cost of living increased?)	*Ya, belanja hidup sudah meningkat.* (Yes, the cost of living has increased.)
Harga barang-barang sudah melambungkah? (Have prices of goods soared?)	*Ya, harga barang-barang sudah melambung.* (Yes, prices of goods have soared.)

Harga minyak sudah merosotkah? (Has the oil price gone down?)	*Ya, harga minyak sudah merosot.* (Yes, the oil price has gone down.)
Berita itu sudah merebakkah? (Has the news spread?)	*Ya, berita itu sudah merebak.* (Yes, the news has spread.)

1. *Penyakit itu sudah menjangkitkah?*
   (Has the disease spread?)
2. *Bom itu belum meledakkah?*
   (Hasn't the bom exploded?)
3. *Angin sedang membadaikah?*
   (Is the wind raging?)
4. *Hujan sudah meredakah?*
   (Has the rain subsided?)
5. *Fajar sedang menyingsingkah?*
   (Is the day breaking?)
6. *Air sedang mendidihkah?*
   (Is the water boiling?)
7. *Kaki budak lelaki itu sedang membengkakkah?*
   (Is the boy's foot swelling?)
8. *Anjing itu sedang menyalakkah?*
   (Is the dog barking?)
9. *Lembu jantan itu sedang mengganaskah?*
   (Is the bull raging?)
10. *Perang sudah meletuskah?*
    (Has a war erupted?)

Exercise 3. Change the following statements into questions.

e.g.

Statement	*Question*
Kapal terbang ***sudah mendarat.*** (The plane has landed.)	***Sudah mendaratkah*** *kapal terbang?* (Has the plane landed?)
Encik Ahmad ***suka*** *mengembara.* (Mr. Ahmad likes to travel.)	***Sukakah*** *Encik Ahmad mengembara?* (Does Mr. Ahmad like to travel?)
Lelaki itu ***selalu*** *melancong ke Jawa.* (The man always travels to Java.)	***Selalukah*** *lelaki itu melancong ke Jawa?* (Does the man always travels to Java?)
Dia ***boleh*** *menumpang di rumah sahabatnya.* (He can lodge in his friend's house.)	***Bolehkah*** *dia menumpang di rumah sahabatnya?* (Can he lodge in his friend's house?)

1. *Budak lelaki itu* ***suka mengaji.***
   (The boy likes to recite [the Quran].)
2. *Dia* ***sudah*** *mengalah.*
   (He has succumbed.)
3. *Adik* ***suka*** *memancing.*
   (Younger brother likes to fish.)
4. *Perempuan itu* ***selalu*** *merajuk.*
   (The woman always sulks.)
5. *Perempuan itu* ***suka*** *membazir.*
   (The woman likes to spend money wastefully.)
6. *Pencuri itu* ***sudah menghilang***.
   (The thief has disappeared.)

7. *Mereka* ***boleh*** *mengundi.*
   (They can vote.)

8. *Mereka* ***boleh*** *mengundur.*
   (They can retreat.)

9. *Orang itu* ***sedang menganggur****.*
   (That person is being unemployed.)

10. *Rakyat negeri itu* ***selalu*** *memberontak.*
    (The people of that country always rebel.)

Exercise 4. Answer the following questions by using the words supplied.

e.g.

Air hujan mangalir ke mana? *- ke dalam longkang* (Where did the rain water flow? -into the drain)	*Air hujan mangalir ke dalam longkang.* (The rain water flowed into the drain.)
Orang itu mengamuk di mana? *- di pasar* (Where did that person run amok? - at the market)	*Orang itu mengamuk di pasar.* (That person ran amok at the market.)
Rumah itu menghadap ke mana? *- ke laut* (Where does the house face? - the sea)	*Rumah itu menghadap ke laut.* (The house faces the sea.)
Bajak itu melanun di mana? *- di Selat Melaka* (Where did the criminal commit piracy? - in the Straits of Malacca)	*Bajak itu melanun di Selat Melaka.* (The criminal committed piracy in the Straits of Malacca.)

1. *Bola itu melambung ke mana? - ke atas air*
   (Where did the ball bounce to? - onto the water)
2. *Air memancar dari mana? - dari paip*
   (From where did the water squirt out? - out of the pipe)
3. *Semut-semut sedang merayap di mana? - di lantai*
   (Where are the ants crawling? - on the floor)
4. *Pekerja itu sudah menetap di mana? - di Singapura*
   (Where has the worker settled down? - in Singapore)
5. *Kassim sedang menuntut di mana? - di universiti*
   (Where is Kassim studying? - at the university)
6. *Ali menoleh ke arah mana? - ke belakang*
   (To which direction did Ali turn his head? - to the rear)
7. *Lelaki itu menyelunduk ke mana? - ke negeri kita*
   (Where did the man smuggle goods? - into our country)
8. *Bom itu meledak di mana? - di tengah bandar.*
   (Where did the bomb explode? - in the town centre.)
9. *Air hujan menitis dari mana? - dari bumbung bocor*
   (From where did the rain water drip? - from the leaking roof)
10. *Budak lelaki itu melangkah ke mana? - ke depan*
    (Where is the boy stepping? - to the front)

8C. Grammar

Numerals

Numerals are number-bearing words used to modify nouns. Numerals always precede nouns. In other words, a numeral signifies that the word following it is a noun. There are two types of numbers in Malay, namely cardinal numbers and ordinal numbers.

Cardinal numbers are further divided into definite cardinal and indefinite cardinal. Examples of definite cardinals are:

0	*kosong*	(zero)	11	*sebelas*	(eleven)
1	*satu*	(one)	21	*dua puluh satu*	(twenty-one)
2	*dua*	(two)	31	*tiga puluh satu*	(thirty-one)
3	*tiga*	(three)	41	*empat puluh satu*	(forty-one)
4	*empat*	(four)	51	*lima puluh satu*	(fifty-one)
5	*lima*	(five)	61	*enam puluh satu*	(sixty-one)
6	*enam*	(six)	71	*tujuh puluh satu*	(seventy-one)
7	*tujuh*	(seven)	81	*lapan puluh satu*	(eighty-one)
8	*lapan*	(eight)	91	*sembilan puluh satu*	(ninety-one)
9	*sembilan*	(nine)	100	*satu ratus/seratus*	(one hundred)
10	*sepuluh*	(ten)	1000	*satu ribu/seribu*	(one thousand)
			100000	*seratus ribu*	(one hundred thousand)

Examples of indefinite cardinal numbers are:

berpuluh-puluh/puluhan	(tens of)
beratus-ratus/ratusan	(hundreds of)
beribu-ribu/ribuan	(thousands of)
tiap/tiap-tiap/setiap	(every)
seluruh	(whole)
segala/sekalian/semua	(all)
sedikit	(few)
beberapa	(several/few/some)
separuh/setengah	(half)

ramai/banyak (many/a lot of)

Cardinal numbers are usually used with what is generally known as numerical co-efficients. Though they are gradually being discarded in Bahasa Indonesia, they are still widely used in Malay. Some of the commonly used numerical co-efficients are:

biji - for fruits

buah - for objects of uncertain shape like house, radio etc.

ekor - for animals

orang - for human beings

keping - for objects that are wide, thin but hard such as picture or biscuit

helai - for objects that are soft and wide such as paper or cloth

bidang - for land

batang - for objects that are long such as pencil, road or river

e.g. *Saya makan **sebiji** telur setiap pagi.*
(I eat an egg every morning.)

*Tiap-tiap pagi Ahmad makan **dua** keping roti.*
(Every morning Ahmad eats two pieces of bread.)

*Sepuluh **orang** kawannya sudah berkumpul di rumahnya.*
(Ten of his friends have gathered at his house.)

*Ibu membeli **seekor** ayam.*
(Mother bought a hen.)

*Orang itu ada dua **buah** lemari buku.*
(That person has two bookcases.)

Ordinal number is formed when ***ke-*** is added to a cardinal number. The ordinal number is followed by the relative pronoun ***yang***, which is, however, often dropped:

e.g. *Ahmad menang* ***tempat [yang] kedua***.
(Ahmad won second place.)

Pemenang [yang] ketiga *menerima hadiah wang tunai.*
(The third winner receives a cash award.)

However, when referring to 'the first' the prefix ***ke-*** cannot be used. Instead, '***pertama***' is used.

e.g. ***Jilid [yang] pertama*** *buku itu sedang dijual*. (not *kesatu*)
(The first volume of the book is on sale.)

Fractions are formed by using the prefix ***per-***.

e.g.	1/2	*satu perdua/setengah*	(half)
	1/3	*satu pertiga*	(one third)
	1/4	*satu perempat/satu suku*	(one quarter)
	3/4	*tiga perempat/tiga suku*	(three quarter)

Exercise 5. Fill in the blanks with suitable numerical co-efficients.

e.g.

Saya makan __________ *telur setiap pagi.* (I eat __________ egg every morning.)	*Saya makan* ***sebiji*** *telur setiap pagi.* (I eat an egg every morning.)
Ahmad makan dua __________ *roti saja.* (Ahmad eats two __________ of bread only)	*Ahmad makan dua* ***keping*** *roti saja.* (Ahmad eats two **pieces** of bread only.)

1. *Semalam saya membeli lima* __________ *pensel.*
   (Yesterday I bought 5 pencils.)

2. *Abdullah ada lima* __________ *kemeja baru.*
   (Abdullah has five new shirts.)

3. *Ada se*__________ *tanah kosong di belakang rumah saya.*
   (There is a __________ of empty land behind my house.)

4. *Adik saya adalah se*__________ *pengakap.*
   (My younger brother is a boy scout.)

5. *Dia memberi saya dua* __________ *roti.*
   (He gives me two __________ of bread.)

6. *Kucing saya menangkap lima* __________ *tikus semalam.*
   (My cat caught five rats last night.)

7. *Di dalam rumah saya ada tiga* __________ *bilik.*
   (In my house there are three rooms.)

8. *Taib sudah makan tiga* __________ *durian sendiri.*
   (Taib ate three durians himself.)

9. *Dia menulis namanya di se*__________ *kertas.*
   (He wrote his name on a __________ of paper.)

10. *Adik saya ada dua* __________ *guli.*
    (My younger brother has two marbles.)

Exercise 6. Fill in the blanks with suitable indefinite cardinal numbers.

e.g.

__________ *orang melihat wayang gambar.* (__________ watch cinema shows.)	***Ramai*** *orang melihat wayang gambar.* (**Many** people watch cinema shows.)
Salih ada __________ *buku di rumah.*	*Salih ada* ***banyak*** *buku di rumah.*

(Salih has __________ books at home.)

(Salih has **many** books at home.)

1. __________ *kehendak Ahmad dipenuhi oleh ibunya.*
   (__________ Ahmad's wishes are fulfilled by his mother.)
2. *Lelaki itu memberi* __________ *daripada hartanya kepada kawannya.*
   (The man gave __________ of his property to his friend.)
3. *Hanya ada* __________ *orang penonton di pertandingan itu.*
   (There is only __________ spectators at the competition.)
4. __________ *orang menghadiri rapat umum itu.*
   (__________ people attended the mass meeting.)
5. *Di dalam hutan ada* __________ *pokok.*
   (In the jungle there are __________ trees.)
6. __________ *murid akan melawat pulau itu.*
   (__________ the pupils will visit the island.)
7. __________ *dunia tahu hal itu.*
   (The __________ world knows about the incident.)
8. __________ *orang akan mati.*
   (__________ people will die.)
9. *Saya hanya ada* __________ *wang di dalam bank.*
   (I have only __________ money in the bank.)
10. *Luas padang itu* __________ *ekar.*
    (The width of the field is __________ acre.)

8D. Word Formation

Prefix *ter-*

Prefix ***ter-***, when added to verbs, will not change the functional form of the root words. The word formed will still remain a verb.

However the prefix will modify its meaning. Prefix ***ter-*** has several functions. The most important of which are:

(a) indicating an accidental (*tiada sengaja*) or sudden (*dengan tiba-tiba*) action, e.g.

Dia ***terpijak*** *ekor kucing itu.* (He accidentally stepped on the cat's tail.)	=	*Dia* ***memijak*** *ekor kucing itu* ***dengan tiada sengaja.***
Motokar itu ***terlanggar*** *tiang.* (The car collided into the pole accidentally.)	=	*Motokar itu* ***melanggar*** *tiang* ***dengan tiada sengaja.***

(b) indicating possibility or practicability, e.g.

Kami tidak ***terdaki*** *gunung tinggi itu.* (We are unable to climb the high mountain.)	=	*Kami tidak* ***dapat mendaki*** *gunung tinggi itu.*
Peti berat itu tidak ***terangkat*** *oleh Ahmad.* (The heavy box could not be lifted by Ahmad.)	=	*Peti berat itu tidak* ***dapat diangkat*** *oleh Ahmad.*

(c) indicating a completed action, e.g.

Makanan sudah ***tersaji*** *di atas meja.* (Food has been served on the table.)	=	*Makanan* ***sudah disaji*** *di atas meja.*
Tingkap rumah itu sudah ***tertutup.*** (The windows of the house have been closed.)	=	*Tingkap rumah itu* ***sudah ditutup.***

Exercise 7. Replace phrases in bold with verbs using the prefix ***ter-*.**

e.g.

*Dia **dengan tiada sengaja dengar** berita itu.* (He heard the news unintentionally.)	*Dia **terdengar** berita itu.*
*Dia **dengan tiada sengaja jumpa** lima puluh dolar di tepi jalan.* (He accidentally found fifty dollars by the roadside.)	*Dia **terjumpa** lima puluh dolar di tepi jalan.*

1. *Budak lelaki itu **jatuh dengan tiada sengaja**.*
   (The boy fell accidentally.)
2. *Lelaki itu **dengan tiada sengaja minum** racun.*
   (The man drank poison accidentally.)
3. *Ali **dengan tiada sengaja nampak** pencuri itu.*
   (Ali saw the thief accidentally.)
4. *Dia **dengan tiada sengaja baca** berita itu.*
   (He read the news accidentally.)
5. *Halimah **dengan tiada sengaja ambil** buku kawannya.*
   (Halimah took her friend's book accidentally.)
6. *Dia **dengan tiada sengaja sepak** kayu itu.*
   (He kicked the wood accidentally.)
7. *Polis itu **dengan tiada sengaja tembak** kawannya.*
   (The policeman shot his friend accidentally.)
8. *Dia **dengan tiba-tiba ingat** hendak pulang ke kampung.*
   (He suddenly thinks of going back to the village.)

9. *Saya* ***dengan tiba-tiba jaga*** *pada pukul lima.*
   (I suddenly woke up at five.)

10. *Dia* ***dengan tiada sengaja tidur*** *di kelas.*
   (He unintentionally fell into sleep in the classroom.)

Exercise 8. Replace phrases in bold with verbs using the prefix ***ter-***.

e.g.

Buku itu tidak ***dapat dibeli*** *oleh Ahmad.* (The book could not be bought by Ahmad.)	*Buku itu tidak* ***terbeli*** *oleh Ahmad.*
Budak lelaki itu ***sudah dipilih*** *menjadi ketua murid.* (The boy was chosen as a prefect.)	*Budak lelaki itu* ***terpilih*** *menjadi ketua murid.*

1. *Soalan itu tidak* ***dapat dijawab*** *oleh Ali.*
   (The question could not be answered by Ali.)
2. *Tulisan itu tidak* ***dapat dibaca*** *oleh guru.*
   (The writing could not be read by the teacher.)
3. *Hutang itu tidak* ***dapat dibayar*** *oleh negara.*
   (The debt could not be paid by the country.)
4. *Kuman tidak* ***dapat dilihat*** *oleh mata kasar.*
   (Germs could not be seen by the naked eyes.)
5. *Suara itu tidak* ***dapat didengar*** *oleh kita.*
   (The voice could not be heard by us.)
6. *Pencuri itu* ***sudah ditangkap.***
   (The thief has been caught.)

7. *Buku-bukunya* ***sudah disusun*** *di atas meja*.
(His books have been arranged on the table.)

8. *Wangnya* ***sudah disimpan*** *dengan baik*.
(His money has been safely kept.)

9. *Pintu* ***sudah dikunci.***
(The door has been locked.)

10. *Pelita belum* ***dipasang.***
(The lamp has not been lit.)

LESSON 9

9A. Conversation

Kegemaran
(Hobbies)

Amin: *Saudara Ali, bolehkah saya bertanya?*
(Mr. Ali, may I ask you a question?)

Ali: *Oh, boleh.*
(Oh, yes.)

Amin: *Apakah kegemaran saudara?*
(What are your hobbies?)

Ali: *Kegemaran saya ialah mengumpul setem.*
(My hobby is collecting stamps.)

Amin: *Mengapa saudara suka mengumpul setem?*
(Why do you like to collect stamps?)

Ali: *Faedah mengumpul setem banyak sekali. Kita akan tahu sejarah sesebuah negeri dan bagaimana rakyatnya hidup. Bagaimana dengan saudara? Apakah kegemaran saudara?*
(There are many advantages of collecting stamps. We can learn about the history of a country and how her people live. What about you? What are your hobbies?)

Amin: *Kegemaran saya banyak. Saya suka melukis, menari dan menyanyi.*
(My hobbies are many. I like to paint, dance and sing.)

Ali: *Lagu-lagu apa yang paling saudara sukai?*
(What songs do you like best?)

Amin: *Saya paling suka lagu Melayu asli.*
(I like Malay folk songs the best.)

Ali: *Oh, saudara ini rupanya seorang pencinta lagu Melayu asli.*
(Oh, apparently you are a lover of Malay folk songs.)

9B. Structure

Read the following sentences carefully.

SUBJECT	VERB + OBJECT	ADVERBIALS
Guru Teacher	*memuji budak lelaki itu* praised the boy	*kelmarin.* yesterday.
Budak lelaki itu The boy	*menolong kawannya* helped his friend	*di sekolah.* in school.
Polis Police	*telah menangkap orang itu* apprehended that person	*dua hari yang lalu.* two days ago.
Orang itu That person	*memukul Ali* beats Ali	*di luar sekolah.* outside the school.
Kita We	*menyokong orang itu* support that person	*dengan sepenuh hati.* whole-heartedly.

Exercise 1. Substitute the verb in the model sentence with the one given.

e.g   *Kita* ***melatih*** *orang itu*
(We train that person.)

membela (to defend)   *Kita* ***membela*** *orang itu.*
(We defend that person.)

memeriksa (to examine)	*Kita **memeriksa** orang itu.* (We examine that person.)
melawat (to visit)	*Kita **melawat** orang itu.* (We visit that person.)
mendidik (to educate)	*Kita **mendidik** orang itu.* (We educate that person.)

1. *mencium* (to kiss)
2. *mendakap* (to embrace)
3. *mendera* (to flog)
4. *mengejek* (to tease)
5. *menelefon* (to telephone)
6. *mengejar* (to chase)
7. *memfitnah* (to slander)
8. *menggaji* (to employ)
9. *menggambar* (to make a picture of)
10. *mengganggu* (to disturb)

Exercise 2. Give negative answers to the following questions.

e.g.

Adakah dia mendakwa orang itu? (Did he sue that person?)	*Tidak, dia tidak mendakwa orang itu.* (No, he did not sue that person.)
Adakah peguam membantu orang itu? (Did the lawyer help that person?)	*Tidak, peguam tidak membantu orang itu.* (No, the lawyer did not help that person.)
Adakah hakim mendenda orang itu? (Did the judge fine that person?)	*Tidak, hakim tidak mendenda orang itu.* (No, the judge did not fine that person.)

Adakah saudara menipu orang itu? (Did you cheat that person?)	*Tidak, saya tidak menipu orang itu.* (No, I did not cheat that person.)

1. *Adakah jururawat merawat orang sakit itu?* (Did the nurse treat the patient?)
2. *Adakah guru itu membimbing muridnya?* (Did the teacher guide his students?)
3. *Adakah perempuan itu mengasuh anaknya?* (Did the woman nurture her child?)
4. *Adakah saudara mengacau gadis itu?* (Did you disturb the girl?)
5. *Adakah saudara menguji budak itu?* (Did you test the child?)
6. *Adakah penyamun menyamun orang itu?* (Did the robber rob that person?)
7. *Adakah polis menembak orang itu?* (Did the policeman shoot that person?)
8. *Adakah peguam itu memanggil saksinya?* (Did the lawyer call his witness?)
9. *Adakah hakim mencela peguam itu?* (Did the judge criticise the lawyer?)
10. *Adakah dia menculik saudagar itu?* (Did he kidnap the businessman?)

Exercise 3. Change the folowing statements into questions.

e.g.

*Hakim **sudah** menyaman orang salah itu.*	***Sudahkah** hakim menyaman orang salah itu?*

(The judge has summoned the criminal.)

(Has the judge summoned the criminal?)

Gurubesar ***mahu*** *menyebat budak itu.*
(The principal wants to beat the child.)

Mahukah *gurubesar menyebat budak itu?*
(Does the principal want to beat the child?)

Dia ***dapat*** *memecat orang itu.*
(He can dismiss that person.)

Dapatkah *dia memecat orang itu?*
(Can he dismiss that person?)

Dia ***dapat*** *memaksa orang itu.*
(He can force that person.)

Dapatkah *dia memaksa orang itu?*
(Can he force that person?)

1. *Ali* ***sudah*** *menjemput orang itu.*
   (Ali has invited that person.)
2. *Amin* ***dapat*** *membayar orang itu.*
   (Amin can pay that person.)
3. *Orang kampung* ***mahu*** *membelasah pencuri itu.*
   (The kampung folk want to cane the thief.)
4. *Doktor* ***mahu*** *membedah pesakit itu.*
   (The doctor wishes to operate on the patient.)
5. *Kita* ***dapat*** *mengepung penjahat itu.*
   (We can surround the criminal.)
6. *Dia* ***sudah*** *menghalau pengemis itu.*
   (He has chased the beggar away.)
7. *Dia* ***mahu*** *menyapa orang itu.*
   (He wishes to speak to that person.)
8. *Perempuan itu* ***mahu*** *memeluk anaknya.*
   (The woman wants to embrace her child.)
9. *Ibu tiri* ***sudah*** *menyeksa anak tirinya.*
   (The step-mother has tortured her step-child.)

10. *Mereka* ***dapat*** *menuduh orang itu.*
(They can accuse that person.)

Exercise 4. Answer the following questions by using the words supplied.

e.g.

Bila dia akan mengundang tamu itu? - *sekarang* (When is he going to invite the guest? - now)	*Dia akan mengundang tamu itu sekarang.* (He is going to invite the guest now.)
Bila dia mengugut orang itu? - *malam tadi* (When did he intimidate the man? - last night)	*Dia mengugut orang itu malam tadi.* (He intimidated the man last night.)
Bila polis akan menyoal orang itu? - *minggu depan* (When will the police question that person? - next week)	*Polis akan menyoal orang itu minggu depan.* (The police will question that person next week.)
Bila lelaki itu membelasah anaknya? - *minggu lalu* (When did that man beat his child? - last week)	*Lelaki itu membelasah anaknya minggu lalu.* (That man beat his child last week.)

1 *Bila dia menyindir orang itu? - pagi tadi*
(When did he make insinuation about the person? - this morning

2. *Bila doktor menyuntik budak itu? - tahun lalu*
(When did the doctor inoculate the child? - last year)

3. *Bila dia mengajar budak itu? - tiap-tiap hari*
(When does he teach the child? - every day)

4. *Bila dia menegur orang itu? - kelmarin*
(When did he greet that person? - yesterday)

5. *Bila dia mencemuh orang itu? - kelmarin dulu*
(When did he insult that person? - the day before yesterday)

6. *Bila dia mencerca orang itu? - semalam*
(When did he abuse that person? - last night)

7. *Bila kerajaan akan melantik orang itu? - minggu depan*
(When will the government appoint that person? - next week)

8. *Bila anjing menggigit orang itu? - minggu lalu*
(When did the dog bite that person? - last week)

9. *Bila Yusuf menggertak orang itu? - kelmarin*
(When did Yusuf threaten that person? - yesterday)

10. *Bila kerajaan akan mengganjar orang itu? - tahun depan*
(When is the government going to reward that person? - next year)

9C. Grammar

Adverbs

An adverb modifies a verb, an adjective or another adverb. It is this function of adverb that distinguishes it from other parts of speech.

e.g.

Bangunan ***tinggi*** *itu bagus.*	*Burung itu terbang* ***tinggi.*** (The bird flies **high**.)

(The **tall** building is beautiful.)
[*tinggi* modifies the noun *bangunan*; it is an adjective.]

[*tinggi* modifies the verb **flies**; it is an adverb.]

Esok *hari Rabu.*
(**Tomorrow** is Wednesday.)
[*Esok* equates the noun phrase hari *Rabu*; it is a noun.]

Esok *saya datang.*
(**Tomorrow** I will come.)
[*Esok* modifies the verb *datang*; it is an adverb.]

Saudara tidak bersungguh -sungguh.
(You are not **serious**.)
[*bersungguh-sungguh* modifies the pronoun *Saudara*; it is an adjective.]

Kita bekerja bersungguh-sungguh.
(We worked **seriously**.)
[*bersungguh-sungguh* modifies the verb *bekerja*; it is an adverb.]

An adverb can be placed at the front, middle or the end of a sentence, e.g.

1. *Budak itu berlari* ***dengan cepat.***
   (The child runs **quickly**.)

   Dengan cepat, *budak itu berlari.*
   (**Quickly**, the child runs.)

   Budak itu, ***dengan cepat****, berlari.*
   (The child **quickly** runs.)

2. *Ia akan ke pejabat pos* ***esok.***
   (He will go to the post office **tomorrow.**)

   Esok *dia akan pergi ke pejabat pos.*
   (***Tomorrow*** he will go to the post office.)

   Dia, ***esok****, akan pergi ke pejabat pos.*
   (He, **tomorrow**, will go to the post office.)

3. *Ibu sedang memasak* ***di dapur***.
(Mother is cooking **in the kitchen**.)

Di dapur, *ibu sedang memasak.*
(**In the kitchen**, mother is cooking.)

Ibu, ***di dapur***, *sedang memasak.*
(Mother, [who is] **in the kitchen**, is cooking.)

The use of adverb is optional. It can be left out altogether. The sentences above can thus be written as follows:

1. *Budak itu berlari.*

2. *Ia akan pergi ke pejabat pos.*

3. *Ibu sedang memasak.*

Types of Adverbs

(a) Adverbs of manner – indicating the manner of action, e.g.

Dia berjalan ***perlahan-lahan***.
(He walks **slowly**.)

Abang bekerja ***keras***.
(Elder brother is working **hard**.)

Hujan turun ***dengan tiba-tiba***.
(Rains fall **suddenly**.)

(b) Adverbs of place – indicating the place of action, e.g.

Dia tinggal di ***sini***.
(He lives **here**.)

Perempuan itu pergi ***ke bandar***.
(The woman goes **to the city**.)

Emak sudah balik ***dari pasar***.
(Mother has returned **from the market**.)

(*c*) Adverbs of time – indicating the time of action, e.g.

Dia tiba ***pagi ini****.*
(He arrived **this morning**.)

Saya berhenti ***sebentar sahaja****.*
(I stop for **only a while.**)

Dia ***selalu*** *membaca buku agama.*
(He **always** reads religious books.)

(*d*) Adverbs of degree – indicating the degree of adjective, e.g.

Malam itu ***sangat*** *gelap.*
(The night is **very** dark.)

Dia sudah gila ***betul****.*
(He is **really** mad.)

Budak itu ***amat*** *pandai.*
(The child is **very** clever.)

Orang itu kaya ***sekali****.*
(That person is **very** rich.)

Exercise 5. Take out the adverbs from the following sentences.

e.g.

Dia sudah bertolak ke Kuala Lumpur. (He has left for Kuala Lumpur.)	*Dia sudah bertolak.* (He has left.)
Budak itu tidur dengan nyenyak. (The child sleeps soundly.)	*Budak itu tidur.* (The child sleeps.)

1. *Ali tidur di rumah kawannya.*
   (Ali slept in his friend's house.)

2. *Yusuf sedang bersiar-siar di kebun bunga itu.*
   (Yusuf is strolling in the garden.)

3. *Bayi itu menangis semalam-malaman.*
   (The baby cried the whole night.)

4. *Saya akan belayar minggu depan.*
   (I will set sail next week.)

5. *Lelaki itu bercakap dahulu.*
   (The man spoke first.)

6. *Dia sudah menerima surat itu daripada abangnya.*
   (He has received the letter from his elder brother.)

7. *Dia meninggalkan tempat itu dengan segera.*
   (He left the place immediately.)

8. *Murid-murid belajar dengan tekun.*
   (The pupils study hard.)

9. *Dia membaca surat itu dengan teliti.*
   (He reads the letter carefully.)

10. *Mereka berbual dengan mesra.*
    (They talked intimately.)

Exercise 6. Underline the adverbs of degree in the following sentences.

e.g.

Saya kurang sihat hari ini. (I am less well today.)	*Saya* ***kurang*** *sihat hari ini.*
Hari ini panas sungguh. (Today is very hot.)	*Hari ini panas* ***sungguh****.*

1. *Gadis itu amat cantik.*
   (The girl is very beautiful.)

2. *Harga buku ini mahal benar.*
(The price of this book is very high.)

3. *Dia sudah gila betul.*
(He is really crazy.)

4. *Harga rumah sangat mahal sekarang.*
(The price of houses is very high now.)

5. *Layanan di kedai itu kurang memuaskan.*
(The service at the shop is less satisfying.)

6. *Saya cukup penat.*
(I am tired enough.)

7. *Rumah itu bagus sekali.*
(The house is very good.)

8. *Budak itu terlalu nakal.*
(The child is extremely naughty.)

9. *Anak itu terlampau manja.*
(The child is too pampered.)

10. *Kerja itu hampir siap.*
(The work is nearly ready.)

9D. Word Formation

Adverb-forming Affixes

Adverbs can be formed by reduplication with or without affixation. The most commonly used affixes are ***ter-***, ***ber-*** and ***se-nya***.

e.g. *Dia berkahwin* ***diam-diam*** *sahaja.*
(He **quietly** married.)

Mereka masuk ke bilik darjah ***dua-dua***.
(They entered the classroom two by two.)

Abang pulang ***tergesa-gesa***.
(Brother goes home **hurriedly**.)

Dia menangis ***terisak-isak.***
(He cried **sobbingly** [sobbed].)

Dia membelanjakan wangnya ***berdikit-dikit***.
(He spent his money **bit by bit**.)

Dia makan ***berjam-jam*** *lamanya.*
(He eats **for hours**.)

Dia tinggal di sana ***selama-lamanya***.
(He lives there **forever**.)

Buku ini akan siap ***selekas-lekasnya*** *dua hari lagi.*
(The book will be ready in two days at **the earliest.**

There are adverbs which are formed by the suffix ***-nya*** or the affix ***se-nya*** without reduplication.

e.g. ***Sebenarnya*** *saya sudah tinggal dua tahun di sini.*
(**Actually**, I have been living here for two years.)

Rupanya *dia tidak ada di rumah.*
(**Apparently**, he was not at home.)

Nampaknya *mereka akan berjaya lagi tahun ini.*
(**Evidently**, they are going to succeed again this year.)

Sepatutnya *engkaulah yang memegang jawatan ini.*
(**By right**, you should be holding this post.)

There are also a few adverbs which take the prefix ***se-*** and the affix ***se-an***.

e.g. *Mereka datang* ***serempak.***
(They came together.)

Peristiwa itu berlaku ***serentak***.
(The incident happened at the same time.)

Mereka tidak tidur ***semalaman***.
(They did not sleep the whole night.)

Dia merasa letih selepas bekerja ***seharian***.
(He feels tired after working the whole day.)

Exercise 7. Take out the adverbs from the following sentences.

e.g.

Mereka membuat kerja itu dengan hati-hati. (They did the work carefully.)	*Mereka membuat kerja itu.* (They did the work.)
Dia pergi berhari-hari lamanya. (He went for days.)	*Dia pergi.* (He went.)

1. *Siang-siang dia sudah datang.*
   (He arrived very early.)
2. *Mereka berdiri tegak-tegak.*
   (They stood upright.)
3. *Dia merenung muka adiknya lama-lama.*
   (He stared at his younger brother for a long time.)
4. *Lelaki itu berjalan terhuyung-huyung.*
   (The man walked unsteadily.)
5. *Pelajar itu belajar dengan rajin.*
   (The student studies diligently.)
6. *Perempuan itu menangis tersedu-sedu.*
   (The woman cried sobbingly.)
7. *Semua permohonan hendaklah sampai selewat-lewatnya pada 1hb. Januari.*
   (All applications should arrive by the first of January at the latest.)

8. *Mereka akan sampai selambat-lambatnya setengah jam lagi.*
   (They will arrive in half an hour at the latest.)
9. *Mereka duduk berkelompok-kelompok.*
   (They sat in groups.)
10. *Kita pergi ke sekolah bersama-sama.*
    (We go to school together.)

Exercise 8. Underline the adverbs in the following sentences.

e.g.

Sebaiknya kita tidak menjawab pertanyaan itu. (It's best that, we do not answer the question.)	***Sebaiknya*** *kita tidak menjawab pertanyaan itu.*
Agaknya dia marah malam tadi. (Perhaps, he was angry last night.)	***Agaknya*** *dia marah malam tadi.*

1. *Barangkali saya tidak dapat datang hari ini.*
   (Perhaps, I cannot come today.)
2. *Semestinya kita taat kepada ibu bapa.*
   (Certainly, we must obey our parents.)
3. *Seharusnya kita menolong lelaki miskin itu.*
   (By right, we must help the poor man.)
4. *Sesungguhnya saya tidak berbohong.*
   (Really, I did not lie.)
5. *Sebetulnya lelaki itu tidak bersalah.*
   (In reality, the man was not guilty.)
6. *Sememangnya dia harus bersukaria.*
   (Indeed, he should be merry.)

7. *Sewajarnya seorang isteri menolong suaminya.*
(Naturally, a wife should help her husband.)

8. *Agaknya betul kata engkau.*
(Perhaps, your words are correct.)

9. *Rupanya kita akan berHari Raya pada hari Sabtu.*
(Apparently, we will celebrate Hari Raya on Saturday.)

10. *Nampaknya kita kalah lagi.*
(Evidently, we will lose again.)

LESSON 10

10A. Conversation

Adik-beradik
(Brothers and sisters)

Yuming: *Saudara Aziz, bolehkah saya tumpang tanya?*
(Mr. Aziz, may I ask a question?)

Aziz: *Boleh, tanyalah.*
(Yes, please ask.)

Yuming: *Berapa umur saudara?*
(How old are you?)

Aziz: *Umur saya dua puluh tahun.*
(I am twenty years old.)

Yuming: *Ada berapa orang di rumah saudara?*
(How many people are there in your house?)

Aziz: *Saya ada seorang datuk, bapa, ibu, abang dan kakak di rumah.*
(I have a grandfather, father, mother, elder brother and elder sister at home.)

Yuming: *Berapa umur datuk saudara? Masih sihatkah beliau?*
(How old is your grandfather? Is he still healthy?)

Aziz: *Datuk saya sudah berumur delapan puluh tahun, tapi beliau masih sihat.*
(My grandfather is already eighty, but he is still healthy.)

Yuming: *Bagaimana dengan bapa dan ibu saudara?*
(How about your father and mother?)

Aziz: *Bapa saya sudah berumur enam puluh tahun dan ibu saya sudah lima puluh lima.*
(My father is already sixty and my mother is fifty-five.)

Yuming: *Berapa umur abang dan kakak saudara?*
(How old are your elder brother and sister?)

Aziz: *Abang saya sudah berumur dua puluh lapan tahun dan kakak saya dua puluh lima tahun.*
(My elder brother is twenty-eight years old and my elder sister is twenty-five.)

Yuming: *Saudara beruntung betul mempunyai kakak dan abang. Saya seorang adik beradik pun tak punya.*
(You are really fortunate to have an elder brother and an elder sister. I do not have a brother or sister at all.)

10B. Structure

Read the following sentences carefully.

SUBJECT	VERB + OBJECT	ADVERBIAL
Saya I	*sudah memesan buku itu* ordered the book	*kelmarin.* yesterday.
Ali Ali	*sudah menerima hadiah itu* received the gift	*dua hari yang lalu.* two days ago.
Ibu Mother	*sedang memasak nasi* is cooking rice	*di dapur.* in the kitchen.
Bapa Father	*membaca suratkhabar* is reading a newspaper	*di bilik duduk.* in the sitting room.
Kakak Elder sister	*akan menjahit baju itu* will sew the dress	*besok.* tomorrow.

Exercise 1. Substitute the word in the model answer with the one given.

e.g.	*Kita akan* ***mengurus*** *perkara itu besok.* (We will take care of the matter tomorrow.)
mencatat (to note down)	*Kita akan* ***mencatat*** *perkara itu besok.* (We will note down the matter tomorrow.)
membahas (to discuss)	*Kita akan* ***membahas*** *perkara itu besok.* (We will discuss the matter tomorrow.)
soal (the question)	*Kita akan membahas* ***soal*** *itu besok.* (We will discuss the question tomorrow.)
mengkaji (to study)	*Kita akan* ***mengkaji*** *soal itu besok.* (We will study the matter tomorrow.)

1. *mendengar* (to hear)
2. *mengupas* (to analyse)
3. *mengusut* (to enquire into)
4. *menyebut* (to mention)
5. *hal* (matter)
6. *menyiasat* (to investigate)
7. *menyelidiki* (to investigate)
8. *meneliti* (to study)
9. *menimbang* (to consider)
10. *meninjau* (to look at)

Exercise 2. Answer the following questions by using the words given.

e.g.

Question	*Answer*
Pengail itu sedang buat apa? - *mengail ikan* (What is the fisherman doing? - fishing)	*Pengail itu sedang mengail ikan.* (The fisherman is fishing.)
Peminjam itu sedang buat apa? - *meminjam wang* (What is the borrower doing? - borrowing money)	*Peminjam itu sedang meminjam wang.* (The borrower is borrowing money.)
Penunggang itu sedang buat apa? - *menunggang basikal* (What is the rider doing? - riding a bicycle)	*Penunggang itu sedang menunggang basikal.* (The rider is riding a bicycle.)

1. *Pemandu itu sedang buat apa? - memandu kereta*
   (What is the driver doing? - driving a car)

2. *Para penonton sedang buat apa? - menonton sandiwara*
   (What are the audience doing? - watching a play)

3. *Pengawal itu sedang buat apa? - mengawal keselamatan*
   (What is the guard doing? - maintaining security)

4. *Pelawat itu sedang buat apa? - melawat sekolah*
   (What is the visitor doing? - visiting schools)

5. *Perompak itu sedang buat apa? - merompak sebuah kedai*
   (What is the robber doing? - robbing a shop)

6. *Peminta sedekah itu sedang buat apa? - meminta sedekah*
   (What is the beggar doing? - begging for alms)
7. *Penjaga itu sedang buat apa? - menjaga rumah*
   (What is the watchman doing? - watching a house)
8. *Penjual itu sedang buat apa? - menjual buku*
   (What is the seller doing - selling books)
9. *Pengumpul itu sedang buat apa? - mengumpul setem*
   (What is the collector doing? - collecting stamps)
10. *Penderma itu sedang buat apa? - menderma wang*
    (What is the donor doing? - donating money)

Exercise 3. Answer the following questions by using the words supplied.

e.g.

Question	*Answer*
Pekebun itu membela apa? - *ayam* (What is the gardener rearing? - chicken)	*Pekebun membela ayam.* (The gardener is rearing chicken.)
Orang itu sedang membelah apa? - *buah betik* (What is the man cutting? - a papaya)	*Orang itu membelah buah betik.* (The man is cutting papaya.)

1. *Peladang itu sedang menganyam apa? - tikar*
   (What is the farmer weaving? - a mat)
2. *Orang itu sedang mengasah apa? - pisau*
   (What is the man sharpening? - a knife)
3. *Petani itu sedang membajak apa? - sawah*
   (What is the farmer ploughing? - a paddy field)

4. *Ibu sedang membancuh apa? - susu*
   (What is mother mixing? - milk)

5. *Kakak sedang membasuh apa? - kain*
   (What is elder sister washing? - clothes)

6. *Ahmad sedang memberus apa? - giginya*
   (What is Ahmad brushing? - his teeth)

7. *Kerajaan sedang membina apa? - perpustakaan baru*
   (What is the government building? - a new library)

8. *Budak lelaki itu sedang membongkar apa? - lacinya*
   (What is the boy ransacking? - his drawer)

9. *Mak Limah sedang mencencang apa? - daging*
   (What is aunt Limah mincing? - meat)

10. *Budak itu sedang mencubit apa? - tangan adiknya*
    (What is the boy pinching? - his younger brother [sister]'s hand)

Exercise 4. Change the following statements into questions.

e.g.

Statement	*Question*
*Dia **mahu** membayar hutangnya.* (He wants to pay his debts.)	***Mahukah** dia membayar hutangnya?* (Does he want to pay his debts?)
*Dia **boleh** menyimpan wang itu.* (He may keep the money?)	***Bolehkah** dia menyimpan wang itu?)* (May he keep the money?)

1. *Dia **mahu** menghantar anaknya ke sekolah.*
   (He wants to send his son to school.)

2. *Dia **boleh** memakai kasut kulit.*
   (He may wear leather shoes.)

3. *Dia* **boleh** *menyanyi lagu Melayu.*
   (He can sing Malay songs.)
4. *Dia* **mahu** *menanam modal di sini.*
   (He wants to invest here.)
5. *Dia* **mahu** *mengulas buku itu.*
   (He wants to review the book.)
6. *Dia* **boleh** *menolak cadangan itu.*
   (He can reject the proposal.)
7. *Dia* **boleh** *mengukir bunga-bungaan.*
   (He can carve flowers.)
8. *Dia* **mahu** *mengkaji masalah itu.*
   (He wants to study the problems.)
9. *Dia* **boleh** *menyadur cerita itu.*
   (He can adapt the story.)
10. *Dia* **boleh** *menyandang jawatan itu.*
   (He can hold the post.)

10C. Grammar

Interrogative Adverbs

Interrogative adverbs are interrogative words which require an adverb or an adverbial as an answer. There are four important interrogative adverbs in Malay: *bagaimana* (how), *di mana* (where), *bila* (when) and *mengapa* (why).

e.g.

Bagaimana *saudara pergi kerja?* (How do you go to work?)	*Saya pergi kerja* ***dengan bas***. (I go to work by bus.)
Bila *saudara sampai?* (When did you arrive?)	*Saya sampai* ***semalam.*** (I arrived yesterday.)

Saudara tinggal ***di mana****?*
(Where do you live?)

Saya tinggal ***di Woodlands****.*
(I live in Woodlands.)

Mengapa *budak lelaki itu menangis?*
(Why did the boy cry?)

Budak lelaki itu menangis ***kerana dimarah****.*
(The boy cried because he was scolded.)

Interrogative adverbs can also be formed by certain prepositions such as *untuk* and *dengan* (followed by *apa* or *siapa*).

e.g.

Untuk apa *dia bekerja keras?*
(For what does he work hard?)

Dia bekerja keras ***untuk mencari rezeki****.*
(He works hard to earn a living.)

Untuk siapa *dia membeli kamus itu?*
(For whom did he buy the dictionary?)

Dia membeli kamus itu ***untuk anak lelakinya****.*
(He bought the dictionary for his son.)

Dengan apa *guru menulis di papan hitam?*
(With what does the teacher write on the blackboard?)

Guru menulis ***dengan kapur*** *di papan hitam.*
(The teacher writes with a chalk on the blackboard.)

Dengan siapa *dia datang?*
(With whom did he come?)

Dia datang ***dengan kawannya****.*
(He came with his friends.)

Please note that *apa sebab* (what is the reason) is often used as a synonym of *mengapa*. *Mengapa* often becomes *kenapa* in colloquial speech. *Untuk apa* is synonymous with *buat apa*.

Exercise 5. Change the following statements into questions by using ***bagaimana***, ***bila***, ***mengapa*** and ***di mana***.

e.g.

Statement	*Question*
Dia mengambil buku itu ***dua hari yang lalu***. (He took the books two days ago.)	***Bila*** *dia mengambil buku itu?* (When did he take the books?)
Dia menjawab soalan itu ***dengan hati-hati.*** (He answered the question carefully.)	***Bagaimana*** *dia menjawab soalan itu?* (How did he answer the question?)
Pensel merah itu ***di atas meja***. (The red pencil is on the table.)	*Pensel merah itu* ***di mana****?* (Where is the red pencil?)
Yusuf tidak datang semalam ***kerana selesema***. (Yusuf did not come yesterday because of a cold.)	***Mengapa*** *Yusuf tidak datang semalam?* (Why did not Yusuf come yesterday?)

1. *Dia berlari* ***dengan pantas***.
   (He runs quickly.)
2. *Ahmad memandu keretanya* ***dengan laju***.
   (Ahmad drives his car fast.)
3. *Mereka akan menjalankan kerja itu* ***esok.***
   (They will carry out the job tomorrow.)
4. *Para tamu sudah sampai pada* ***pukul dua belas***.
   (The guests arrived at twelve o'clock.)
5. *Rumahnya* ***di luar kota***.
   (His house is outside the city.)

6. *Mereka berkelah* ***di pantai.***
(They are picnicking at the seaside.)

7. *Dia tinggal di rumah* ***kerana hujan***.
(He stayed at home because of the rain.)

8. *Dia mengantuk* ***kerana kurang tidur malam tadi***.
(He was sleepy because of insufficient sleep last night.)

9. *Dia tidak datang* ***sebab sakit***.
(He did not come because of illness.)

10. *Kamil tidak membeli barang itu* ***sebab terlalu mahal***.
(Kamil did not buy the thing because it was too expensive.)

Exercise 6. Change the following statements into questions by using ***dengan apa/siapa*** or ***untuk apa/siapa***.

e.g.

Statement	*Question*
Dia mengarang bunga itu ***untuk ibunya***. (She arranges the flowers for her mother.)	***Untuk siapa*** *dia mengarang bunga itu?* (For whom does she arrange the flowers?)
Lelaki tua itu berjalan ***dengan tongkat.*** (The old man walked with a stick.)	***Dengan apa*** *lelaki tua itu berjalan?* (With what did the old man walk?)

1. *Ahmad selalu berkelahi* ***dengan temannya***.
(Ahmad is always fighting with his friends.)

2. *Azman tinggal di rumah* ***dengan kakaknya***.
(Azman stays at home with his elder sister.)

3. *Dewi makan nasi* ***dengan kari***.
(Dewi eats rice with curry.)

4. *Dia membelah kayu* ***dengan kapak***.
   (He splits the wood with an axe.)

5. *Dia pergi ke bandar* ***untuk membeli kasut***.
   (He went to town to buy shoes.)

6. *Dia mencari duit* ***untuk anak-anaknya***.
   (He obtains money for his children.)

7. *Dia menelefon kawannya* ***untuk meminta nasihat***.
   (He telephoned his friend to ask for advice.)

8. ***Untuk tuanlah*** *lelaki itu datang kemari*.
   (It is for you that the man comes here.)

9. *Dia pergi ke sekolah* ***dengan bas***.
   (He goes to school by bus.)

10. *Dia memotong daging* ***dengan pisau***.
    (He cuts the meat with a knife.)

10D. Word Formation

Suffix *-kan*

Suffix ***-kan*** is an important suffix used to form transitive verbs. It is often used together with the prefix ***me-***, forming ***me-kan***. There is very little difference between ***-kan*** and ***me-kan***. The only difference may be that suffix ***-kan*** is often omitted in conversation and imperative sentences.

Suffix ***-kan*** can be added to nouns, adjectives and verbs. When it is added to nouns, it has four important functions:

(a) causative: to make the object adopt the characteristics of the root word (*menjadikan sebagai*)

e.g.

Mereka akan ***mencalonkan*** *Ahmad dalam pilihan raya ini.* (*calon*: candidate) (They will nominate Ahmad as a candidate in the general election.)	=	*Mereka akan m**enjadikan*** ***Ahmad sebagai calon*** *dalam pilihan raya ini.*
Dia ***mewakilkan*** *orang lain ke persidangan itu.* (*wakil:* representative) (He sent a representative to the meeting.)	=	*Dia* ***menjadikan orang lain sebagai wakil*** *ke persidangan itu.*

(b) to produce (*menghasilkan*)

e.g.

Percubaan itu tidak ***menelurkan*** *hasil*. (*telur*: an egg)
(The attempt does not produce any result.)

Bumi kita banyak ***membuahkan*** *padi*. (*buah*: fruit)
(Our land produces paddy in abundance.)

(c) to put the object into the noun represented by the root word (*memasukkan ke dalam*)

e.g.

Dia ***menyekolahkan*** *adik perempuannya.* (*sekolah*: school) (He sends his younger sister to school.)	=	*Dia* ***memasukkan*** *adik perempuannya* ***ke sekolah.***
Panglima Hitam ***menyarungkan*** *kerisnya.* (*sarung*: sheath) (Commander Hitam put his kris into the sheath.)	=	*Panglima Hitam* ***memasukkan ke dalam sarung*** *kerisnya.*

(d) to give the object something mentioned in the root word (*memberi*)

e.g.

Orang itu telah ***mendermakan*** *gajinya untuk anak-anak yatim*. (*derma*: donation)
(The man gave, as a donation, his salary to the orphans.)

Guru itu ***menghadiahkan*** *sebuah jam tangan kepada muridnya*. (*hadiah*: gift)
(The teacher gave, as a gift, a watch to his student.)

When ***me-kan*** is added to an adjective, it also has a causative effect and makes the object acquire the charateristics of the root word (*menyebabkan*, *menjadikan*).

e.g.

Lelaki itu akan ***membesarkan*** *rumahnya*. (*besar*: large)
(The man will enlarge his house.)

Adik selalu ***mengotorkan*** *meja saya*. (*kotor*: dirty)
(Younger brother always dirties my table.)

Exercise 7. Replace phrases in bold with verbs using the affix ***me-kan***.

e.g.

Orang-orang kampung ***menjadikan*** *orang baru itu* ***sebagai imam.*** (*imam*: Islamic religious leader) (The villagers make the newcomer an imam.)	=	*Orang-orang kampung* ***mengimamkan*** *orang baru itu.*
Polis telah ***memasukkan*** *orang jahat itu* ***ke dalam***	=	*Polis telah* ***memenjarakan*** *orang jahat itu.*

penjara.
(*penjara*: prison)
(The Police imprisoned the criminal.)

1. *Dia telah dapat* ***memasukkan*** *4 gol ke* ***dalam jaring***. (*jaring*: net)
   (He netted 4 goals.)

2. *Budak itu* ***memasukkan*** *wang sakunya* ***ke dalam tabung***. (*tabung*: money-box)
   (The child puts his pocket money into the money-box.)

3. *Mereka* ***memasukkan*** *buah-buah tempatan* ***ke dalam tin***. (*tin*: tin)
   (They put local fruits into the tin.)

4. *Gembala itu* ***memasukkan*** *lembu-lembunya* ***ke dalam kandang***. (*kandang*: pen)
   (The shepherd put his cows into the pen.)

5. *Perbuatan pemuda itu* ***memberi aib kepada*** *jirannya*. (*aib*: shame)
   (The young man's behaviour shames his neighbour.)

6. *Dia selalu* ***memberi nasihat kepada*** *adik lelakinya*. (*nasihat*: advice)
   (He always gives advice to his younger brother.)

7. *Dia tidak pernah* ***menaruh dendam terhadap*** *lelaki itu*. (*dendam*: grudge)
   (He never bore any grudge against the man.)

8. *Saya tidak pernah* ***mengeluarkan kata tentang*** *hal itu kepadanya*. (*kata*: word)
   (I have never said a word about the matter to him.)

9. *Asia Tenggara* ***mengeluarkan hasil*** *bijih timah yang banyak. (hasil*: produce)
   (Southeast Asia produces tin ore in abundance.)

10. *Budak-budak semua* ***menjadikan*** *Ahmad* ***sebagai tuan***.
(*tuan:* boss)
(All the children make Ahmad their boss.)

Exercise 8. Replace phrases in bold with verbs using the affix ***me-kan***.

e.g.

Dia sengaja ***menjadikan*** *suaminya* ***malas***. (She purposefully made her husband lazy.)	=	*Dia sengaja* ***memalaskan*** *suaminya*.
Berita itu tentu akan ***menjadikan suka*** *orang tua saya*. (The news will certainly make my parents happy.)	=	*Berita itu tentu akan* ***menyukakan*** *orang tua saya*.

1. *Pengangguranlah yang* ***menjadikan*** *saya* ***susah***.
(Unemployment made my life hard.)

2. *Jawapan itu* ***menjadikan*** *Ahmad* ***gusar***.
(The answer angered Ahmad.)

3. *Tindakan majikan* ***menjadikan*** *para pekerja* ***kecewa***.
(The employer's action disappointed the workers.)

4. *Ubat itu boleh* ***menjadikan*** *badan kita* ***kuat.***.
(The medicine can strenghten our body.)

5. *Kurang tidur boleh* ***menjadikan*** *badan* ***kurus***.
(Lack of sleep can cause loss of weight.)

6. *Orang kampung beramai-ramai* ***menjadikan*** *jalan itu* ***lapang***.
(The villagers work together to widen the road.)

7. *Senaman boleh* ***menjadikan*** *badan* ***cergas****.*
   (Exercise can activate the body.)

8. *Dia cuba* ***menjadikan*** *tanah itu* ***keras****.*
   (He tried to harden the soil.)

9. *Kita boleh* ***menjadikan*** *api dapur* ***kecil*** *dengan serta-merta.*
   (We can make the fire of the stove small immediately.)

10. *Sukan boleh* ***menjadikan*** *tubuh* ***cerdas****.*
    (Sports can make the body healthy.)

LESSON 11

11A. Conversation

Waktu
(Time)

Yaming: *Pukul berapa sekarang?*
(What is the time now?)

Yunus: *Sekarang sudah pukul lapan.*
(It is eight o'clock now.)

Yaming: *Tidak mungkin, jam saya baru menunjukkan pukul tujuh setengah. Jam saudara mungkin cepat.*
(Impossible, my watch shows just seven thirty. Your watch may be fast.)

Yunus: *Tidak mungkin. Jam saya ini jam baru. Pukul berapa kuliah saudara?*
(Impossible. My watch is new. When is your lecture?)

Yaming: *Kuliah saya mulai pukul sembilan. Marilah kita pergi sarapan, kemudian kita pergi kuliah bersama-sama. Kuliah saudara jam berapa?*
(My lecture begins at nine o'clock. Let us go for breakfast, and later go to lectures together. When is your first lecture?)

Yunus: *Kuliah saya jam sepuluh. Kuliah saudara sampai pukul berapa?*
(My lecture is at ten o'clock. Until what time are your lectures?)

Yaming: *Kuliah saya sampai pukul lima hari ini. Ada apa?*
(My lectures end at five o'clock. Is there anything?)

Yunus: *Tidak apa-apa. Kalau saudara lapang, saya ingin mengajak saudara berjalan-jalan di kampung Melayu.*
(Nothing. If you are free, I would like to ask you out for a trip to a Malay village.)

Yaming: *Oh, saya senang sekali berjalan-jalan di kampung Melayu. Pukul berapa kita pergi?*
(Oh, I am very keen on going for a trip to a Malay village. At what time shall we go?)

Yunus: *Pukul tujuh malam ini.*
(Seven o'clock tonight.)

Yaming: *Baik, saya akan tunggu saudara di bilik asrama saya.*
(Fine, I shall wait for you at my room in the hostel.)

11B. Structure

Read the following sentences carefully.

SUBJECT	VERB	OBJECT	ADVERBIAL
Dia He	*sudah menerima* has received	*surat itu.* the letter.	
Dia She	*sedang menjerang* is boiling	*air.* water.	
Halimah Halimah	*memotong* cuts	*kain* the cloth	*dengan gunting.* with a pair of scissors.
Perempuan itu The woman	*membungkus* wraps	*nasi* the rice	*dengan daun.* with leaves.
Dia He	*memberi* gives	*derma* a donation	*kepada sekolah itu.* to the school.

Exercise 1. Substitute the phrase given in the model sentence with the one given.

e.g.		*Dia sudah* ***membalas surat*** *itu.* (He has replied to the letter.)
	menjawab (to answer)	*Dia sudah* ***menjawab surat*** *itu.* (He has answered the letter.)
	mengoyak (to tear)	*Dia sudah* ***mengoyak surat*** *itu.* (He has torn the letter.)
	buku (a book)	*Dia sudah* ***mengoyak buku*** *itu.* (He has torn the book.)
	memesan (to order)	*Dia sudah* ***memesan buku*** *itu.* (He has ordered the book.)

1. *mencetak* (to print)
2. *mengutip* (to quote)
3. *menyemak* (go check)
4. *meminjam* (to borrow)
5. *kereta* (a car)
6. *menyewa* (to rent)
7. *rumah* (a house)
8. *menghuni* (to live in)
9. *mengunci* (to lock)
10. *mengetuk* (to knock)

Exercise 2. Answer the following questions by using the words supplied.

e.g.

Question	*Answer*
Dengan apa perempuan itu membungkus nasi? - *dengan daun* (With what did the woman	*Perempuan itu membungkus nasi dengan daun.* (The woman wrapped the rice with leaves.)

wrap the rice?
- with leaves)

Dengan apa lelaki itu menconteng mukanya?
- dengan arang
(With what did the man smear his face?
- with charcoal)

Lelaki itu menconteng mukanya dengan arang.
(The man smeared his face with charcoal.)

1. *Dengan apa lelaki itu menggaul nasinya? - dengan kuah*
(With what did the man mix his rice? - with gravy)
2. *Dengan apa dia menyumbat mulut botol itu? - gabus*
(With what did he stop up the mouth of the bottle? - a cork)
3. *Dengan apa dia menetak pokok itu? - sebilah kapak*
(What did he use to chop down the tree? - an axe)
4. *Dengan apa emak menudung hidangan itu? - tudung saji*
(What did mother use to cover the food? -a food cover)
5. *Dengan apa pekedai itu menimbang gula? - dacing*
(What did the shopkeeper use to weigh the sugar? - a weighing scale)
6. *Dengan apa dia menimbus lubang itu? - tanah*
(What did he use to fill the hole? - soil)
7. *Dengan apa lelaki itu menangkap burung? - jerat*
(What did the man use to catch birds? - a trap)
8. *Dengan apa kakak menapis air kopi? - penapis*
(What did elder sister use to filter the coffee? - a filter)
9. *Dengan apa lelaki itu menyisir rambut? - sikat*
(What did the man use to comb his hair? - a comb)
10. *Dengan apa emak menyapu lantai? - penyapu*
(What did mother use to sweep the floor? - a broom)

Exercise 3. Answer the following questions by using the words given.

e.g.

Question	*Answer*
Untuk apa pelajar-pelajar mendaki gunung itu? *- berkhemah* What did the students climb the mountain for ? - to camp)	*Pelajar-pelajar mendaki gunung itu untuk berkhemah.* (The students climbed the mountain to camp there.)
Untuk apa lelaki itu menggali lubang? *- menanam pokok* (What did the man dig the hole for? - to plant a tree)	*Lelaki itu menggali lubang untuk menanam pokok.* (The man dug the hole to plant a tree.)

1. *Untuk apa orang itu menderma wang? - membantu anak-anak yatim*
   (What did the man donate the money for? - to help the orphans)
2. *Untuk apa polis menggeledah rumah itu? - mencari senjata*
   (What did the police search the house for? - to search for weapons)
3. *Untuk apa kakak menggubah bunga? - perhiasan*
   (What did elder sister arrange the flowers for? - decoration)
4. *Untuk apa kakak menghiris bawang? - menggoreng telur*
   (What did elder sister slice the onion for? - to fry eggs)
5. *Untuk apa emak menjerang air? - membuat kopi*
   (What is mother boiling the water for? - to make coffee)
6. *Untuk apa orang itu mengembara? - mencari rezeki*
   (What is the man travelling for? - to look for a livelihood)

7. *Untuk apa kerajaan mengerah para pemuda? - berkhidmat dalam tentera*
(What did the government calling up the young men for? - to serve in the army)

8. *Untuk apa ibu memerah kelapa? - mengambil santannya*
(What is mother squeezing the coconut for? - to extract its milk)

9. *Untuk apa mereka menyingsing baju? - bekerja*
(What did they roll up their sleeves for? - to work)

10. *Untuk apa emak meramas tepung itu? - membuat kuih*
(What is mother kneading the flour for? - to make cake)

Exercise 4. Answer the following questions by using the words given.

e.g.

Question	*Answer*
Kepada siapa dia mengirim surat itu? - *emaknya.* (To whom did he send the letter? - his mother)	*Dia mengirim surat itu kepada emaknya.* (He sent the letter to his mother.)
Ke mana dia menghantar anak lelakinya? - *sekolah* (Where did he send his son to? - school)	*Dia menghantar anak lelakinya ke sekolah.* (He sent his son to school.)

1. *Kepada siapa dia memberi wang itu? - ketuanya*
(To whom did he give the money? - his boss)

2. *Kepada siapa dia mengucap terima kasih? - bapa Hasyim*
(To whom did he express his thanks? - Hasyim's father)

3. *Kepada siapa dia menulis surat itu? - orang tuanya*
   (To whom did he write the letter? - his parents)

4. *Kepada siapa dia meminta bantuan? - gurunya*
   (From whom did he ask for assistance? - his teacher)

5. *Kepada siapa dia melempar bola? - budak lelaki itu*
   (To whom does he throw the ball? - the boy)

6. *Ke mana dia mengutus surat itu? - Jakarta*
   (Where did he send the letter to? - Jakarta)

7. *Ke mana Ahmad membawa makanan itu? - rumah sakit*
   (Where did Ahmad bring the food to? - hospital)

8. *Ke mana anak lelaki itu mengikut ibunya? - pasar*
   (Where did the boy follow his mother to? - market)

9. *Ke mana dia mendayung sampannya? - tengah laut*
   (Where did he paddle his boat to? - the open sea)

10. *Ke mana dia memandang? - bukit itu*
    (Where was he looking to? - the hill)

11C. Grammar

Preposition

A preposition is a word which is placed before a noun or a pronoun to show its relationship with other words. Based on its function, a preposition can be classified into different classes.

(a) time: *pada* (on), *dalam* (in), *dari* (from), *hingga/sampai* (until/till), *semenjak/sejak* (since), *selama* (for).

e.g. ***Pada*** *hari Ahad, kita tidak bekerja.*
(On Sundays, we do not work.)

Dalam *masa dua jam, dia akan sampai.*
(In two hours' time, he will arrive.)

***Dari** sekarang, kita tidak boleh main-main lagi.*
(From now onwards, we cannot play any more.)

***Hingga** kini, saya tidak mahu bercakap dengan adik lelaki saya.*
(Until now, I do not wish to speak to my younger brother.)

***Sampai** hari ini, kami tidak mempedulikan dia lagi.*
(Until today we do not bother about him any more.)

*Dia berada di sini **sejak** dua hari yang lalu.*
(He has been here since two days ago.)

*Dia berkursus **selama** tiga bulan.*
(He attends the course for three months.)

(b) place: *di* (at), *ke* (to), *dari* (from), *pada* (with), *kepada* (to), *daripada* (from) and *dalam* (in).

e.g. *Saya tinggal **di** Bedok.*
(I live in Bedok.)

*Ahmad sudah pergi **ke** sekolah.*
(Ahmad has gone to school.)

*Surat itu datang **dari** Malaysia.*
(The letter came from Malaysia.)

*Saya menerima surat itu **daripada** Yusuf.*
(I received the letter from Yusuf.)

*Surat itu ada **pada** saya sekarang.*
(The letter is with me now.)

*Dia sudah mengirim bungkusan itu **kepada** emaknya.*
(He has sent the parcel to his mother.)

*Dia tidak berkata apa-apa **dalam** surat terakhirnya.*
(He did not say anything in his last letter.)

(c) accompaniment: *dengan* (with).

e.g. *Dia pergi* **dengan** *kawannya.*
(He went with his friend.)

Dia menunggu di pejabat **dengan** *Wahid.*
(He waits in the office together with Wahid.)

Ahmad sudah bernikah **dengan** *gadis itu.*
(Ahmad has contracted a marriage with the girl.)

(d) goal/purpose: *untuk* (for), *bagi* (for).

e.g. *Buku ini* **untuk** *kamu.*
(This book is for you.)

Dia pergi ke bandar **untuk** *mencari kerja.*
(He went to the city [in order] to look for a job.)

Kamus ini **bagi** *adik lelaki kamu.*
(This dictionary is for your younger brother.)

(e) cause/reason: *kerana* (because of), *sebab* (due to).

e.g. *Mati semut* **kerana** *gula.*
(Ants die because of sugar.)

Yamin tidak pergi **sebab** *sakit.*
(Due to illness, Yamin did not go.)

(f) instrument: *oleh* (by), *dengan* (by/with).

e.g. *Cerita ini dikarang* **oleh** *cikgu kita.*
(The story was written by our teacher.)

Ibu pergi ke pasar **dengan** *bas.*
(Mother goes to the market by bus.)

Ibu memotong kain **dengan** *gunting.*
(Mother cuts the cloth with a pair of scissors.)

(g) manner: *seperti/bagai* (is/like).

e.g. *Gadis itu cantik **seperti** bidadari.*
(The girl is beautiful as a nymph.)

*Lelaki itu menjerit **bagai** orang gila.*
(The man shouts like a mad man.)

A preposition is often used together with a noun phrase to form what is generally known as a prepositional phrase. Prepositional phrases can function as adverbials as shown in the examples above. Besides, they can also function as modifiers.

e.g. *Buku di **atas meja** itu buku saya.*
(The book on the table is my book.)

*Buku-buku **dalam almari** itulah kawan saya setiap hari.*
(The books in the cupboard are my friends every day.)

*Surat **daripada ayahnya** masih belum diterima.*
(The letter from his father has not been received.)

*Dia melihat jam **di dinding**.*
(He looked at the clock on the wall.)

Exercise 5. Fill in the blanks with suitable prepositions from the box below.

di	*pada*	*daripada*	*ke*	*dari*
kepada	*dalam*	*dengan*	*untuk*	*kerana*

1. *Mahmud sekarang bekerja ___________ Kuala Lumpur.*
   (Mahmud is working ___________ Kuala Lumpur.)

2. ___________ *hari Rabu, dia keluar dengan teman-temannya.*
   (___________ Wednesday, he went out with his friends.)

3. *Surat ini datang ___________ abang saya.*
   (The letter came ___________ my elder brother.)

4. *Mereka sudah pindah __________ rumah pangsa bulan lepas.*
   (They moved __________ a flat last month.)
5. *Saudara datang __________ mana?*
   (Where do you come __________?)
6. *Kita mesti memberi hormat __________ guru kita.*
   (We must give our respect __________ our teacher.)
7. *Dia tidak dapat tidur __________ keretapi.*
   (He cannot sleep __________ train.)
8. *Saya selalu pergi ke Kuala Lumpur __________ keretapi.*
   (I always go to Kuala Lumpur __________ train.)
9. *Dua helai baju ini __________ kakak kamu.*
   (These two dresses are __________ your elder sister.)
10. *Lelaki itu mati __________ sakit.*
    (The man died __________ illness.)

Exercise 6. Underline the prepositions in the following sentences.

1. *Ramai orang sedang bersembahyang di masjid.*
   (Many people are praying in the mosque.)
2. *Dia mengirim surat kepada orang tuanya.*
   (He sent a letter to his parents.)
3. *Mak Minah baru balik dari pasar.*
   (Mrs. Minah just returned from the market.)
4. *Dia tinggal bersama neneknya sejak kecil lagi.*
   (He has stayed with his grandmother since [he was] small.)
5. *Bapa bekerja sampai jauh malam.*
   (Father works until late at night.)
6. *Rumah itu dibeli oleh seorang saudagar.*
   (The house was bought by a businessman.)

7. *Hubungannya dengan saudagar itu amat mesra.*
(His relationship with the businessman is very close.)

8. *Keputusan untuk bersara sudah diambil.*
(The decision to retire has already been made.)

9. *Penjelasan dari ayahnya masih belum diperoleh.*
(An explanation from his father has not yet been acquired.)

10. *Hutangnya kepada kawan-kawannya sudah selesai dibayar.*
(His debts to his friends have been settled.)

11D. Word Formation

Suffix *-kan*

Suffix ***-kan***, when added to verbs, has two important meanings. When added to intransitive verbs, its function is causative; it causes the object to adopt the characteristics of the root word, (*menyebabkan*, *membuat*, *menjadi*).

e.g.

*Polis **membiarkan lepas** orang yang disyaki itu.* (*lepas*: to free) {The police freed the suspect.)	=	*Polis **melepaskan** orang yang disyaki itu.*
*Lagu itu **membuat** kita **jadi kantuk.*** (*kantuk:* sleepy) (The song makes us sleepy.)	=	*Lagu itu **mengantukkan** kita.*

When added to transitive verb, however, ***-kan*** means 'doing something for other people' (*membuat untuk orang lain*).

e.g.

*Ayah **membelikan** adik kasut baru.* (Father bought younger	=	*Ayah **membeli** kasut baru **untuk adik.*** (Father bought [a pair of]

brother [a pair of] new shoes.)		new shoes for younger brother.)
Saya ***membacakan*** *dia laporan itu.* (I read [to] him the report.)	=	*Saya* ***membaca*** *laporan itu* ***untuk dia***. (I read the report for him.)

This type of sentence is comparable to the 'Subject V(erb), O(object), O(object)' clause mentioned by Randolph Quirk in his *A University Grammar of English* (Longman, 1979, p. 169).

Exercise 7. Replace phrases in bold with verbs using the affix ***me-kan.***

e.g.

Seorang perompak telah membawa lari wang tunai kedai itu. (*lari*: to run) (A robber has run away with cash from the shop.)	=	*Seorang perompak* ***melarikan*** *wang tunai kedai itu.*
Dia ***membawa masuk*** *mesin taip ke dalam bilik.* (*masuk*: to enter) (He brought the typewriter into the room.)	=	*Dia* ***memasukkan*** *mesin taip ke dalam bilik.*

1. *Dia* ***membawa keluar*** *kotak rokok itu.* (*keluar*: to go out) (He took out the cigarette box.)
2. *Dia* ***membawa turun*** *layang-layang itu.* (*turun*: to come down) (He brought down the kite.)
3. *Dia* ***membawa pulang*** *motokar itu kepada tuannya.* (*pulang*: to return) (He brought back the car to its owner.)

4. *Kerajaan* ***membawa datang*** *guru-guru dari luar negeri.* (*datang*: to come)
(The government brought in teachers from overseas.)

5. *Para doktor tidak dapat* ***membuat supaya hidup*** *orang mati itu.* (*hidup*: to live)
(The doctors could not bring back to life the dead man.)

6. *Kuli-kuli sedang* ***membawa naik*** *barang-barang itu ke kapal.* (*naik:* to go up)
(The labourers are loading the goods onto the ship.)

7. *Sebuah bom telah* ***menjadikan runtuh*** *seluruh bandar.* (*runtuh*: to collapse)
(A bomb has caused the collapse of the city.)

8. *Setiap pagi ibu* ***menyuruh*** *saya* ***bangun*** *pada pukul enam.* (*bangun*: to wake up)
(Every morning mother wakes me up at six.)

9. *Ribut telah* ***menjadikan tumbang*** *pokok itu.* (*tumbang*: to fall)
(The storm has caused the tree to fall.)

10. *Letupan bom itu telah* ***menjadikan hancur*** *pertahanan musuh.* (*hancur*: to be destroyed)
(The explosion of the bomb destroyed the enemy's defence.)

Exercise 8. Replace phrases in bold with verbs using the affix **me-kan.**

e.g.

Ali ***mencari*** *pekerjaan* ***untuk*** *adik lelakinya.* (Ali finds a job for his younger brother.)	=	*Ali* ***mencarikan*** *adik lelakinya pekerjaan.*
Guru ***memberi*** *kerja rumah* ***kepada*** *kami.*	=	*Guru* ***memberikan*** *kami kerja rumah.*

(The teacher gives [to] us homework.)

1. *Ahmad* ***membawa*** *beg* ***untuk*** *ayahnya.*
   (Ahmad carries the bag for his father.)
2. *Ibu* ***memasak*** *nasi* ***untuk*** *ayah.*
   (Mother is cooking rice for father.)
3. *Dia* ***menulis*** *sepucuk surat* ***untuk*** *kawannya.*
   (He wrote a letter for his friend.)
4. *Aminah* ***membasuh*** *kain* ***untuk*** *ibunya.*
   (Aminah washes the clothes for her mother.)
5. *Osman* ***membeli*** *baju* ***untuk*** *isterinya.*
   (Osman bought a dress for his wife.)
6. *Yusuf* ***membuat*** *rumah* ***untuk*** *orang tuanya di kampung.*
   (Yusuf built a house for his parents in the village.)
7. *Kakak* ***mengikat*** *tali kasut* ***untuk*** *adik.*
   (Elder sister is tying the shoe lace for younger brother.)
8. *Dia* ***membuka*** *pintu* ***untuk*** *tamu.*
   (He opened the door for the guest.)
9. *Dia* ***menuang*** *secawan kopi* ***untuk*** *kawannya.*
   (He poured a cup of coffee for his friend.)
10. *Dia* ***menyimpan*** *cincin itu* ***untuk*** *kawannya.*
    (She kept the ring for her friend.)

LESSON 12

12A. Conversation

Hari
(Day)

Ailing: *Hari ini hari apa?*
(What day is today?)

Helen: *Hari ini hari Rabu. Ada apa?*
(Today is Wednesday. Is there anything.)

Ailing: *Saya ada ujian bahasa Inggeris pada hari Khamis. Saya masih belum belajar.*
(I have an English test on Thursday. I have not studied yet.)

Helen: *Jangan khuatir, kamu pasti lulus. Kamu senang belajar bahasa?*
(Do not worry, you are sure to pass. Do you like to study languages?)

Ailing: *Ya, saya suka sekali belajar bahasa. Bahasa Inggeris mata pelajaran utama saya. Bahasa Melayu mata pelajaran 'minor' saya.*
(Yes, I like to study languages. English is my major subject. Malay is my minor subject.)

Helen: *Hari apa kamu belajar bahasa Inggeris?*
(On what days do you study English?)

Ailing: *Hari Senin, Rabu dan Khamis.*
(Mondays, Wednesdays and Thursdays.)

Helen: *Jadi, kamu tidak ada kuliah pada hari Selasa dan Jumaat?*
(So, you have no lectures on Tuesdays and Fridays?)

Ailing: *Tidak, hari Selasa, saya ada bahasa Melayu dan hari Jumaat, saya mengikuti kelas bahasa Perancis.*
(No, I have Malay on Tuesdays and on Fridays I attend a French language class.)

Helen: *Kamu memang seorang pakar bahasa.*
(You are really a language expert.)

12B. Structure

Read the following sentences carefully.

SUBJECT	PREDICATE
Saya I am	*takut kepada anjing itu* afraid of that dog.
Ibu Mother	*sayang kepada anaknya.* loves her children.
Kejadian itu The incident	*sungguh mengejutkan.* is extremely shocking.
Anaknya The number of children he has (literally 'His children')	*dua orang.* are two.
Ada buku There ia a book	*di atas meja.* on the table.

Note: Sometimes *kepada* can be substituted by *akan* with no change in meaning. See the first and second sentences above.

Exercise 1. Substitute the word in bold, in the model sentence with the one given.

e.g.	*Mereka **sayang** akan kawan kita.* (They love our friends.)
hormat (respect)	*Mereka **hormat** akan kawan kita.* (They respect our friends.)
ingat (remember)	*Mereka **ingat** akan kawan kita.* (They remember our friends.)
benci (to hate)	*Mereka **benci** akan kawan kita.* (They hate our friends.)
perlu (need)	*Mereka **perlu** akan kawan kita.* (They need our friends.)

1. *kasih* (to love)
2. *rindu* (to long for)
3. *kenal* (to know)
4. *gusar* (to be angry with)
5. *malu* (to be ashamed of)
6. *marah* (to be angry with)
7. *percaya* (to trust)
8. *patuh* (to obey)
9. *cinta* (to love)
10. *suka* (to be fond of)

Exercise 2. Answer the following questions. Use the words given.

e.g.

Question	*Answer*
***Bagaimana** pandangan lelaki itu?* *- membingungkan Hilmi* (How is the man's view? - confuses Hilmi)	*Pandangan lelaki itu **membingungkan Hilmi**.* (The man's view confuses Hilmi.)

Bagaimana *kejadian itu?*
- sungguh mengejutkan
(How is the incident?
- very shocking)

Kejadian itu ***sungguh mengejutkan***.
(The incident is very shocking.)

1. ***Bagaimana*** *peristiwa itu? - menghebohkan seluruh kampung*
   (How is the incident? - causing an uproar in the whole village)
2. ***Bagaimana*** *akibatnya? - sangat memalukan*
   (What was the consequence? - very shameful)
3. ***Bagaimana*** *pertanyaan itu? - sungguh memusykilkan*
   (How is the question? - very perplexing)
4. ***Bagaimana*** *pekerjaan itu? - sungguh memenatkan*
   (How is the job? - very tiring)
5. ***Bagaimana*** *layanan kedai itu? - sangat memuaskan*
   (How is the shop's service? - very satisfactory)
6. ***Bagaimana*** *syarahan lelaki itu? - sangat menjemukan*
   (How is the man's lecture? - very boring)
7. ***Bagaimana*** *angin malam di pergunungan? - sangat menyegarkan*
   (How is the night wind on the mountain range? - very refreshing)
8. ***Bagaimana*** *kemalangan itu? - sungguh menakutkan*
   (How is the accident? - very frightening)
9. ***Bagaimana*** *keadaan orang-orang miskin di bandar? - sangat menyedihkan*
   (How is the condition of the poor in town? - very saddening)
10. ***Bagaimana*** *cuaca hari ini? - baik*
    (How is the weather today? - good)

Exercise 3. Answer the following questions. Use the words given.

e.g.

Question	*Answer*
Apa yang *sungguh mengkagumkan?* *- kepandaian ahli silap mata itu* (What is really astonishing? - the cleverness of the magician)	***Kepandaian ahli silap mata itu*** *sungguh mengkagumkan.* (The cleverness of the magician is really astonishing.]
Apa yang *sungguh mengerikan?* *- kematiannya* (What is really frightening? - his death)	***Kematiannya*** *sungguh mengerikan.* (His death is really frightening.)

1. ***Apa yang*** *mengecewakan para pekerja? - tindakan majikan itu*
   (What disappointed the workers? - the employer's action)
2. ***Apa yang*** *menggemparkan seluruh dunia? - berita itu*
   (What shocked the whole world? - the news)
3. ***Apa yang*** *membimbangkan hatinya? - ugutan perempuan itu*
   (What is troubling him [literally 'his heart']? - the woman's threat)
4. ***Apa yang*** *menggoncangkan dunia? - pembunuhan itu*
   (What shook the world? - the killing)
5. ***Apa yang*** *menghairankan para penonton? - kepintaran akrobat itu*
   (What suprises the audience? - the acrobat's skilfulness)
6. ***Apa yang*** *dapat mengenyangkan saya? - sepinggan nasi*
   (What can satisfy me? - a plate of rice)

7. ***Apa yang*** *membingungkan dia? - leteran ibunya*
   (What confuses him? - his mother's grumbling)

8. ***Apa yang*** *menggentarkan orang kampung - berita orang minyak*
   (What shook the villagers? - news of the 'oily man')

9. ***Apa yang*** *dapat mengharukan perasaan penonton? - muzik*
   (What moves the audience? - music)

10. ***Apa yang*** *memuakkan kita? - bau makanan itu*
    (What disgusts us? - the smell of the food)

Exercise 4. Answer the following questions. Use the words given.

e.g.

Question	*Answer*
Berapa orang anak Ahmad? - *dua* (How many children does Ahmad have? - two)	*Anak Ahmad dua orang.* (Ahmad has two children.)
Berapa tinggi lelaki itu? - *enam kaki* (How tall is the man? - six feet)	*Tinggi lelaki itu enam kaki.* (The man's height is six feet.)

1. *Berapa orang anak Cik Limah? - lima*
   (How many children has Mrs. Limah? - five)

2. *Berapa buah rumah orang kaya itu? - sepuluh*
   (How many houses has the rich man? - ten)

3. *Berapa ekor lembu Pak Haji itu? - tujuh*
   (How many cows has the Haji? - seven)

4. *Berapa harga buku itu? - sebelas dolar*
   (How much does the book cost? - eleven dollars)

5. *Berapa umur murid itu? - dua belas tahun*
   (How old is the student? - twelve years old)

6. *Berapa banyak penduduk kota itu? - satu juta*
   (What is the population of the town? - one million)

7. *Berapa orang adik-beradik saudara? - empat*
   (How many brothers and sisters have you? - four)

8. *Berapa berat badan lelaki itu? - empat puluh lima kilogram*
   (What is the weight of the man? - forty-five kilogrammes)

9. *Berapa dalam sungai itu? - dua puluh meter*
   (How deep is the river? - twenty metres.)

10. *Berapa tinggi gunung itu? - seribu meter*
    (How high is the mountain? - one thousand metres)

12C. Grammar

Conjunctions

Conjunctions are words which join words or groups of words. There are two types of conjunctions: (a) co-ordinating conjuntions and (b) subordinating conjunctions.

(a) Co-ordinating Conjunctions

Co-ordinating conjunctions are used to join words, phrases or clauses which are of the same type. The most common co-ordinating conjunctions are *dan* (and), *serta* (and/together with), *atau* (or), *tetapi* (but), *melainkan/kecuali* (except), *sambil/seraya* (while), *lagi* (more) and *lalu* (then).

e.g. *Aminah* ***dan*** *Fatimah mesti pergi ke pasar.*
(Aminah and Fatimah must go to the market.)

Aminah cantik ***tetapi*** *sombong.*
(Aminah is beautiful but arrogant.)

Kanak-kanak menari ***sambil*** *menyanyi.*
(The children are dancing while singing.)

Tuan pengerusi bangun ***lalu*** *bercakap.*
(The chairman stood up [and] then gave a speech.)

Pejabat pos dibuka setiap hari ***kecuali*** *hari Ahad.*
(The post office is open every day except on Sundays.)

Badannya belum sihat ***tetapi*** *dia pergi juga.*
(He [literally 'His body'] was not healthy but he still went.)

(b) Subordinating Conjunctions

Subordinating conjunctions join two sentences together. The sentence preceded by the conjunction becomes the subordinating clause and the conjunction becomes subordinating conjunction.

Subordinating conjunctions can be grouped according to the kinds of clauses formed.

(a) **clauses of time** are introduced by *ketika/apabila* (when), *sesudah* (after), *sejak* (since), *selama* (during), *sebelum* (before), *sehingga* (until) and *sementara* (while).

e.g. *Ayahnya meninggal* ***ketika*** *dia masih kecil.*
(His father passed away when he was still small.)

Apabila *mereka datang, saya tidak ada di rumah.*
(When they came, I was not at home.)

Sikapnya berubah ***sejak*** *dia menjadi wakil rakyat.*
(His attitude has changed since he became the people's representative.)

Sementara *ibu memasak, saya membasuh pinggan.*
(While mother is cooking, I wash the dishes.)

(b) **clauses of condition** are introduced by *jika/kalau/jikalau* (if).

e.g. ***Jika*** *saya tidak salah, orang itu memang ayahnya.*

(If I am not mistaken, that man is really his father.)

Permainan itu tidak dapat dijalankan ***kalau*** *hari hujan.*
(The game cannot be continued if it rains.)

(c) **clauses of concession** are introduced by *walaupun/sungguhpun/meskipun/biarpun* (although/though).

e.g. *Lelaki tua itu masih bekerja* ***walaupun*** *dia uzur.*
(The old man still works although he is sick.)

Sungguhpun *mulut orang itu manis hatinya jahat.*
(Although his words are pleasant to the ears, his intentions are bad.)

(d) **clauses of reason and cause** are introduced by *kerana/sebab* (because/as).

e.g. *Bayi itu menangis* ***kerana*** *perutnya lapar.*
(The baby cried because he was hungry.)

Budak lelaki itu sakit perut ***sebab*** *terlalu banyak makan pisang.*
(The boy has stomach upset because he has eaten too many bananas.)

(e) **clauses of purpose** are introduced by *agar/supaya* (so that, so as to)

e.g. *Belajarlah sungguh-sungguh* ***agar*** *kamu naik darjah.*
(Study seriouly so that you will be promoted to the next class.)

Saudara mesti berfikir dahulu ***supaya*** *tidak menyesal kelak.*
(You must think beforehand so as not to regret later.)

(f) **clauses of analogy** are introduced by *seperti/sebagai/seolah-olah seumpama/semacam* (as if/though).

e.g. *Dia berjalan tergopoh-gapah* ***seolah-olah*** *dia sedang*

diekori.
(He walks hurriedly as though he is being followed.)

Encik Leman berlagak ***seperti*** *dia baru sahaja kenal orang itu.*
(Mr. Leman behaves as if he has just known that person.)

Exercise 5. Underline the conjunctions in the following sentences.

e.g. *Saya bangun* ***lalu*** *keluar dari rumah.*
(I get up [and] then go out of the house.)

Lelaki itu kaya ***tetapi*** *kedekut.*
(The man is rich but stingy.)

1. *Saya tidak ada di rumah ketika dia datang.*
(I was not at home when he came.)
2. *Datuk saya masih sihat walaupun usianya sudah lanjut.*
(My grandfather is still healthy though he is advanced in age.)
3. *Apabila hujan mereka tidak dapat menoreh getah.*
(When it rains they cannot tap rubber.)
4. *Dia baru sampai sesudah mesyuarat selesai.*
(He only arrived after the meeting had ended.)
5. *Selama tinggal di sini dia tidak pernah menjenguk kita.*
(During his stay here, he never visited us.)
6. *Lelaki itu bekerja keras supaya lekas naik pangkat.*
(The man works hard in order to get a promotion fast.)
7. *Semua murid lulus kecuali Yusuf seorang.*
(All the pupils passed except Yusuf alone.)
8. *Saya akan pergi besok atau lusa.*
(I will go tomorrow or the day after tomorrow.)

9. *Sejak umurnya tujuh tahun, dia tidak pernah meninggalkan sembahyang.*
(Since he was seven years old, he had never neglected his prayers.)

10. *Kita mesti bekerja keras jikalau kita hendakkan kemajuan.*
(We must work hard if we want progress.)

Exercise 6. Fill in the blanks with suitable conjunctions given in the box below.

melainkan	*sambil*	*sampai*	*supaya*	*jikalau*
seperti	*agar*	*kecuali*	*sementara*	*walaupun*

e.g.

Salim makan __________ *bercakap.* (Salim eats __________ he talks.)	*Salim makan* ***sambil*** *bercakap.* (Salim eats while [he] talks.)
Fatimah bercakap __________ *tersenyum.* (Fatimah talks __________ smiles.)	*Fatimah bercakap* ***serta*** *tersenyum.* (Fatimah talks and smiles.)

1. *Dia membaca* __________ *kepalanya sakit.*
(He reads __________ his head aches.)

2. *Bacalah surat ini dengan kuat* __________ *saya dapat dengar.*
(Read this letter loudly __________ I can hear.)

3. __________ *saudara tidak memegang janji, tentu saya akan marah.*

(__________ you do not keep your promise, certainly I will be angry.)

4. __________ *dia kaya, dia tidak sombong.*
   (__________ he is rich, he is not arrogant.)

5. *Bibirnya bergerak-gerak* __________ *dia hendak berkata sesuatu.*
   (His lips move __________ he wishes to say something.)

6. *Belajarlah kuat-kuat* __________ *saudara lekas pandai.*
   (Study hard __________ you will soon be clever.)

7. *Semua orang pergi* __________ *saya seorang.*
   (All go __________ I alone.)

8. __________ *menunggu guru datang, murid-murid membaca buku.*
   (__________ waiting for the teacher to come, the pupils read books.)

9. *Pemuda itu berjalan* __________ *menyanyi.*
   (The young man is walking __________ singing.)

10. *Tiada seorang pun yang boleh masuk ke dalam bilik itu* __________ *saya.*
    (No one can enter the room __________ I.)

12D. Word Formation

Verb-forming Suffix *-i*

Suffix ***-i*** is an important suffix used to form verbs from nouns and adjectives. It is often used with the prefix ***me-***, forming ***me-i***. It can also be added to verbs.

When added to nouns, the suffix ***-i*** has two important functions.

(a) to give or fix the thing mentioned by the root word (*memberi, membuat*)

e.g.

Kita mesti ***menghormati*** *ibu bapa kita.* (We must respect our parents.)	=	*Kita mesti* ***memberi*** *hormat* ***kepada*** *ibu bapa kita.*
Pak Man ***memagari*** *kebunnya dengan kawat berduri.* (Pak Man fenced his garden with barbed wire.)	=	*Pak Man* ***membuat pagar pada*** *kebunnya dengan kawat berduri.*

(b) to become or to act as something mentioned in the root word (*menjadi atau bertindak sebagai*)

e.g.

Bahri ingin menganggotai pertubuhan itu. (Bahri is anxious to become a member of that organization.)	=	*Bahri ingin* ***menjadi anggota*** *pertubuhan itu.*
Ahmad telah membintangi filem itu. (Ahmad starred in the film.)	=	*Ahmad telah* ***bertindak sebagai bintang dalam*** *filem itu.*

Please note that suffix ***-i*** sometimes may acquire the meaning of 'to remove' as in the following sentences:

e.g. *Kakak sedang* ***membului*** *ayam di dapur*. (*bulu*: feather)
(Elder sister is removing feathers from a chicken in the kitchen.)

Adik sudah pandai ***menyisiki*** *ikan*. (*sisik*: scales of fish)
(Younger brother is good at removing fishs' scales.)

When added to an adjective, suffix ***-i*** acquires a causative effect and causes the verb formed to acquire the characteristics of the root word (*menyebabkan, membuat, membuat menjadi*).

e.g.

Ayah akan ***membaiki*** *rumah kami yang buruk.* (Father will repair our dilapidated house.)	=	*Ayah akan* ***membuat menjadi baik*** *rumah kami yang buruk.*
Fatimah sedang ***memanasi*** *makanan.* (Fatimah is heating up the food.)	=	*Fatimah sedang* ***membuat*** *panas makanan.*

Exercise 7. Replace phrases in bold with verbs using the affix ***me-i.***

e.g.

Tukang masak lupa ***membubuh garam pada*** *ikan.* (*garam*: salt) (The cook forgot to salt the fish.)	=	*Tukang masak lupa* ***menggarami*** *ikan.*
Lelaki itu ***memberi harga*** *rumahnya terlalu rendah.* (*harga*: price) (The man priced his house too low.)	=	*Lelaki itu* ***menghargai*** *rumahnya terlalu rendah.*

1. *Dia* ***membubuh tanda pada*** *rumah itu.* (*tanda*: sign)
   (He marks the house.)

2. *Dia selalu* ***memberi nasihat kepada*** *temannya.* (*nasihat*: advice)
   (He always advises his friend.)

3. *Rosminah sedang* ***memberi minum air susu kepada*** *anaknya.* (*susu*: milk)
(Rosminah is giving milk to her child.)

4. *Doktor* ***memberi ubat kepada*** *orang sakit itu.* (*ubat*: medicine)
(The doctor gave medicine to the patient.)

5. *Dia* ***memberi belanja kepada*** *adik lelakinya setiap bulan.* (*belanja*: allowance)
(He gives an allowance to his younger brother every month.)

6. *Kata-katanya* ***memberi ilham kepada*** *pengarang itu.* (*ilham*: inspiration)
(His words gave inspiration to the writer.)

7. *Lelaki itu tidak* ***memberi nafkah kepada*** *isterinya.* (*nafkah*: sustenance)
(The man does not provide sustenance for his wife.)

8. *Aku tak sudi* ***memberi sedekah kepada*** *orang pemalas.* (*sedekah*: alms)
(I am unwilling to give alms to a lazy person.)

9. *Dia* ***memberi upah kepada*** *mereka membakar rumah itu.* (*upah*: payment for service rendered)
(He paid them to burn the house.)

10. *Dia* ***memberi naungan kepada*** *pelarian itu.* (*naung*: refuge)
(He provides shelter for the refugee.)

Exercise 8. Replace phrases in bold with verbs using the affix ***me-i***.

e.g.

Seorang ahli parlimen ***menjadi kepala kepada*** *lembaga baru itu.* (*kepala*: head) (A Member of Parliament	=	*Seorang ahli parlimen* ***mengepalai*** *lembaga baru itu.*

heads the new Board.)

Pekerja-pekerja sedang ***membuat baru*** *jambatan itu.* (*baru*: new) (Workers are renovating the bridge.)	=	*Pekerja-pekerja sedang* ***membarui*** *jambatan itu.*

1. *Dia* ***menjadi wakil kepada*** *saudagar itu.* (*wakil*: representative)
   (He represents the businessman.)
2. *Dia yang* ***menjadi orang pengantara*** *dalam perselisihan itu.* (*antara*: middle)
   (He is the one who mediates in the quarrel.)
3. *Siapa yang* ***menjadi dalang kepada*** *pemberontakan itu?* (*dalang*: secret force)
   (Who is the secret force behind the rebellion?)
4. *Dia* ***menjadi ketua kepada*** *majlis itu.* (*ketua*: head)
   (He heads the meeting.)
5. *Dia* ***menjadi raja*** *di negeri itu.* (*raja*: a ruler)
   (He rules that country.)
6. *Lampu minyak itu* ***memberi terang*** *biliknya.* (*terang*: light)
   (The oil lamp lights up his room.)
7. *Gadis itu* ***membuat merah*** *kukunya.* (*merah*: red)
   (The girl reddens her finger-nails.)
8. *Sebuah kipas* ***membuat sejuk*** *bilik itu.* (*sejuk*: cold)
   (A fan cools the room.)
9. *Setiap malam binatang-binatang liar* ***menjadikan rosak*** *tanamannya.* (*rosak*: be destroyed)
   (Every night wild animals destroy the crop.)
10. *Air mata* ***menyebabkan basah*** *pipinya.* (*basah:* wet)
    (The tears wet her cheeks.)

LESSON 13

13A. Conversation

Haribulan
(Dates)

Suyin: *Tahukah kamu berapa haribulan hari ini?*
(Do you know today's date?)

Halimah: *Hari ini empat belas haribulan, bulan Mei.*
(Today is the fourteenth of May.)

Suyin: *Tahun berapa sekarang?*
(What is the year now?)

Halimah: *Tahun sembilan belas delapan puluh lapan. Ada apa?*
(Year nineteen eighty-eight. Is there anything?)

Suyin: *Sepuluh hari lagi adalah hari jadi saya.*
(Ten days more is my birthday.)

Halimah: *Jadi, dua puluh empat haribulan, bulan Mei adalah hari jadi kamu? Hari jadi yang keberapa?*
(So, the twenty-fourth of May is your birthday. Which birthday will it be?)

Suyin: *Hari jadi saya yang kedua puluh satu. Bila hari jadi kamu?*
(My twenty-first birthday. When is your birthday?)

Halimah: *Sembilan haribulan Ogos.*
(The nineth of August.)

Suyin: *Yang keberapa?*
(How many years?)

Halimah: *Oh, itu rahsia. Saya sudah tua. Kamu akan mengadakan majlis hari jadi?*
(Oh, that's secret. I am old already. Are you going to organise a birthday party?)

Suyin: *Sudah tentu. Saya harap kamu sudi datang ke majlis hari jadi saya. Mungkin kamu akan bertemu dengan orang yang kamu senangi.*
(Certainly. I hope you can come to my birthday party. Perhaps you will meet someone you like.)

13B. Structure

Read the following sentences carefully.

SUBJECT	PREDICATE
Dia He	*akan menggembirakan orang tuanya.* will make his parents happy.
Dia He	*boleh mengecewakan saudara-maranya.* can disappoint his relatives.
Dia He	*telah menyampingkan diri dari masyarakat.* isolated himself from society.
Ahmad Ahmad	*menewaskan seorang johan dalam pertandingan itu.* defeated a champion in the competition.
Perempuan itu The woman	*boleh membaringkan anaknya di atas katil.* can lay her child down on the bed.

Exercise 1. Substitute the words in the model sentence with the one given.

e.g.	*Dia akan* ***mendamaikan*** *kawan-kawan kita*. (He will reconcile our friends.)
membosankan (to bore)	*Dia akan* ***membosankan*** *kawan-kawan kita*. (He will bore our friends.)
mengutamakan (to pay special attention to)	*Dia akan* ***mengutamakan*** *kawan-kawan kita*. (He'll pay special attention to our friends.)
handai taulan (companions)	*Dia akan* ***mengutamakan*** *handai taulan kita*. (He'll pay special attention to our companions.)
membinasakan (to destroy)	*Dia akan membinasakan handai taulan kita*. (He will destroy our friends.)

1. *membahagiakan* (to make happy)
2. *mengejutkan* (to startle)
3. *memencilkan* (to isolate)
4. *menguntungkan* (to benefit)
5. *rakan sejawat* (colleagues)
6. *menyatukan* (to unite)
7. *mengistimewakan* (to give privilege to)
8. *mendiamkan* (to silence)
9. *membahayakan* (to endanger)
10. *merugikan* (to bring loss(es) to)

Exercise 2. Change the following statements into questions.

e.g.

Statement	*Question*
Lelaki itu sudah menghimpunkan ***semua pengikutnya*** *di padang.* (The man has gathered all his followers in the field.)	*Lelaki itu sudah menghimpunkan* ***siapa*** *di padang?* (Whom did the man gather in the field?)
Perbuatannya menjengkelkan ***ayahnya.*** (His action annoyed his father.)	*Perbuatannya menjengkelkan* ***siapa****?* (Whom did his action annoy?)

1. *Syarahan itu menjemukan* ***para penonton.***
   (The lecture bored the audience.)
2. *Dia selalu mengenangkan* ***kekasihnya****.*
   (He always remembers his beloved.)
3. *Dia jarang mengetawakan* ***orang cacat.***
   (He seldom laughs at the disabled.)
4. *Fatimah sedang memandikan* ***adik perempuannya.***
   (Fatimah is bathing her younger sister.)
5. *Ucapannya memarahkan* ***kaum keluarganya.***
   (His speech angered his family.)
6. *Dia tidak dapat memaafkan* ***pemberita itu.***
   (He cannot forgive the reporter.)
7. *Racun itu boleh mematikan* ***sesiapa****.*
   (The poison can kill anyone.)
8. *Orang itu memburukkan nama* ***ketuanya.***
   (The man slanders his boss' name.)

9. *Lelaki itu sudah menemberangkan* ***sahabat handainya***.
(The man has lied to his friends.)

10. *Ibu itu sedang menidurkan* ***anaknya***.
(The mother is putting her child to sleep.)

Exercise 3. Answer the following questions. Use the words given.

e.g.

Question	*Answer*
Ahmad menewaskan ***siapa*** *dalam pertandingan itu?* - *seorang johan* (Whom did Ahmad defeat in the competition? - a champion)	*Ahmad menewaskan* ***seorang johan*** *dalam pertandingan itu.* (Ahmad defeated a champion in the competition?
Budak lelaki itu menyusahkan ***siapa*** *tiap-tiap hari?* - *orang tuanya* (Whom does the boy get into trouble every day?)	*Budak lelaki itu menyusahkan* ***orang tuanya*** *tiap-tiap hari.* (The boy get his parents into troubles every day.)

1. *Dia sudah menyingkirkan* ***siapa*** *dari jawatan? - pegawai tadbir*
(Whom did he remove from appointment?
- administrative officer)

2. *Ramli menundukkan* ***siapa*** *dalam permainan itu?*
- kawannya
(Whom did Ramli beat in the game? - his friend)

3. *Dia sudah mencalonkan* ***siapa*** *untuk jawatan itu? - iparnya*
(Whom did he nominate for the post/position? - his brother/sister-in-law)

4. *Dia meraikan* ***siapa*** *dalam majlis itu? - kakitangannya*
(Whom did he entertain in the party? - his staff)

5. *Dia menjatuhkan* ***siapa*** *dalam perlawanan tinju? - lawannya*
(Whom did he defeat in the boxing match? - his opponent)

6. *Ahmad menumpangkan* ***siapa*** *di rumah sahabat? - anaknya*
(Whom did Ahmad lodge at a friend's house? - his child)

7. *Razak menyelimutkan* ***siapa*** *dengan selimut? - adiknya*
(Whom did Razak cover with a blanket? - his younger brother/sister)

8. *Dia menyedarkan* ***siapa*** *dari lalainya? - pengawal itu*
(Whom did he arouse from negligence? - the guard)

9. *Dia menjagakan* ***siapa*** *dari tidurnya? - abangnya*
(Whom did he wake up from sleep? - his elder brother)

10. *Kerajaan telah memberhentikan* ***siapa*** *dari jawatan? - guru itu*
(Whom did the government dismiss from office?
- the teacher)

Exercise 4. Give affirmative answers to the following questions.

e.g.

Question	*Answer*
Bolehkah *perempuan itu membaringkan anaknya di atas katil?* (Can the woman lay her child down on the bed?)	*Boleh, perempuan itu boleh membaringkan anaknya di atas katil.* (Yes, the woman can lay her child down on the bed.)
Dapatkah *dia membebaskan lelaki itu dari tahanan?* (Can he free the man from detention?)	*Dapat, dia dapat membebaskan lelaki itu dari tahanan.* Yes, he can free the man from detention.)

1. ***Bolehkah** dia memenjarakan lelaki itu di rumah*?
   (Can he imprison the man at home?)

2. ***Dapatkah** dia memulaukan orang itu dari masyarakat?*
   (Can he segregate the man from society?)

3. ***Bolehkah** dia menyelamatkan lelaki itu daripada mati lemas?*
   (Can he save the man from drowning?)

4. ***Dapatkah** dia menukarkan pegawai itu ke tempat lain?*
   (Can he transfer the officer to another place?)

5. ***Bolehkah** dia menurunkan kita di depan masjid?*
   (Can he drop us off in front of the mosque?)

6. ***Dapatkah** pengetua itu mendatangkan guru-guru dari luar?*
   (Can the principal bring in teachers from outside?)

7. ***Bolehkah** seorang gadis mendedahkan mukanya kepada pelanggan?*
   (Can a girl expose her face to her client?)

8. ***Dapatkah** dia memasukkan anaknya ke sekolah itu?*
   (Can he enroll his child in that school?)

9. ***Bolehkah** dia menitipkan anaknya kepada jirannya?*
   (Can he entrust his child to his neighbour?)

10. ***Bolehkah** dia menyewakan rumahnya kepada kita?*
    (Can he rent out his house to us?)

13C. Grammar

Simple Sentence

Sentences can be structurally divided into three types, i.e. (a) Simple sentences, (b) Complex sentences, and (c) Compound sentences.

(a) Simple Sentences

A simple sentence is a sentence which contains only one subject and one predicate.

e.g. *Ali murid.*
(Ali is a pupil.)

Budak lelaki itu berdiri.
(The boy is standing.)

Encik Ahmad menyewa rumah itu.
(Mr. Ahmad rented the house.)

Bilik itu gelap.
(The room is dark.)

A simple sentence may be expanded and still be regarded as a simple sentence. For example, the above sentences can be expanded as follows:

Ali murid ***sekolah.***
(Ali is a school pupil.)

Budak lelaki itu berdiri ***di depan pintu.***
(The boy is standing in front of the door.)

Encik Ahmad menyewa rumah itu ***dua bulan yang lalu.***
(Mr. Ahmad rented the house two months ago.)

Bilik ***besar*** *itu gelap.*
(The big room is dark.)

Indeed, a simple sentence may be very long. The late Za'ba gave the following example as an illustration.

Pada suatu hari yang sangat panas dalam bulan puasa yang baru ini ***saya*** *telah* ***terjumpa*** *seorang* ***peminta sedekah*** *terbaring dengan terlalu amat letih dan dahaganya di tepi suatu parit dalam bandar Singapura.*
(On a very hot day in the last fasting month **I came across** a **beggar** lying very tired and thirsty by the side of a ditch in the city of Singapore.)

This long sentence is considered as a simple sentence because it contains one subject, *saya* (I), and one predicate, *terjumpa peminta sedekah* (came across [a] beggar).

Exercise 5. Expand the following sentences. Use the words given.

e.g.

Guru itu abang saya. *- bahasa Melayu* (The teacher is my brother. - Malay language)	*Guru* ***bahasa Melayu*** *itu abang saya.* (The Malay language teacher is my brother.)
Mereka berjalan. *- perlahan-lahan* (They walked. - slowly)	*Mereka berjalan* ***perlahan-lahan.*** (They walked slowly.)

1. *Latiff pemuda. - Melayu*
   (Latiff is a youth. - Malay)
2. *Umurnya lima belas tahun. - pada bulan Ogos ini*
   (He is fifteen years old. - this August)
3. *Dia berbakat. - di dalam bidang perniagáan*
   (He has talent. - in the field of business)
4. *Saudagar itu kedekut. - kaya*
   (The man is miserly. - rich)
5. *Guru itu pengarang. - Bahasa Melayu kita*
   (The teacher is a writer. - our Malay language teacher)
6. *Orang berkumpul. - di kedai Pak Sudin*
   (People gathered. - in Pak Sudin's shop)
7. *Ahmad mencuci keretanya. - setiap hari*
   (Ahmad washes his car. - every day)
8. *Murid-murid duduk. - di dalam darjah*
   (The pupils sit. - in the class room)

9. *Budak itu menangis. - kecil*
(The child cried. - small)

10. *Lembu makan rumput di padang. - ketua kampung*
(The cow eats grass in the field. - the village chief)

Exercise 6. Fill in the blanks with suitable words.

e.g.

Budak __________ sakit perut. (The __________ child has a stomach ache.)	*Budak* ***nakal*** *itu sakit perut.* (The **naughty** child has a stomach ache.)
Halimah murid __________. (Halimah is a __________ pupil.)	*Halimah murid* ***sekolah****.* (Halimah is a **school** pupil.)

1. *Pelajar __________ itu rajin.*
(The __________ student is diligent.)

2. *Arif pengarang __________ .*
(Arif is __________ writer.)

3. *Sekolah __________ itu baik.*
(The __________ school is good.)

4. *Musim __________ sudah tiba.*
(The __________ season has arrived.)

5. *Bapa __________ sudah kaya sekarang.*
(__________ father is rich now.)

6. *Cerita __________ itu menarik.*
(The __________ story is interesting.)

7. *Ahmad suka membaca buku __________.*
(Ahmad likes to read __________ books.)

8. *Anjing* __________ *itu menyalak.*
(The __________ dog barks.)

9. *Budak* __________ *pandai.*
(The __________ child is clever.)

10. *Lembu-lembu* __________ *makan rumput di padang.*
(The __________ cows eat grass in the field.)

13D. Word Fomation

Suffix *-i*

Suffix ***-i,*** when added to verbs, has two important functions. Its first and most important function is to show location or direction.

e.g.

Dia masuk dan ***menduduki*** *tempat saya.* (He entered and sat in my place.)	=	*Dia masuk dan* ***duduk*** *di tempat saya.*
Ahmad tiada berani ***memasuki*** *gua itu.* (Ahmad dared not enter the cave.)	=	*Ahmad tiada berani* ***masuk ke*** *dalam gua itu.*

Perhaps, verb phrases ending with *dengan*, *pada* or *kepada* should also be regarded as having the meaning of location and direction, as these kinds of phrases can be replaced by single verbs with the affix ***me-i***.

e.g.

Tuhan ***berserta dengan*** *orang yang sabar.* (God is with people who are patient.)	=	*Tuhan* ***menyertai*** *orang yang sabar.*

Rakyat mesti ***patuh pada*** *undang-undang negeri.* (The people must obey the laws of the country.)	=	*Rakyat mesti* ***mematuhi*** *undang-undang negeri.*
Dia ***bertanya kepada*** *maksud lelaki itu.* (He enquired about the man's intention.)	=	*Dia* ***menanyai*** *maksud lelaki itu.*

Another function of ***me-i*** is to indicate intensity, denoting that the action is done by many people or is done repeatedly.

e.g.

Dia ***memukuli*** *budak lelaki itu.* (He beat the boy repeatedly.)	=	*Dia* ***memukul*** *budak lelaki itu berulang-ulang.*
Semut mengerumuni *gula-gula itu.* (Ants surrounded the sweet.)	=	*Semut* ***datang beramai-ramai berkerumun*** *pada gula-gula itu.*

It should be pointed out here that there is a number of words which can take both ***me-kan*** and ***me-i.*** Such words are like *duduk* (to sit), *tidur* (to sleep), *masuk* (to enter), *jalan* (road/movement), *turun* (to go down) and *naik* (to go up) etc.

e.g.

Perempuan itu ***mendudukkan*** *anaknya di atas tikar.* (The woman seated her child on the mat.)	*Anak itu sudah* ***menduduki*** *tikar itu.* (The child has already sat on the mat.)
Kuli-kuli sedang ***menaikkan*** *barang-*	*Mereka* ***menaiki*** *bas yang datang.*

barang kapal.
(The coolies are loading the goods onto the ship.)

(They boarded the bus that came.)

Ia ***memasukkan*** *mesin taip ke dalam bilik.*
(He put the typewriter into the room.)

Saya tidak berani ***memasuki*** *rumah itu.*
(I dare not enter the house.)

Dia tidak dapat ***menjalankan*** *kereta itu.*
(He cannot move the car.)

Dia telah ***menjalani*** *beberapa ujian.*
(He has gone through a few tests.)

From the examples above, it is clear that both ***-kan*** and ***-i*** indicate action and location. The difference between ***-kan*** and ***-i*** is found in the reaction of the object towards the action. In a verb with suffix ***-kan*** the object moves to another place. On the other hand, the object remains in its position when suffix ***-i*** is used.

Exercise 7. Replace phrases in bold with verbs using the affix ***me-i.***

e.g.

Siapa yang ***diam*** *di rumah itu sekarang?*
- diam
(Who stays in that house now?
- to stay)
= *Siapa yang* ***mendiami*** *rumah itu sekarang?*

Dia sudah ***berkuasa atas*** *syarikat itu sekarang.*
- kuasa
(He has gained control of the company now.
- control)
= *Dia sudah* ***menguasai*** *syarikat itu sekarang.*

1. *Ramai sungguh orang* ***datang ke*** *rumahnya. - datang*
   (Many people came to his house. - to come)

2. *Dia tidak* ***hadir dalam*** *majlis perkahwinan sahabatnya. - hadir*
   (He did not attend his friend's wedding celebration. - to attend)

3. *Dia selalu* ***lalu di*** *jalan itu. - lalu*
   (He always passed through the road. - to pass by)

4. *Mereka tidak pernah* ***singgah di*** *pelabuhan itu. - singgah*
   (They have never called at that port. - to call at)

5. *Jerawat* ***tumbuh di*** *mukanya. - tumbuh*
   (Pimples grow on his face. - to grow)

6. *Siapa yang* ***bertempat di*** *rumah itu sekarang? - tempat*
   (Who occupies the house now? - place)

7. *Dia tidak mahu* ***bercampur dengan*** *orang itu. - campur*
   (He does not wish to mix with that person. - to mix)

8. *Perbuatan itu* ***bersalahan dengan*** *undang-undang. - salah*
   (The action is against the law. - wrong)

9. *Dia* ***menikam*** *lelaki itu* ***berturut-turut.*** *- tikam*
   (He stabs the man repeatedly. - to stab)

10. *Dia* ***menembak*** *orang jahat itu* ***berkali-kali****. - tembak*
    (He shoots the criminal repeatedly. - to shoot)

Exercise 8. Add the affix ***me-kan*** or ***me-i*** to the verbs in bold.

e.g.

Pencuri itu ***masuk*** *rumahnya semalam.* (The thief entered his house yesterday.)	=	*Pencuri itu* ***memasuki*** *rumahnya semalam.*

Ramai ibu bapa ***masuk*** *anak-anak mereka ke sekolah ini.* (Many parents enrolled their children in this school.)	=	*Ramai ibu bapa* ***memasukkan*** *anak-anak mereka ke sekolah ini.*

1. *Sejak itu dia tidak mahu* ***diam*** *kampung itu lagi.*
   (Since then, he did not wish to stay in the village.)
2. *Dia* ***diam*** *adiknya yang menangis dengan gula-gula.*
   (He silences his crying younger brother/sister by [giving] sweets.)
3. *Perempuan itu sedang* ***tidur*** *anaknya.*
   (The woman is putting her child to sleep.)
4. *Kemudian dia pergi* ***tidur*** *katil itu.*
   (Then he went to sleep on the bed.)
5. *Setiap pagi, saya* ***naik*** *bas itu ke sekolah.*
   (Every morning, I take the bus to school.)
6. *Pekedai itu telah* ***naik*** *harga barang-barangnya.*
   (The shopkeeper has increased the prices of his goods.)
7. *Lelaki itu berlari-lari* ***turun*** *tangga hotel itu.*
   (The man runs down the hotel's staircase.)
8. *Pemerintah boleh membuat undang-undang untuk menaikkan atau* ***turun*** *cukai.*
   (The government can pass laws to increase or decrease taxes.)
9. *Apabila dia pulang ke rumah, dia* ***dapat*** *ibunya sedang tidur.*
   (When he returned home, he found his mother sleeping.)
10. *Anak itu berlari-lari* ***dapat*** *ibunya yang pulang dari pasar.*
    (The child runs to meet his mother who is returning from the market.)

LESSON 14

14A. Conversation

Di Kedai Buku Melayu
(In a Malay Bookshop)

Johnny: *Maafkan saya Encik Lim. Encik Lim tahukah di mana ada kedai buku Melayu?*
(Excuse me, Mr. Lim. Do you know where there is a Malay bookshop?)

Lim: *Oh, kedai buku Melayu. Pergilah ke Geylang Serai. Di sana ada beberapa buah kedai buku Melayu.*
(Oh, a Malay bookshop. Go to Geylang Serai. There are several Malay bookshops there.)

[*Di kedai buku.*]
(In the bookshop.)

Pekedai: *Sila masuk, encik.*
(Please come in, sir.)

Johnny: *Di sini ada jual kamuskah? Saya hendak membeli sebuah kamus Melayu-Inggeris.*
(Are dictionaries sold here? I want to buy a Malay-English dictionary.)

Pekedai: *Inilah kamus Melayu-Inggeris yang paling baik. Ia disusun oleh seorang pensyarah universiti.*
(This is the best Malay-English dictionary. It was compiled by a university lecturer.)

Johnny: *Berapa harga kamus itu?*
(What is the price of the dictionary?)

Pekedai: *Dua belas ringgit.*
(Twelve dollars.)

Johnny: *Tidak boleh kurang sedikitkah?*
(Can't it be slightly reduced?)

Pekedai: *Tidak boleh. Saya sudah beri encik potongan sepuluh peratus.*
(No, it cannot. I have already given you a ten percent discount.)

Johnny: *Terima kasih.*
(Thank you.)

Pekedai: *Sama-sama.*
(You are welcome.)

14B. Structure

Read the following sentences carefully.

SUBJECT	PREDICATE
Kita We	*mesti mengadakan wang untuk membeli rumah.* must produce the money to buy a house.
Dia She	*menghulurkan segelas air kepada suaminya.* passes a glass of water to her husband.
Dia He	*dapat menyudahkan pekerjaan itu dalam seminggu.* can complete the job in a week.
Kerajaan The government	*telah meluluskan undang-undang itu minggu lepas.* has passed the bill last week.
Ahmad Ahmad	*telah menterjemahkan buku itu ke dalam bahasa Melayu.* has translated the book into Malay.

Exercise I. Substitute the word in bold, in the model sentence with the one given.

e.g.		*Kita mesti* ***mengadakan*** *wang untuk membeli rumah.* (We must produce the money to buy a house.)
	mendapatkan (to get)	*Kita mesti* ***mendapatkan*** *wang untuk membeli rumah.* (We must get the money to buy a house.)
	mendermakan (to donate)	*Kita mesti* ***mendermakan*** *wang untuk membeli rumah.* (We must donate the money to buy a house.)
	menyediakan (to prepare)	*Kita mesti* ***menyediakan*** *wang untuk membeli rumah.* (We must prepare the money to buy a house.)
	kereta (a car)	*Kita mesti menyediakan wang untuk membeli* ***kereta.*** (We must produce the money to buy a car.)
	menabung (to save)	*Kita mesti* ***menabungkan*** *wang untuk membeli kereta.* (We must save money to buy a car.)

1. *mengeluarkan* (to withdraw)
2. *mengadakan* (to supply)
3. *menyumbangkan* (to contribute)
4. *mengumpulkan* (to collect)
5. *bangunan baru* (a new building)
6. *sebidang tanah* (a piece of land)
7. *meninggalkan* (to leave behind)

8. *menyerahkan* (to hand over)
9. *menjimatkan* (to save [literally 'to economise'])
10. *mencarikan* (to find)

Exercise 2. Answer the following questions. Use the words given.

e.g.

Question	*Answer*
Abas mengadukan peristiwa itu kepada siapa? - *polis* (To whom did Abas complain about the incident? - the police)	*Abas mengadukan peristiwa itu kepada polis.* (Abas complained about the incident to the police.)
Dia membocorkan rahsia itu kepada siapa? - *musuh* whom did he leak the secret? - the enemy)	*Dia membocorkan rahsia itu kepada musuh.* (He leaked the secret to the enemy.)

1. *Dia menjanjikan pertolongan kepada siapa? - mangsa-mangsa kebakaran*
   (To whom did he promise assistance? - the fire victims)
2. *Dia menjelaskan perkara itu kepada siapa? - para pekerja*
   (To whom did he explain the matter? - the workers)
3. *Dia mengemukakan pertanyaan itu kepada siapa? - seorang menteri*
   (To whom did he put forward the question? - a minister)
4. *Dia mengajukan usul itu kepada siapa? - ketua pejabatnya*
   (To whom does he put forward the proposal? - the head of his office)

5. *Dia mengucapkan terima kasih kepada siapa? - sahabat handainya*
(To whom did he say 'thank you'? - to all his friends)
6. *Fatimah menghidangkan makanan untuk siapa? - para tamu*
(To whom did Fatimah serve the food? - the guests)
7. *Dia menunjukkan cincin itu kepada siapa? - kekasihnya*
(To whom did he show the ring? - his love)
8. *Datuk Tan menyampaikan hadiah kepada siapa? - para pemenang*
(To whom did Datuk Tan give away the prizes? - the winners)
9. *Lelaki tua itu meninggalkan hartanya kepada siapa? - anak-anaknya*
(To whom did the old man leave his property? - his children)
10. *Dia mengembalikan surat itu kepada siapa? - pengirimnya*
(To whom did he return the letter? - its sender)

Exercise 3. Answer the following questions. Use the words given.

e.g.

Question	*Answer*
***Apa yang** telah memusnahkan rumah-rumah itu?* - *api* (What destroyed the houses? - fire)	*Api telah memusnahkan rumah-rumah itu.* (Fire destroyed the houses.)
***Siapa yang** telah mententeramkan keadaan itu?* - *tentera* (Who pacified the situation? - the army)	*Tentera telah mententeramkan keadaan itu.* (The army pacified the situation.)

1. ***Apa yang** telah meruntuhkan rumah itu? - bom*
(What has caused the house to collapse? - a bomb)

2. ***Siapa yang** telah mendirikan persatuan itu? - guru*
(Who founded the association? - teachers)

3. ***Apa yang** menghanyutkan pondok itu? - air bah*
(What washed away the hut? - a flood)

4. ***Siapa yang** telah menggadaikan rumahnya? - jurujual itu*
(Who mortgaged his house? - the salesman)

5. ***Siapa yang** mengharamkan perjudian? - kerajaan*
(Who banned gambling? - the government)

6. ***Apa yang** menenggelamkan kapal itu? - kapal selam*
(What sank the ship? - a submarine)

7. ***Siapa yang** mengelolakan kursus bahasa itu? - Kementerian Pelajaran*
(Who organized the language course? - the Ministry of Education)

8. ***Siapa yang** telah mempengerusikan sidang mingguan itu? - Perdana Menteri*
(Who chaired the weekly meeting? - the Prime Minister)

9. ***Siapa yang** telah menyuraikan pertemuan itu? - polis*
(Who dispersed the gathering? - the police)

10. ***Siapa yang** menubuhkan perpustakaan di mana-mana? - pemerintah*
(Who establishes libraries everywhere? - the government)

Exercise 4. Form questions from the following statements.

e.g.

*Dia **boleh** membuktikan kesalahan lelaki itu.* (He can prove the man's guilt.)	***Bolehkah** dia membuktikan kesalahan lelaki itu?* (Can he prove the man's guilt?)

Dia **dapat** *melaksanakan tugas itu.*
(He can carry out the task.)

Dapatkah *dia melaksanakan tugas itu?*
(Can he carry out the task?)

1. *Dia* **boleh** *melaksanakan kewajipannya.*
(He can accomplish his responsibilities.)
2. *Ali* **dapat** *menjalankan kerjanya.*
(Ali can carry out his job.)
3. *Dia* **boleh** *menjayakan usaha itu.*
(He can make the effort a success.)
4. *Dia* **dapat** *mengemaskan rumah itu sendiri.*
(He can tidy up the house himself.)
5. *Anak perempuan itu* **boleh** *mengemudikan perusahaan ayahnya.*
(The girl can manage her father's business.)
6. *Anak itu* **boleh** *mengkhatamkan Quran dalam tiga bulan.*
(The child can complete reading the Quran in three months' time.)
7. *Ubat itu* **boleh** *menguatkan badan.*
(The medicine can strengthen the body.)
8. *Hadiah percuma* **boleh** *melariskan barang dagangan.*
(Free gifts can make merchandise saleable.)
9. *Dia* **dapat** *menyalakan api itu.*
(He can light the fire.)
10. *Dia* **dapat** *memadamkan api itu.*
(He can extinguish the fire.)

14C. Grammar

Expansion of Simple Sentence

Simple sentences are the basic sentences in any language. They can be expanded or combined to form all the sentences in a language. In previous lesson we have already learnt that simple sentences can be expanded. In this lesson we intend to go into more details about the expansion of simple sentences.

The most common way of expanding a simple sentence is by expanding the noun that functions as a subject into noun phrase. A noun phrase is a group of words that can function as a noun:

e.g. ***Gadis itu*** *menyanyi.*
(**The girl** is singing.)

Gadis kecil itu *menyanyi.*
(**The small girl** is singing.)

Gadis Melayu itu *menyanyi.*
(**The Malay girl** is singing.)

Lima orang gadis itu *menyanyi.*
(**Five girls** are singing.)

Gadis di dalam bilik itu *menyanyi.*
(**The girl in the room** is singing.)

Lima orang gadis kecil Melayu di dalam bilik itu *menyanyi.*
(**Five small Malay girls in the room** are singing.)

All the phrases in bold are noun phrases, because they are expansion of the head noun *gadis* (the girl). These noun phrases are formed through the addition of the adjective *kecil*, the noun *Melayu*, the numeral *lima orang*, the prepositional phrase, *di dalam bilik* and a combination of all these modifiers. Below are some additional examples of noun phrases:

Buku ***tebal*** *itu mahal.*
(The **thick** book is expensive.)

Murid-murid ***sekolah*** *sedang menyanyi.*
(**School** children are singing.)

Kedua-dua *kejadian itu berlaku serentak.*
(The **two** incidents happened at the same time.)

Buku-buku ***di dalam almari buku*** *itulah kawan saya tiap-tiap hari.*
(The books **in the bookcase** are my friends every day.)

Ramai *murid tidak hadir hari ini.*
(**Many** pupils did not turn up today.)

It should be pointed out here that a noun functioning as an object can also be expanded in the same way.

e.g. *Dia menyetujui cadangan* ***Sudin.***
(He agrees to **Sudin's** suggestion.)

Saya kenal saudagar ***kaya*** *itu.*
(I know the **rich** merchant.)

Ali menaiki perahu ***lanun*** *itu.*
(Ali boarded the **pirate's** ship.)

Dia melihat jam ***di dinding***.
(He looked at the clock **on the wall**.)

All the words modifying the nouns are called modifiers.

Exercise 5. Underline the modifiers in the following sentences.

e.g.

Rumah Encik Rahman jauh dari sini. (Mr. Rahman's house is far from here.)	*Rumah* ***Encik Rahman*** *jauh dari sini.*

Rahim pergi mengambil beberapa bungkusan. (Rahim went to get a few packets.)	*Rahim pergi mengambil* ***beberapa*** *bungkusan.*

1. *Rumah Ahmad jauh dari sekolah.*
(Ahmad's house is far from school.)

2. *Angin laut telah memulihkan kesihatan saya.*
(The sea breeze has cured me [literally 'my health']).

3. *Bahasa Melayu mustahak.*
(Malay language is important.)

4. *Pelajaran sekolah itu tinggi.*
(The educational standard [literally 'lesson'] of the school is high.)

5. *Orang kaya patut menolong orang miskin.*
(Rich men should help poor men.)

6. *Tin kosong berbunyi kuat.*
(An empty vessel makes the loud noise.)

7. *Semua murid berkumpul di padang sekolah.*
(All the pupils gathered at the school field.)

8. *Gaji saya seribu dolar sebulan.*
(My salary is one thousand dollars a month.)

9. *Ali sudah menjadi ahli Persatuan Bahasa Melayu.*
(Ali became a member of the Malay Language Society.)

10. *Dia selalu bermain dengan kanak-kanak di dalam kampung.*
(He always played with the children in the village.)

Exercise 6. Expand the following sentences by adding suitable modifiers (from the box below) to the nouns.

di atas meja	*dari Jepun*	*dalam keluarga*	*di dalam air*
ramai	*banyak*	*segala*	*kencang*
cerdik	*lebat*		

e.g.

Anjing __________ itu telah menggigit seorang budak lelaki.
(The dog has bitten a boy.)

Anjing ***garang*** *itu telah menggigit seorang budak lelaki.*
(The fierce dog has bitten a boy.)

__________ *kawan-kawan berkumpul di rumahnya.*
(__________ the friends gathered at his house.)

Sekalian *kawan-kawan berkumpul di rumahnya.*
(All the friends gathered at his house.)

1. __________ *orang di situ.*
   (__________ people are there.)
2. *Salleh ada* __________ *buku.*
   (Salleh has __________ books.)
3. __________ *kehendaknya dipenuhi ibunya.*
   (__________ his wishes were satisfied by his mother.)
4. *Ribut* __________ *telah bertiup semalam.*
   (A __________ wind blew last night.)
5. *Hujan* __________ *telah turun.*
   (__________ rain fell.)
6. *Ikan* __________ *itu sedang bermain-main.*
   (The fish __________ is playing.)

7. *Buku* __________ *itu buku saya.*
   (The book __________ is my book.)

8. *Budak* __________ *disukai guru-guru.*
   (An __________ child is liked by teachers.)

9. *Tamu-tamu* __________ *sudah pulang.*
   (The guests __________ have returned home.)

10. *Masalah* __________ *itu susah diselesaikan.*
    (The problem __________ is difficult to solve.)

14D. Word Formation

ada, ajar, angkat, baik, bangun

We have learnt about noun-forming, verb-forming and adjective-forming prefixes and suffixes. From this lesson onwards, we are going to learn the different prefixes and suffixes that a root word may take. Below are examples on prefixes and suffixes commonly used. Observe their uses carefully.

(a) ***ada: berada, mengadakan, keadaan, adakan, berkeadaan***

e.g. *Emak saya tidak* ***ada*** *di rumah.*
(My mother **is** not at home.)

Ketika itu saya ***berada*** *di Malaysia.*
(At that time I **was** in Malaysia.)

Azman anak orang ***berada****.*
(Azman is a **rich** man's son.)

Mereka ***mengadakan*** *pertemuan itu di sebuah restoran.*
(They **organized** the meeting in a restaurant.)

Keadaan bilik itu sangat bersih.
(The **condition** of the room is clean.)

Adakan *dia hendak membeli rumah itu; sedangkan dia bergaji rendah.*
(**How can** he buy that house; he earns a low salary.)

Negara itu ***berkeadaan*** *kacau-bilau kerana serangan-serangan pemberontak.*
(That country **is in a state** of chaos as a result of the attacks by rebels.)

(b) ***ajar: berajar, belajar, mengajar, mengajari, mengajarkan, mempelajari, ajaran, pengajaran, pelajar, pelajaran, berpelajaran, pembelajaran, pengajar, terpelajar***

e.g. *Budak-budak itu tidak* ***berajar.***
(Those children have not been **educated.**)

Adik lelaki sedang ***belajar*** *berenang.*
(Younger brother is **learning** to swim.)

Fatimah ***mengajar*** *anaknya membaca dan menulis.*
(Fatimah **teaches** her child to read and write.)

Guru yang ***mengajari*** *murid-murid itu tidak hadir hari ini.*
(The teacher who **teaches** those students is not present today.)

Emak sedang ***mengajarkan*** *cara-cara membuat kek kepada kakak.*
(Mother is **teaching** the methods of making cake to sister.)

Ia sedang ***mempelajari*** *ilmu kimia.*
(He is **studying** chemistry.)

Dia tidak pernah melupakan ***ajaran*** *gurunya.*
(He never forgets the **teaching** of his teacher.)

Pengajaran *bahasa Melayu di sekolah itu kurang baik.*
(**The teaching** of Malay language in that school is not [literally 'less'] good.)

Budak lelaki itu ***pelajar*** *sekolah menengah.*
(The boy is a secondary school **student**.)

Pelajaran*nya bagus sekali.*
(His **studies** are very good. = He is very good at his studies.)

Hanya orang-orang yang ***berpelajaran*** *sahaja dijemput.*
(Only persons **of learning** are invited.)

Pembelajaran *bahasa Melayu memerlukan banyak masa.*
(The study of Malay language requires a lot of time.)

Pada masa ini ***pengajar-pengajar*** *sangat berkurangan.*
(At present, **teachers** are in short supply.)

Golongan ***terpelajar*** *memang dihormat dalam masyarakat kami.*
(The **learned** are respected in our society.)

(c) angkat: berangkat, memberangkatkan, keberangkatan, mengangkat, mengangkati, mengangkatkan, angkatan, pengangkatan, pengangkat

e.g. *Rombongan itu akan* ***berangkat*** *ke Pulau Pinang.*
(The group will **depart** for Penang.)

Usaha untuk ***memberangkatkan*** *rombongan itu ke London telah dibuat.*
(Efforts at **despatching** the group to London have been made.)

Keberangkatan *rombongan itu telah dirahsiakan.*
(The **departure** of the group has been kept secret.)

Seorang murid ***mengangkat*** *tangannya untuk menjawab soalan guru itu.*

(A pupil **raised** his hand in order to answer the teacher's question.)

Pertubuhan itu hendak ***mengangkat*** *Rahmat sebagai pengerusinya.*
(The organization wishes **to appoint** Rahmat as its Chairman.)

Mereka ***mengangkati*** *barang-barang muatan itu sejak pagi tadi.*
(They **have been unloading** the cargoes since this morning.)

Dia ***mengangkatkan*** *topinya untuk memberi hormat.*
(He **took off** his cap in order to salute.)

Perselisihan terjadi antara ***angkatan*** *muda dan* ***angkatan*** *tua.*
(A misunderstanding occurs between the younger **generation** and the older **generation**.)

Pengangkatan *beliau sebagai duta telah disahkan.*
(His **appointment** as ambassador has been officially confirmed.)

Pengangkat *beg tadi tidak dapat dikesan.*
(The **person who carried** the bag cannot be traced.)

(d) ***baik: baik-baik, sebaik, berbaik-baik, membaiki, kebaikan, pembaikan, membaikkan, pembaik***

e.g. *Baca* ***baik-baik*** *surat itu.*
(Read **carefully** the letter.)

Pensel kamu tidak ***sebaik*** *pensel saya.*
(Your pencil is not **as good as** my pencil.)

Saya tidak tahu mengapa ia ***berbaik-baik*** *dengan orang jahat itu.*
(I do not know why he **befriends** that criminal.)

*Osman sedang **membaiki** radionya yang rosak.*
(Osman was **repairing** his radio which was broken.)

*Saya tidak sanggup membalas **kebaikan** hati saudara.*
(I am unable to repay your **kindness**.)

*Buku ini merupakan **pembaikan** daripada buku yang terdahulu.*
(This book is a **revision** of the previous one.)

*Dia **membaikkan** kelakuan anaknya.*
(He **corrects** his child's behaviour.)

***Pembaik** kereta itu mengenakan kami bayaran yang tinggi untuk perkhidmatannya.*
(The car **repairman** charges us highly for his services.)

(e) ***bangun: membangun, membangunkan, terbangun, bangunan, pembangunan***

e.g. *Saya sudah **bangun** pukul enam pagi.*
(I **woke up** at six o'clock in the morning.)

*Kita mesti berusaha **membangun** negara kita.*
(We must try **to build** our country.)

*Ibu **membangunkan** saya tiap-tiap pagi.*
(Mother **wakes** me up every morning.)

*Dia **terbangun** di tengah malam.*
(He **woke up** [**unintentionally**] in the middle of the night.)

***Bangunan** itu sudah tua.*
(The **building** is already old.)

***Pembangunan** bandar mendapat perhatian pemerintah.*
(Urban development gets the government's attention.)

LESSON 15

15A. Conversation

Sejarah Melayu
(The Malay Annals)

Anita: *Eh, Jamilah, apa saudari buat di sini?*
(Hey, Jamilah, what are you doing here?)

Jamilah: *Saya sedang membaca sebuah buku yang sangat menarik.*
(I am reading a very interesting book.)

Anita: *Apa namanya buku itu?*
(What is the name of the book?)

Jamilah: *'Sejarah Melayu'.*
(The 'Malay Annals'.)

Anita: *'Sejarah Melayu'?*
(The 'Malay Annals'?)

Jamilah: *Mengapa saudari hairan?*
(Why are you surprised?)

Anita: *Saya pernah membaca buku itu. Buku itu ditulis dalam bahasa lama yang membosankan. Sebab itulah saya merasa hairan bila saudari berkata buku itu menarik.*
(I have read the book. It is written in classical language which is boring. That is why I am surprised to hear you say that the book is interesting.)

Jamilah: *Itu hanya pendapat saudari sendiri. Pendapat saya lain. Saya fikir buku ini patut dibaca oleh semua orang.*
(That is your opinion. My opinion is different. I think the book should be read by everyone.)

Anita: *Mengapa saudari berkata demikian?*
(Why do you say so?)

Jamilah: *'Sejarah Melayu' banyak mengandungi kisah-kisah yang menarik tentang Singapura. Di samping itu ia juga mengisahkan asal-usul kerajaan Melayu dan keagungannya pada zaman dahulu.*
(The 'Malay Annals' has many interesting stories about Singapore. Besides, it also narrates the origins of the Malay kingdom and its glory in times gone by.)

Anita: *Betulkah raja-raja Melayu berasal dari Iskandar Zulkarnain?*
(Is it true that the Malay rulers are descended from Alexander the Great?)

Jamilah: *Betul atau tidak, itu tidak penting. Yang penting orang Melayu percaya raja mereka berasal dari Iskandar Zulkarnain.*
(Whether it is true or not is not important. What is important is that the Malays believe their rulers are descended from Alexander the Great.)

Anita: *Wah, saudari ini pandai sekali. Saudari bercakap seperti seorang pensyarah universiti.*
(Wah, you are very clever. You speak like a university lecturer.)

Jamilah: *Oh, tidak. Saya tahu hanya sedikit sahaja.*
(Oh, no. I know only a little.)

15B. Structure

Read the following sentences carefully.

SUBJECT	PREDICATE
Dia He	*selalu melawati sahabat-sahabatnya.* always visits his friends.
Dia He	*sentiasa menghujani lelaki itu dengan pertanyaan.* always showers the man with questions.
Dia He	*menjumpai lelaki itu di bandar.* met the man in town.
Pekerja pejabat itu The office worker	*boleh mengatasi rakan-rakan sekerjanya.* can excel his colleagues.
Pengguna The consumer	*mendekati jurujual itu dengan hati-hati.* approaches the salesman(woman) cautiously.

Exercise 1. Substitute the verb in bold, in the model sentence with the one given.

e.g.	*Dia tidak mahu* ***memarahi*** *rakannya.* (He does not want to scold his colleague.)
menyebelahi (to side with)	*Dia tidak mahu* ***menyebelahi*** *rakannya.* (He does not want to side with his colleague.)

menyaingi (to compete with)	*Dia tidak mahu* ***menyaingi*** *rakannya.* (He does not want to compete with his colleague.)
menyetujui (to agree with)	*Dia tidak mahu* ***menyetujui*** *rakannya.* (He does not want to agree with his colleague.)
menyalahi (to blame)	*Dia tidak mahu* ***menyalahi*** *rakannya.* (He does not want to blame his colleague.)

1. *menghabisi* (to finish off)
2. *menyumpahi* (to curse)
3. *menyertai* (to join)
4. *menyekutui* (to form an alliance with)
5. *meramahi* (to please)
6. *memusuhi* (to antagonize)
7. *menanyai* (to ask)
8. *menyakiti* (to hurt)
9. *menakuti* (to frighten)
10. *mempercayai* (to believe)

Exercise 2. Answer the following questions. Use the words given.

e.g.

Question	*Answer*
Dia mengunjungi siapa di kampung? - *saudara-maranya* (Whom did he visit in the village? - his relatives)	*Dia mengunjungi saudara-maranya di kampung.* (He visited his relatives in the village.)

Dia sangat mencintai siapa? *- isterinya*	*Dia sangat mencintai isterinya.*
(Whom did he love deeply? - his wife)	(He loved his wife deeply.)

1. *Allah selalu melindungi siapa? - orang yang salih*
   (Whom does God protect? - pious persons)
2. *Jururawat itu sedang mengubati siapa? - orang sakit*
   (Whom is the nurse treating? - the patient)
3. *Dia akan mewakili siapa dalam pertemuan itu? - ketua pejabatnya*
   (Whom will he be representing at the meeting? - his office chief)
4. *Pihak polis telah menghubungi siapa petang semalam? - usahawan itu*
   (Whom did the police contact yesterday afternoon? - the industrialist)
5. *Dia sangat mengasihi siapa? - sahabatnya*
   (Whom did he love very much? - his friend)
6. *Ramlan mengasihani siapa? - orang miskin*
   (Whom did Ramlan pity? - the poor)
7. *Rosminah sedang menyusui siapa? - anaknya*
   (Whom is Rosminah giving milk to? - her child)
8. *Dia mengesyaki siapa? - saudara kandungnya sendiri*
   (Whom did he suspect? - his own brother/sister)
9. *Orang itu telah mengkhianati siapa? - bangsanya sendiri*
   (Whom did the man betray? - his own race)
10. *Dia sanggup mengahwini siapa? - gadis itu*
    (Whom is he willing to marry? - the girl)

Exercise 3. Answer the following questions. Use the words given.

e.g.

Question	*Answer*
Siapa yang *menghormati pahlawan?* *- masyarakat* (Who honours heroes? - the society)	***Masyarakat*** *menghormati pahlawan.* (The society honours heroes.)
Siapa yang *akan menyarai anak-anak yang malang itu?* *- tiada seorang pun* (Who will support the poor children.) - no one)	***Tiada seorang*** *pun akan menyarai anak-anak yang malang itu.* (No one will support the poor children?

1. ***Siapa yang*** *enggan menikahi gadis kaya itu? - tiada orang*
   (Who is unwilling to marry the rich girl? - no one)

2. ***Siapa yang*** *sangat menyayangi isterinya? - lelaki itu*
   (Who loves his wife dearly? - that man)

3. ***Siapa yang*** *menyegani lelaki itu? - kita semua*
   (Who feel respectful towards the man? - all of us)

4. ***Siapa yang*** *masih mencurigai lelaki itu? - pihak polis*
   (Who is still suspicious of the man? - the police)

5. ***Siapa yang*** *suka mencampuri orang-orang jahat? - ramai budak nakal*
   (Who like to associate with bad people? - many deliquents)

6. ***Siapa yang*** *selalu mendampingi adiknya ke pekan? - penulis itu*
   (Who is always accompanying his brother to the town? - the writer)

7. ***Siapa yang*** *mengerumuni pengarang itu? - murid-murid sekolah*
   (Who surrounded the writer? - the school pupils)

8. ***Siapa yang*** *pulang menemui kaum keluarganya? - ahli bahasa itu*
   (Who returned to meet his family? - the linguist)

9. ***Siapa yang*** *dapat menandingi Ahmad dalam permainan itu? - tiada seorang pun*
   (Who can be a formidable opponent to Ahmad in the game? - no one)

10. ***Siapa yang*** *menanyainya tentang hal itu? - ahli sejarah*
    (Who asked him about the matter? - the historian)

Exercise 4. Answer the following questions. Use the words given.

e.g.

Question	*Answer*
Bagaimana *dia menghadapi musuh-musuhnya?* *- dengan berani* (How did he confront his enemies? - bravely)	*Dia menghadapi musuh-musuhnya* ***dengan berani.*** (He confronted his enemies **bravely**.)
Bagaimana *dia menyudahi suratnya?* *- dengan salam hormat* (How did he conclude the letter? - with greetings)	*Dia menyudahi suratnya* ***dengan salam hormat.*** (He concluded the letter with greetings.)

1. ***Bagaimana*** *dia menistai lawannya? - dengan kata-kata menghina*
   (How did he insult his opponent?- with abusive words)

2. ***Bagaimana*** *dia memberkati anak lelakinya? - dengan membaca mantera*
   (How did he bless his son? - by reading a charm)

3. ***Bagaimana*** *hakim mengadili lelaki itu? - dengan bijaksana*
   (How did the judge pass his judgement on the man?
   - wisely)

4. ***Bagaimana*** *dia menghadapi lelaki tua itu? - dengan hati yang berdebar-debar*
   (How did he confront the old man? - with a beating heart)

5. ***Bagaimana*** *dia mempengaruhi pegawai itu? - dengan wang*
   (How did he influence the officer? - with money)

6. ***Bagaimana*** *dia menyuapi pegawai itu? - dengan hadiah*
   (How did he bribe the officer? - with gifts)

7. ***Bagaimana*** *dia menziarahi ibunya? - dengan senang hati*
   (How was he when he visited his mother? - happily)

8. ***Bagaimana*** *dia menyirami bunga? - dengan getah paip*
   (How did he water the flowers? - with a rubber hose)

9. ***Bagaimana*** *dia melayani pelanggan-pelanggannya? - dengan ramah*
   (How did he serve his customers? - courteously)

10. ***Bagaimana*** *teguh dia mempercayai lelaki itu? - dengan sepenuh hati*
    (How much did he trust the man? - whole-heartedly)

15C. Grammar

Expansion of Simple Sentences (continuation)

We have discussed the expansion of nouns in simple sentences. Adjectives and verbs can also be expanded. The best way to expand adjectives is to add words denoting various degrees of comparison.

e.g. *Anak itu **agak** manja sekarang.*
(The child is **rather** pampered now.)

*Anak itu **sangat** manja sekarang.*
(The child is **very** pampered now.)

*Anak itu **kurang** manja sekarang.*
(The child is **less** pampered now.)

Verbs, on the other hand, can be modified by auxiliary verbs. There are two types of auxiliary verbs: (a) aspect auxiliaries e.g. *sudah, telah, masih, sedang,* and *akan* and (b) modal auxiliary e.g. *boleh, dapat, hendak, mahu, ingin, mesti, wajib, harus.* A simple sentence may contain more than one auxiliary verb.

e.g. *Saya **sudah** makan pagi tadi.*
(I **have** eaten this morning.)

*Saya **akan** belajar bahasa Arab.*
(I **will** study Arabic.)

*Dia **belum** hendak pergi.*
(He **does not wish** to go.)

*Dia **masih belum hendak** pergi.*
(He **is still not willing** to go.)

*Bapa kamu **belum tentu boleh** datang.*
(Your father **may not be** [literally 'is not certain to be'] **able to** come.)

Perhaps adverbs or adverbials are most important in the expansion of simple sentences.

e.g. ***Sesungguhnya** saudara kawan yang setia.*
(**Indeed**, you are a loyal friend.)

*Usman sakit **barangkali.***
(Usman is sick **perhaps**.)

Mereka berkahwin ***diam-diam sahaja***.
(They married **quietly.**)

Dia membuat kerja itu ***dengan hati-hati.***
(He does the job **cautiously**.)

Similarly, a simple sentence may contain more than one adverb or adverbial.

e.g. *Mereka tinggal* ***di sini sejak perang dulu.***
(They have been staying **here since the last war**.)

Mereka masuk ***dengan diam-diam ke dalam bilik itu.***
(They entered **quietly into the room**.)

Pada suatu hari dalam bulan puasa*, saya berjumpa seorang pengemis* ***di sebuah pusat membeli-belah di Singapura.***
(**One day in the fasting month**, I [accidentally] met a beggar **in a shopping centre in Singapore**.)

Exercise 5. Delete the modifiers in the following sentences.

e.g.

Jalan raya itu sibuk sekali. (The highway is very busy.)	*Jalan raya itu sibuk.* (The highway is busy.)
Siang-siang dia sudah datang. (He came very early.)	*Dia sudah datang.* (He came.)

1. *Cerita itu terlalu panjang.*
(The story is too long.)

2. *Bubur itu kurang manis.*
(The porridge is not sweet [enough].)

3. *Saudagar itu lokek benar.*
   (The businessman is really stingy.)

4. *Pekerjaan itu amat susah.*
   (The job is very difficult.)

5. *Mereka masuk ke bilik darjah dua-dua.*
   (They entered the classroom two by two.)

6. *Dia merenung muka adik lelakinya lama-lama.*
   (He stares at his younger brother's face for a long time.)

7. *Kamu akan menyesal kelak.*
   (You will regret later.)

8. *Ayah sudah pergi ke Jakarta dengan kapal terbang.*
   (Father went to Jakarta by plane.)

9. *Saya tidak akan masuk sekolah esok.*
   (I will not go to school tomorrow.)

10. *Tiap-tiap pagi dia pergi ke pejabat dengan bas.*
    (Every day, he goes to office by bus.)

Exercise 6. Expand the following sentences by adding modifying words to the adjectives or verbs.

e.g.

Baunya harum. (The smell is fragrant.)	*Baunya harum* ***sekali.*** (The smell is **very** fragrant.)
Dia bercakap. (He talked.)	*Dia bercakap* ***dahulu***. (He talked **first**.)

1. *Airnya jernih.*
   (The water is clear.)

2. *Udaranya bersih.*
   (The air is fresh.)

3. *Budak itu degil.*
(The child is stubborn.)

4. *Pelabuhan itu besar.*
(The harbour is big.)

5. *Lelaki itu berjalan.*
(The man walks.)

6. *Bayi itu menangis.*
(The baby cried.)

7. *Ali datang.*
(Ali came.)

8. *Keretapi bergerak.*
(The train moves.)

9. *Angin bertiup.*
(The wind blows.)

10. *Hujan turun.*
(Rains fall.)

15D. Word Formation

benar, boleh, buat, dapat, datang

(a) ***benar: benar-benar, sebenarnya, membenarkan, kebenaran, pembenaran, dibenarkan***

e.g. *Ejaan perkataan itu tidak* ***benar.***
(The spelling of that word is not **correct**.)

Kata-katanya itu meninggalkan kesan ***benar-benar*** *di hatiku.*
(His words have [literally 'leave'] **a great** effect on my feelings [literally 'heart'].)

Sebenarnya *saya suka makan durian.*
(**Actually**, I like to eat durian.)

Yang empunya rumah tidak ***membenarkan*** *kami masuk.*
(The house owner does not **allow** us to enter.)

Kedai itu didirikan tanpa ***kebenaran*** *kerajaan.*
(The shop was built without a **permit** from the government.)

Kebenaran *khabar itu masih disangsikan.*
(The **validity** of the news is still doubted.)

Pembenaran *berita itu dilakukan oleh pemerintah.*
(The **validation** of the news is made by the government.)

Kami ***dibenarkan*** *pulang awal hari ini.*
(We **are allowed** to go back early today.)

(b) ***boleh: seboleh-bolehnya, membolehkan, kebolehan, berkebolehan***

e.g. *Kamu* ***boleh*** *melihat dengan mata kamu sendiri.*
(You **can** see with your own eyes.)

Seboleh-bolehnya *dia tidak mahu berjumpa dengan lelaki itu.*
(**As far as possible**, he does not wish to meet that man.)

Kekayaan ayahnya ***membolehkan*** *dia melanjutkan pelajaran ke luar negeri.*
(His father's wealth **allows** him to further his studies abroad.)

Saya tidak menyangsikan ***kebolehan*** *lelaki itu.*
(I do not doubt the man's **ability**.)

Pelajar itu ***berkebolehan*** *masuk belajar di universiti.*
(The student **has the ability** to study in the university.)

(c) ***buat: berbuat, membuat, membuatkan, terbuat, buatan, perbuatan, pembuatan, pembuat***

e.g. *Dia tidak **berbuat** apa-apa.*
(He did not **do** anything.)

*Emak **membuat** kuih di dapur.*
(Mother **is making** cake in the kitchen.)

*Mereka hendak **membuatkan** kita sebuah masjid baru.*
(They intend to **make [build]** us a new mosque.)

*Dinding rumah itu **terbuat** daripada papan.*
(The walls of the house **are made** of wood.)

*Kasut itu **buatan** tempatan.*
(The shoes are a local **made**.)

***Perbuatan** lelaki itu tidak betul.*
(The man's **doing** [action] is not correct.)

***Pembuatan** kapal bukanlah hal yang sukar.*
(**The making [building]** of ships is not a difficult matter.)

***Pembuat** cerita itu tidak dapat diketahui.*
(The story **teller [maker]** is not known.)

(d) ***dapat: sedapat-dapatnya, mendapat, mendapati, mendapatkan, terdapat, pendapat, berpendapat, pendapatan, berpendapatan, kedapatan***

e.g. *Saya **dapat** sepuluh ribu dolar kerana menang loteri.*
(I **get** ten thousand dollars for winning the lottery.)

*Semua pihak telah berusaha **sedapat-dapatnya** untuk menyelesaikan masalah itu.*
(All parties **to their utmost capabilities** have endeavoured to solve the problem.)

Peniaga itu ***mendapat*** *keuntungan yang lumayan.*
(The businessman **gets** satisfactory profits.)

Para doktor ***mendapati*** *ramai penduduk di situ menghidap penyakit malaria.*
(Doctors **discover** many residents there are suffering from malaria.)

Wan Intan berlari ***mendapatkan*** *suaminya.*
(Wan Intan runs **to meet** her husband.)

Di belakang rumahnya ***terdapat*** *pokok buah-buahan.*
(At the back of his house **are** fruit trees.)

Pada ***pendapat*** *saya, eloklah kita sokong projek itu.*
(In my **opinion**, it is good that we support the project.)

Saya ***berpendapat*** *bahawa dia seorang yang jujur.*
(I **am of the opinion** that he is an honest person.)

Dia tidak mampu membeli rumah kerana ***pendapatannya*** *kecil.*
(He cannot afford to buy a house because **his income** is small.)

Golongan yang ***berpendapatan*** *rendah sering mempunyai lebih masalah.*
(The group **with** a low **income** often has more problems.)

Manakala dia balik, ***kedapatan*** *rumahnya kosong dan sunyi.*
(When he returned, his house **was found** to be empty and quiet.)

(e) ***datang: datang-datang, mendatang, mendatangkan, mendatangi, pendatang, kedatangan***

e.g. *Barang-barang itu* ***datang*** *dari luar negeri.*
(The goods **came** from abroad.)

Datang-datang *dia ke mari hendak makan.*
(**No sooner has he arrived** [literally **'come'**] here, than he wants to eat.)

Pada masa itu satu fikiran yang baik ***mendatang****.*
(At that time a good idea **emerges suddenly**.)

Peniaga itu ***mendatangkan*** *berbagai jenis kain dari Jepun.*
(The businessman **imported** various kinds of cloths from Japan.)

Ramai cucunya ***mendatanginya*** *pada Hari Raya.*
(Many of his grandchildren **visited him** on Hari Raya.)

Banyak ***pendatang*** *haram di kampung itu.*
(There are many illegal **immigrants** in that village.)

Kedatangan*nya disambut dengan meriah oleh orang-orang kampung.*
(His **arrival** was merrily greeted by the villagers.)

LESSON 16

16A. Conversation

Kemalangan
(An Accident)

Rahman: *Saya dengar kereta saudara berlanggar dengan lori, betulkah?*
(I heard that your car collided with a truck, is it true?)

Lin: *Kira-kira begitulah.*
(It is more or less so.)

Rahman: *Di manakah kemalangan itu berlaku?*
(Where did the accident happen?)

Lin: *Kemalangan itu berlaku dekat Kulai, Johor.*
(The accident happened near Kulai, Johore.)

Rahman: *Bagaimana kemalangan itu berlaku? Sebab saudara tidak jaga-jagakah atau sebab saudara melarikan kereta terlampau cepat?*
(How did the accident happen? Was it because you were careless or because you drove too fast?)

Lin: *Oh, tidak. Kalau saya cuai atau larikan kereta cepat-cepat, saudara tidak dapat jumpa saya lagi.*
(Oh, no. If I had been careless or had driven too fast, you could not have seen me any more.)

Rahman: *Jadi, bagaimana kemalangan itu boleh berlaku?*
(So, how did the accident happen?)

Lin: *Saya melanggar sebuah lori yang berhenti di tepi jalan. Tetapi bukan saya yang salah. Badan lori itu menyerong ke tengah jalan. Tidak ada lampu pula.*

Hari pun sudah gelap. Bagaimana saya boleh nampak?
(I ran into a stationary lorry at the road side. But it was not my fault. The body of the truck was slanting towards the middle of the road. In addition, there was no light. The day was getting dark too. How could I see?)

Rahman: *Apa saudara buat selepas kemalangan itu?*
(What did you do after the accident?)

Lin: *Saya telefon ke balai polis. Polis datang dan mengukur jalan. Kemudian kami dibawa ke balai polis.*
(I telephoned the police station. The police came and measured the road. Later, we were taken to the police station.)

Rahman: *Apa yang terjadi di balai polis?*
(What happened at the police station?)

Lin: *Nama, alamat dan nombor kad pengenalan saya dicatat. Demikian juga nombor polisi insuran saya.*
(My name, address and identity card number were noted down. So was my insurance policy number.)

Rahman: *Saya gembira sekali saudara selamat.*
(I am happy that you are safe.)

16B. Structure

Read the following sentences carefully.

SUBJECT	PREDICATE
Dia He	*sedang menikmati nasi minyak itu.* is savouring the *nasi minyak* [literally 'oily rice'; name of a dish].
Tukang kayu The carpenter	*sedang mendindingi rumah itu.* is walling up the house.
Dia He	*sedang melubangi pintu itu.* is making a hole in the door.
Pengurus itu The manager	*sudah membaiki rumahnya.* has renovated his house.
Mereka They	*sudah memiliki rumah sendiri.* possessed a house [of their own].

Exercise 1. Substitute the word in bold, in the model sentence with the one given.

e.g.	*Dia sedang* ***menikmati*** *nasi minyak itu.* (He is **savouring** the *nasi minyak* [literally 'oily rice'; name of a dish].)
gulai (curry soup)	*Dia sedang menikmati* ***gulai*** *itu.* (He is savouring the **curry soup**.)
masakan (the dish)	*Dia sedang menikmati* ***masakan*** *itu.* (He is savouring the **dish**.)
merempahi (to spice)	*Dia sedang* ***merempahi*** *masakan itu.* (He is **spicing** the dish.)

daging (meat)	*Dia sedang merempahi* ***daging*** *itu.* (He is spicing the **meat**.)

1. *menggarami* (to salt)
2. *telur rebus* (boiled egg)
3. *lauk* (cooked meat with gravy)
4. *merasai* (to taste)
5. *gado-gado* (vegetable salad)
6. *soto ayam* (chicken soup)
7. *memanasi* (to heat up)
8. *sayur-sayuran* (vegetable)
9. *nasi goreng* (fried rice)
10. *minuman* (the drinks)

Exercise 2. Answer the following questions. Use the words given.

e.g.

Question	*Answer*
Hakim itu sedang ***membuat*** *apa?* - *mengadili perkara pembunuhan* (What is the judge doing? - hearing a murder case)	*Hakim itu sedang* ***mengadili perkara pembunuhan.*** (The judge is hearing a murder case.)
Kita mesti ***membuat apa****?* - *memerangi jenayah* (What must we do? - to fight against crime)	*Kita mesti* ***memerangi jenayah.*** (We must fight against crime.)

1. *Mereka sedang* ***membuat apa****? - menikmati pertunjukan itu*
   (What are they doing? - enjoying the show)

2. *Murid-murid sedang* ***membuat apa****? - menjalani peperiksaan*
   (What are the pupils doing? - sitting for an examination)

3. *Lelaki itu sudah* ***membuat apa****? - mengakui kesalahannya*
   (What has the man done? - to admit his guilt)
4. *Kita mesti* ***membuat apa****? - mengatasi kesukaran kita*
   (What must we do? - to overcome our difficulties)
5. *Mereka mesti* ***membuat apa****? - mendalami pengetahuan mereka*
   (What must they do? - to widen their knowledge)
6. *Kakak mesti* ***membuat apa*** *hari ini? - mengemasi rumah*
   (What must elder sister do today? - to tidy up the house)
7. *Anak-anak patut* ***membuat apa****? menghargai usaha orang tua mereka*
   (What should children do? - to appreciate their parents' efforts)
8. *Mereka sudah* ***membuat apa*** *tahun lepas? - mengelilingi dunia*
   (What did they do last year? - to travel round the world)
9. *Mereka sedang* ***membuat apa****? - menghalangi pekerjaan kita*
   (What are they doing? - to obstruct our work)
10. *Mereka disuruh* ***membuat apa****? - menjauhi budak-budak nakal*
   (What are they told to do? - to keep away from delinquents)

Exercise 3. Answer the following questions. Use the words given.

e.g.

Question	*Answer*
Siapa *dapat memasuki kawasan itu?* *- pengawal keselamatan* (Who can enter the area? - the security guard)	***Pengawal keselamatan*** *dapat memasuki kawasan itu.* (The security guard can enter the area.)

Siapa *sudah menduduki rumah itu?*
- pengurus kita
(Who has occupied the house?
- our manager)

Pengurus *kita sudah menduduki rumah itu.*
(Our manager has occupied the house.)

1. ***Siapa*** *sudah memanasi makanan itu? - emaknya*
(Who has heated up the food? - his mother)
2. ***Siapa*** *dapat menaiki kereta itu? - semua orang*
(Who can ride in that car? - everyone)
3. ***Siapa*** *sudah memungkiri janjinya? - saksi*
(Who has broken his promise? - the witness)
4. ***Siapa*** *akan menepati janjinya? - peguam itu*
(Who is going to keep his promise? - the lawyer)
5. ***Siapa*** *sudah melawati sekolah baru itu? - inspektor sekolah*
(Who has visited the new school? - the school inspector)
6. ***Siapa*** *sudah mengurangi harga beras? - pekedai itu*
(Who has reduced the price of rice? - the shopkeeper)
7. ***Siapa*** *dapat mengharungi sungai itu? - orang-orang kampung*
(Who can cross the river? - the villagers)
8. ***Siapa*** *sudah membaiki jalan itu? - pekerja-pekerja*
(Who has repaired the road? - the workers)
9. ***Siapa*** *dapat menghabisi kerja itu dalam seminggu? - abang saya*
(Who can finish the job in a weeks' time? - my elder brother)
10. ***Siapa*** *sudah menghiasi bilik itu dengan gambar-gambar? - kakak saya*
(Who has decorated the room with pictures? - my elder sister)

Exercise 4. Answer the following questions. Use the words given.

e.g.

Question	*Answer*
***Bilakah** mereka akan memulai perniagaan baru?* *- tahun depan* (When are they going to start a new business? - next year)	*Mereka akan memulai perniagaan baru **tahun depan**.* (They are going to start a new business next year.)
***Sejak bilakah** mereka sudah memiliki rumah sendiri?* *- dua tahun yang lalu* (Since when have they owned a house [of their own]? - two years ago)	*Mereka sudah memiliki rumah sendiri sejak **dua tahun yang lalu.*** (They have owned a house [of their own] since two years ago.)

1. ***Bilakah** dia akan mengetuai rombongan ke Kuala Lumpur?*
   - minggu depan
   (When is he going to lead the mission to Kuala Lumpur?
   - next week)

2. *Sejak **bilakah** Pak Man sudah memagari kebunnya? - bulan lalu*
   (Since when has Pak Man fenced up his farm? - last month)

3. *Sejak **bilakah** dia sudah menganggotai syarikat itu? - lima tahun yang lalu*
   (Since when has he become a member of the company?
   - five years ago)

4. ***Bilakah** dia akan mengepalai syarikat itu? - dalam dua tahun*
   (When is he going to head the company? - in two years' time)

5. *Sejak* ***bilakah*** *dia sudah mendiami rumah itu? - dua minggu yang lalu*
(Since when has he stayed in that house? - two weeks ago)

6. ***Bilakah*** *Razak akan menduduki peperiksaannya? - minggu ini*
(When is Razak going to sit for his examination? - this week)

7. *Sejak* ***bilakah*** *dia banyak menghadiri seminar? - setahun yang lalu*
(Since when does he often attend seminars? - one year ago)

8. *Sejak* ***bilakah*** *dia selalu menuruti permintaan anak lelakinya? - tiga tahun yang lalu*
(Since when has he always granted his son's requests? - three years ago)

9. ***Bilakah*** *pelajar-pelajar akan memasuki universiti? - pada bulan Julai nanti*
(When will the students enter the university? - in July)

10. *Sejak* ***bilakah*** *Ali sudah mematuhi cakap ibunya? - malam tadi*
(Since when has Ali obeyed his mother [literally 'mother's words'?] - last night)

16C. Grammar

Expansion of Simple Sentences (continuation)

Adverbs or adverbial phrases are the most important group of words used to expand simple sentences. Indeed, there are very few simple sentences without the accompaniment of adverbs or adverbial phrases. Most sentences are accompanied by adverbs or adverbial phrases which can be classified into at least four groups:

(a) Adverbial phrases of time

e.g. *Dia datang pada* ***waktu malam.***
(He came at night.)

Dalam masa dua jam *dia akan sampai.*
(In two hours' time, he will arrive.)

Sepanjang tahun *dia tidak membaca sebuah buku pun.*
(Throughout the whole year, he has not read even a book.)

Dia belajar bahasa Mandarin ***seminggu sekali.***
(He studies Mandarin once a week.)

(b) Adverbial phrases of place

e.g. *Dia berjalan* ***ke perpustakaan****.*
(He walks to the library.)

Ali sudah berjaya ***di lapangan sukan.***
(Ali was successful in the field of sports.)

Dia juga maju ***dalam pelajarannya****.*
(He was also successful in his studies.)

Saya suka duduk ***di belakang rumah saya****.*
(I like to sit at the back of my house.)

(c) Adverbial phrases of manner

e.g. *Dia menjawab pertanyaan itu* ***dengan berang****.*
(He answered the question angrily.)

Majlis perkahwinan itu telah diadakan ***secara besar-besaran.***
(The wedding party was organized on a grand scale.)

Dia menjumpai cincin isterinya ***secara kebetulan****.*
(He found his wife's ring accidentally.)

Pemuda-pemudi sedang menari ***dengan rancak.***
(The young men and women are dancing to a fast beat.)

(d) Other classes of adverbial phrases

e.g. *Banyak tanaman rosak* ***kerana banjir.***
(A lot of agricultural produce was spoilt because of the flood.)

Dia mengorbankan wang dan tenaga ***untuk kepentingan negara.***
(He sacrificed money and energy in the country's interest.)

Dia membuka pintu itu ***dengan kunci.***
(He opened the door with a key.)

Exercise 5. Delete the adverbial phrases in the following sentences.

e.g.

Mesyuarat itu telah berjalan mengikut agenda. (The meeting proceeded according to the agenda.)	*Mesyuarat itu telah berjalan.* (The meeting proceeded.)
Pada akhir tahun ini saya akan melancong. (At the end of this year I will be touring.)	*Saya akan melancong.* (I will be touring.)

1. *Majlis perkahwinan itu telah dilakukan mengikut adat orang Melayu.*
(The wedding ceremony was carried out according to Malay customs.)

2. *Emaknya mengalas meja dengan sehelai kain putih.*
(Her mother covers the table with a piece of white cloth.)

3. *Aliran tenaga elektrik terputus kerana suatu kerosakan.*
   (The electrical supply was disrupted because of a fault.)

4. *Firma itu akan mengambil kakitangan baru tahun hadapan.*
   (The firm will recruit new staff next year.)

5. *Dia berangan menjadi pensyarah sejak di sekolah rendah.*
   (He dreamt of becoming a lecturer since primary school day.)

6. *Jemaah haji telah berangkat ke Mekah dari pelabuhan Kelang.*
   (The pilgrims left for Mecca from the port of Kelang.)

7. *Tiap-tiap pagi murid-murid beratur di padang.*
   (Every morning, the pupils queue up in the field.)

8. *Pada awal bulan depan saya akan ke Jakarta.*
   (At the beginning of next month, I will go to Jakarta.)

9. *Sebagai seorang Islam, dia berpuasa dalam bulan Ramadan.*
   (As a Muslim, he fasts in the month of Ramadan.)

10. *Semalam bapa balik dari pekan pada pukul sepuluh malam.*
    (Last night, father returned from town at 10.00 p.m.)

Exercise 6. Expand the following sentences with suitable adverbial phrases given in the box.

dengan usaha kita sendiri
(with our own efforts)

pada 10hb. Ogos nanti
(on the 10th of August)

pada pendapatnya
(in his opinion)

mengenai perkara itu
(about the matter)

dengan nyaring
(loudly and clearly)

hingga larut malam
(till late at night)

dengan penuh kasih sayang
(with [great] love)

sejak dua tahun dahulu
(since two years ago)

di Taman Bunga pada hari Ahad yang lalu
(in the Botanical Garden last Sunday)

dengan panjang lebar dalam mesyuarat itu
(at length at the meeting)

e.g.

Dia tidak berkata apa-apa.
(He did not say anything.)

Dia tidak berkata apa-apa ***di dalam kereta****.*
(He did not say anything **in the car.**)

Dia memukul anjing itu.
(He beats the dog.)

Dia memukul anjing itu ***dengan sebatang kayu****.*
(He beats the dog **with a piece of wood.**)

1. *Dia sakit batuk.*
   (He has a cough.)
2. *Saya bersiar-siar.*
   (I took a stroll.)
3. *Dia membela anaknya.*
   (He brings up his child.)
4. *Haji Ali membentang pendapatnya.*
   (Haji Ali expounds his opinion.)
5. *Ahli jawatankuasa telah berbincang.*
   (The committee members discussed something.)
6. *Dia menyanyi.*
   (He sings.)
7. *Dia telah menyatakan pendapatnya.*
   (He expressed his opinion.)
8. *Perkara itu mudah saja.*
   (The matter is easy [to solve].)
9. *Dia akan datang.*
   (He will come.)
10. *Kita mesti menambah harta.*
    (We must increase [our] property.)

16D. Word Formation

dekat, dengar, diam, diri, duduk

(a) ***dekat: berdekat, berdekatan, mendekat, mendekati, mendekatkan, terdekat, pendekatan***

e.g.

Penghulu kampung itu ***dekat*** *benar dengan anak buahnya.*
(The village chief is very **close** to his subjects.)

Mereka berdua tidak boleh ***berdekat.***
(They cannot be **close to each other**.)

Rumah saya ***berdekatan*** *dengan balai polis.*
(My house is **close to** a police station.)

Basikal penjual mi goreng itu semakin ***mendekat.***
(The bicycle of the fried mee seller **is coming nearer**.)

Usianya sudah ***mendekati*** *empat puluh tahun.*
(His age is **approaching** forty.)

Dia ***mendekatkan*** *kuih-muih kepada tetamunya.*
(He **places** the cakes **near** his guests.)

*Jiran Singapura yang t**erdekat** ialah Malaysia.*
(Singapore's **closest** neighbour is Malaysia.)

Pensyarah itu menggunakan ***pendekatan*** *baru untuk mengkaji bahasa.*
(The lecturer uses a new **approach** to study languages.)

(b) ***dengar: mendengar, mendengarkan, memperdengarkan, terdengar, kedengaran, pendengaran, pendengar***

e.g.

Saya ***mendengar*** *orang mengetuk pintu.*
(I **hear** someone knocking at the door.)

Dia melekapkan telinganya ke dinding untuk ***mendengarkan*** *perbualan ayahnya.*
(He leans against [literally 'puts his ear near'] the wall in order **to listen to** his father's conversation.)

Ia ***memperdengarkan*** *suaranya yang merdu kepada orang-orang kampung.*
(He **sang** [literally 'let his sweet voice be heard'] beautifully to the villagers.)

Di tengah malam dia ***terdengar*** *bunyi orang membuka pintu rumahnya.*

(In the middle of the night, he **heard [suddenly]** the noise of someone opening the door of his house.)

Bunyi loceng sayup-sayup ***kedengaran*** *dari jauh.*
(The ringing of a bell **can** softly **be heard** from afar.)

Kalau ***pendengaran****mu rosak, tentu kamu tidak boleh mendengar lagi.*
(If your **hearing** is damaged, you certainly cannot hear anymore.)

Para ***pendengar*** *bertepuk tangan.*
(The **audience** clapped [their] hands.)

(c) ***diam: diam-diam, berdiam, mendiami, mendiamkan, terdiam, pendiam, kediaman***

e.g.

Dia ***diam*** *sahaja apabila ditanya.*
(He **kept quiet** when he was asked.)

Saya ***diam*** *di rumah kakak saya di Singapura.*
(I **stay** in my elder sister's house in Singapore.)

Dengan ***diam-diam*** *dia keluar dari rumah.*
(**Quietly**, he went out of the house.)

Mereka berdua ***berdiam*** *sebentar.*
(The two of them **keep quiet** for a while.)

Siapa yang ***mendiami*** *rumah itu sekarang?*
(Who is **staying** in that house now?)

Saya tidak berani ***mendiamkan*** *orang yang membuat bising itu.*
(I dare not **silence** the noise-maker.)

Semua orang ***terdiam*** *apabila mendengar pekikan meminta tolong itu.*
(All the people **kept quiet [suddenly]** on hearing the shout for help.)

Zaini seorang murid yang ***pendiam****.*
(Zaini is a **quiet** pupil.)

*Tempat **kediaman** saya jauh dari sini.*
(My place of **residence** is far from here.)

(d) ***diri: berdiri, mendirikan, terdiri, pendirian, berpendirian***

e.g.

*Mereka terpaksa **berdiri** kerana kekurangan tempat duduk.*
(They were forced **to stand** because of a shortage of seats.)

*Dewan Bahasa dan Pustaka sudah **berdiri** sejak tahun 1956.*
(Dewan Bahasa dan Pustaka has been **established** since 1956.)

*Penduduk-penduduk berkerjasama **mendirikan** sebuah surau di kampung.*
(The residents work together to **build** a mosque in the village.)

*Penduduk-penduduk kampung itu **terdiri** daripada berbagai bangsa.*
(The village residents **consist of** various races.)

*Kita mesti mempunyai **pendirian** sendiri.*
(We must have our own **stand-point**.)

*Saya masih **berpendirian** bahawa perbuatannya itu harus dipuji.*
(I still **make the stand** that his action should be praised.)

(e) ***duduk: terduduk, menduduki, mendudukkan, kedudukan, berkedudukan, sekedudukan, pendudukan, penduduk, kependudukan***

e.g.

*Kami **duduk** di atas rumput di padang bola itu.*
(We **sit** on the grass in the football field.)

*Sudah bertahun-tahun mereka **duduk** di rumah itu.*
(For years they have **stayed** in that house.)

*Emak **terduduk** apabila mendengar berita yang mengejutkan itu.*
(Mother **sat down [unexpectedly]** on hearing the shocking news.)

Orang-orang Portugis pernah ***menduduki*** *Melaka.*
(The Portuguese did **occupy** Malacca.)

Mahasiswa-mahasiswa akan ***menduduki*** *peperiksaan akhir bulan ini.*
(The undergraduates will **sit for** their examination at the end of this month.)

Pengerusi itu ***mendudukkan*** *saya di sebelahnya.*
(The chairman **seated** me beside him.)

Seorang guru mempunyai ***kedudukan*** *yang tinggi dalam masyarakat kampung.*
(A teacher has a high **position** in the rural society.)

Dia ***berkedudukan*** *tinggi di dalam masyarakat.*
(He **has a** high **position** in society.)

Pemuda itu hanya mahukan seorang isteri yang ***sekedudukan*** *dengannya.*
(The young man only wants a wife of the same **standing** as his.)

Dalam masa ***pendudukan*** *Jepun saya bekerja di 'Malay Mail'.*
(During the Japanese **occupation**, I worked in the 'Malay Mail'.)

Sekarang ***penduduk-penduduk*** *kampung sudah maju.*
(Now, the **inhabitants** of villages have progressed.)

Aspek ***kependudukan*** *dibincangkan dalam seminar itu.*
(The **population** aspect was discussed in the seminar.)

LESSON 17

17A. Conversation

Tinggal di Rumah Pangsa
(Living in Flats)

Amin: *Betulkah saudara sudah pindah ke rumah pangsa? Bila saudara pindah?*
(Is it true that you have moved to a flat? When did you move?)

Ahmad: *Betul saya sudah pindah ke rumah pangsa. Saya pindah kira-kira enam bulan yang lalu.*
(It is true that I have moved to a flat. I moved about six months ago.)

Amin: *Mengapa saudara pindah? Dulu saudara kata saudara tidak mahu pindah dari rumah kampung saudara itu.*
(Why did you move? Previously, you said you did not want to move out of your village house.)

Ahmad: *Apa hendak buat? Kampung saya itu hendak dibangun semula. Jiran-jiran saya di kampung semua sudah pindah.*
(What can I do? My village will be re-developed. All my neighbours in the village have moved.)

Amin: *Bagaimana perasaan saudara tinggal di rumah pangsa?*
(How do you feel living about in a flat?)

Ahmad: *Lebih baik daripada yang saya sangka. Di kawasan rumah pangsa tempat saya tinggal sekarang itu ada masjid, padang permainan, kolam renang dan segala kemudahan untuk kehidupan moden.*

(Better than I thought. In the housing estate where I live now, there is a mosque, a playground, a swimming pool and all the facilities for modern living.)

Amin: *Tidak adakah kekurangan dalam hidup di rumah pangsa?*
(Are there no shortcomings in living in a flat?)

Ahmad: *Kekurangan itu memang ada. Lebih-lebih lagi kalau tinggal sebelah-menyebelah dengan orang yang tidak bertimbang rasa dan terlalu mementingkan diri sendiri. Tetapi ini bukanlah masalah yang tidak boleh diatasi.*
(Of course, there are shortcomings. More so if you are living next to someone who is inconsiderate and egoistic. But these are not problems that cannot be solved.)

Amin: *Saya senang sekali mendengar bahawa saudara dapat menyesuaikan diri dengan kehidupan di rumah pangsa.*
(I am very glad to hear that you have adjusted yourself to living in a flat.)

17B. Structure

Read the following sentences carefully.

SUBJECT	VERB	INDIRECT OBJECT	DIRECT OBJECT
Ibu	*memberikan*	*adik [lelaki]*	*sebungkus biskut.*
Mother	gave	younger brother	a packet of biscuits.
Salina	*membawakan*	*anak lelakinya*	*segelas kopi.*
Salina	brought	her son	a glass of coffee.
Mahamah	*menjahitkan*	*anaknya*	*sehelai baju.*
Mahamah	sewed for	her child	a dress.
Perempuan itu	*memasakkan*	*suaminya*	*sayur.*
The woman	cooked for	her husband	vegetables.
Lelaki itu	*menghadiahi*	*tamunya*	*sebuah cenderamata.*
The man	presented	his guest	with a souvenir.

Exercise 1. Substitute the word in the model sentence with the one given.

e.g. *Saya **mintakan** Ali pekerjaan.*
(I asked for Ali a job.)

mencarikan *Saya **mencarikan** Ali pekerjaan.*
(to look for) (I found Ali a job.)

payung (an umbrella)	*Saya memintakan Ali* ***payung****.* (I asked an umbrella for Ali.)
memegangkan payung itu (to hold for __________ the umbrella)	*Saya* ***memegangkan*** *Ali* ***payung*** *itu.* (I hold the umbrella for Ali.)
meminjami (to lend)	*Saya* ***meminjami*** *Ali* ***payung*** *itu.* (I lend Ali an umbrella.)

1. *menyerahi* (to hand over)
2. *kereta baru* (a new car)
3. *membelikan* (to buy for)
4. *memesankan* (to order for)
5. *menjualkan* (to sell for)
6. *mendapatkan* (to get for)
7. *tugas baru* (a new task)
8. *membebani* (to burden with)
9. *memberikan* (to give)
10. *segelas minuman* (a glass of drink)

Exercise 2. Answer the following questions. Use the words given and add ***-kan*** where appropriate.

e.g.

Question	*Answer*
Aminah sedang ***membuat apa?*** - *menjahit baju untuk adik perempuannya* What is Aminah doing? - sewing a dress for her younger sister)	***Aminah sedang menjahit baju untuk adik perempuannya.*** (Aminah is sewing a dress for her younger sister.)

Dia sedang ***membuat apa****?*
- menghitung telur ayam untuk kawan-kawannya
(What is he doing?
- counting the chicken eggs for his friends)

Dia sedang ***menghitung telur tayam untuk kawan-kawannya.***
(He is counting the chicken eggs for his friends.)

1. *Perempuan itu sedang* ***membuat apa****? - memasak sayur untuk suaminya*
   (What is the woman doing? - cooking vegetables for her husband)
2. *Dia sedang* ***membuat apa****? - memanggil teksi untuk kawannya*
   (What is he doing? - hailing a taxi for his friend)
3. *Guru itu sudah* ***membuat apa****? - memesan buku untuk murid-muridnya*
   (What has the teacher done? - ordered books for his students)
4. *Dia* ***membuat apa*** *semalam? - memilih sebuah kereta untuk sahabat*
   (What did he do last night? - chose a car for a friend)
5. *Salina sedang* ***membuat apa****? - membawa kopi untuk anak lelakinya*
   (What is Salina doing? - bringing coffee to her son)
6. *Dia jarang* ***membuat apa****? - membeli barang perhiasan untuk isterinya*
   (What does he seldom do? - buy adornments for his wife)
7. *Dia* ***membuat apa****? - membeli sebuah buku cerita untuk adik lelakinya*
   (What is he doing? - buying a story book for his younger brother)
8. *Dia sedang* ***membuat apa****? - membuat segelas minuman untuk adik lelakinya*
   (What is he doing? - making a glass of drink for his younger brother)

9. *Dia sudah* ***membuat apa****? - mencari pekerjaan untuk sahabatnya*
   (What has he done? - looked for a job for his friend)

10. *Lelaki itu sedang* ***membuat apa****? - mengambil buah-buahan untuk anaknya*
    (What is the man doing? - taking fruits for his child)

Exercise 3. Answer the following questions. Use the words given.

e.g.

Question	*Answer*
Dia menghitungkan ibunya ***apa****?* - *telur-telur itu* (What does he count his mother for? - the eggs)	*Dia menghitungkan ibunya* ***telur-telur itu****.* (He counts for his mother the eggs.)
Setiap bulan dia mengirimi ibunya ***apa****?* - *wang* (Every month, what does he send to his mother? - money)	*Setiap bulan dia mengirimi ibunya* ***wang****.* (Every month, he sends his mother money.)

1. *Ali membangunkan orang tuanya* ***apa*** *di kampung? - sebuah rumah batu*
   (What did Ali build for his parents in the village? - a concrete house)

2. *Aminah menghantarkan ayahnya* ***apa*** *setiap hari? - makanan yang lazat*
   (What does Aminah send to her father every day? - delicious food)

3. *Guru menghadiahi murid itu **apa**? - sebatang pena*
(What did the teacher present to the pupil? - a pen)

4. *Lelaki itu membuatkan anak lelakinya **apa**? - layang-layang*
(What did the man make for his son? - a kite)

5. *Guru itu akan mengajarkan **apa** kepada kita? - bahasa Melayu*
(What will the teacher teach us? - Malay language)

6. *Kerani itu memberikan Ahmad **apa**? - dua helai borang kosong*
(What did the clerk give to Ahmad? - two empty forms)

7. *Dia memberikan adik lelakinya **apa**? - sebuah buku cerita*
(What did he give to his younger brother? - a story book)

8. *Murid itu menyanyikan teman-temannya **apa**? - sebuah lagu yang merdu*
(What did the student sing to his friends? - a melodious song)

9. *Ali mengikatkan adik lelakinya **apa**? - tali kasut*
(What did Ali tie for his younger brother? - the shoe lace)

10. *Saudagar itu mendapatkan Amir **apa** di bandar? - satu pekerjaan*
(What did the businessman get for Amir in town? - a job)

Exercise 4. Answer the following questions. Use the words given.

e.g.

Question	*Answer*
*Dia menanyai lelaki itu **apa**?* - *satu soalan* (What did he ask the man? - a question)	*Dia menanyai lelaki itu **satu soalan**.* (He asked the man a question.)

Guru itu menghadiahi muridnya ***apa****?*
- sebuah jam tangan
(What did the teacher give to his pupil [as a gift]?
- a watch)

Guru menghadiahi muridnya ***sebuah jam tangan***.
(The teacher gave his pupil [as a gift] a watch.)

1. *Dia mengirimi ibunya* ***apa****? - wang*
(What did he send to his mother? - money)

2. *Dia meminjami lelaki itu* ***apa****? - keretanya*
(What did he lend to the man? - his car)

3. *Guru bahasa menyerahi pelajar itu* ***apa****? - tugas yang berat itu*
(What did the language teacher give to the student? - the heavy task)

4. *Encik Ali mengajar budak-budak lelaki itu* ***apa****? - bahasa Melayu*
(What did Mr. Ali teach the boys? - Malay language)

5. *Ibu memberi adik* ***apa****? - sebungkus biskut*
(What did mother give to younger brother/sister? - a packet of biscuits)

6. *Ali membawakan adik lelakinya* ***apa****? - buah anggur*
(What did Ali bring for his younger brother? - grapes)

7. *Hang Mahmud telah membungkuskan anak lelakinya* ***apa****? - beberapa gantang beras*
(What did Hang Mahmud pack for his son? - a few gantangs [1 gantang = about 3.1 kg].

8. *Fatimah membelikan adik lelakinya* ***apa****? - sepasang kasut kulit*
(What did Fatimah buy for her younger brother? - a pair of leather shoes)

9. *Tuhan telah mencurahi kami* ***apa****? - kurnia dan rahmat-Nya*
(What has God given us? - His gift and grace)

10. *Suami itu menghantari isterinya* ***apa****? - surat*
(What did the husband send to his wife - a letter)

17C. Grammar

Expansion of Simple Sentences (continuation)

Another way to expand a simple sentence is by inserting a phrase preceded by *yang* into the sentence. This phrases is termed by grammarians as dependent clause.

e.g.

Budak itu sakit. (The child is sick.)	*Budak* ***yang gemuk*** *itu sakit.* (The **fat** child is sick.)
Saya kenal guru itu. (I know the teacher.)	*Saya kenal guru* ***yang baru pulang dari London*** *itu.* (I know the teacher **who has just returned from London**.)
Buku itu buku saya. (The book is mine [my book].)	*Buku* ***yang terletak di atas meja*** *itu buku saya.* (The book **which is placed on the table** is mine.)
Saya suka makan kuih. (I like to eat cakes.)	*Saya suka makan kuih yang* ***dijual oleh budak lelaki itu****.* (I like to eat cakes **which are sold** by the boy.)

These phrases have the same function as adjectives. There are therefore termed as adjective clauses.

e.g.

Hasnah seorang gadis ***yang berumur tiga belas tahun****.*	*Hasnah seorang gadis* ***tiga belas tahun****.*

(Hasnah is a girl **who is thirteen years old**)

(Hasnah is a **thirteen-year-old-girl**.)

*Hasnah seorang gadis **yang cantik.***
(Hasnah is a girl **who is beautiful**.)

*Hasnah seorang gadis **cantik.***
(Hasnah is a **beautiful** girl.)

*Anjing **yang garang** itu sudah ditangkap oleh polis.*
(The dog **which is fierce** has been caught by the police.)

*Anjing **garang** itu sudah ditangkap oleh polis.*
(The **fierce** dog has been caught by the police.)

Exercise 5. Underline the adjective clauses in the following sentences.

e.g.

Pemandu-pemandu yang menggunakan jalan raya hendaklah berhati-hati.
(Drivers who use the highway should be careful.)

*Pemandu-pemandu **yang menggunakan jalan raya** hendaklah berhati-hati.*

Ikan-ikan yang di dalam air itu sedang bermain-main.
(The fish (which are) in the water are playing.)

*Ikan-ikan **yang di dalam air** itu sedang bermain-main.*

1. *Saya sedang mencari orang yang dapat menolong saya.*
   (I am looking for someone who can help me.)
2. *Orang-orang kampung sedang mengejar pencuri yang mencuri jam tangan saya.*
   (The villagers are chasing after the thief who has stolen my watch.)
3. *Abang saya seorang guru yang bertanggungjawab.*
   (My elder brother is a responsible teacher.)

4. *Rumah yang terletak di tepi jalan itu sudah terbakar.*
(The house which was situated at the side of the road was burnt down.)

5. *Buku yang saudara pinjamkan kepada saya itu sudah hilang.*
(The book which you lent me was lost.)

6. *Dia telah mengambil lukisan yang saya letakkan di atas meja.*
(He has taken the painting which I put on the table.)

7. *Wang yang disimpannya di dalam bank itu berjumlah lima ratus dollar.*
(The money [which has been] kept by him in the bank totals five hundred dollars.)

8. *Pengantin laki-laki itu ialah pemuda yang berumur dua puluh lima tahun.*
(The bridegroom is a young man of twenty-five years.)

9. *Cik Aminah seorang guru yang terlatih.*
(Miss Aminah is a trained teacher.)

10. *Hasnah bekerja di sebuah kilang yang berhampiran dengan rumahnya.*
(Hasnah works in a factory which is near her house.)

Exercise 6. Insert suitable adjective clauses into the following sentences.

e.g.

Surat itu sangat penting. (The letter is very important.)	*Surat* ***yang tiba tadi*** *itu sangat penting.* (The letter **which arrived just now** is very important.)
Inilah surat. (This is a letter.)	*Inilah surat* ***yang tiba pagi tadi.*** (This is the letter **which arrived this morning**.)

1. *Guru itu sudah meninggal dunia.*
   (The teacher has passed away.)

2. *Saya mengenangkan Encik Rahim.*
   (I recall Mr. Rahim.)

3. *Wang itu tidaklah banyak.*
   (The money was not much.)

4. *Dia hampir-hampir menghabiskan wang itu.*
   (He almost spent the money.)

5. *Pelajar-pelajar akan tiba.*
   (The students will arrive.)

6. *Guru kami suka kepada pelajar itu.*
   (Our teacher likes the student.)

7. *Suatu peristiwa telah terjadi pada hari itu.*
   (An incident happened that day.)

8. *Saya telah mendengar peristiwa itu.*
   (I have heard about the incident.)

9. *Buku-buku itu masih belum sampai.*
   (The books have not arrived yet.)

10. *Saya masih belum menerima surat itu.*
    (I have not received the letter yet.)

17D. Word Formation

ganti, guna, harga, hati, hubung

(a) ***ganti: berganti, berganti-ganti, menggantikan, pengganti***

e.g. ***Ganti****lah baju anda yang kotor itu.*
(Please **change** your dirty shirt.)

Lelaki itu sudah ***berganti*** *nama.*
(The man has **changed** [his] name.)

Mereka ***berganti-ganti*** *pergi ke rumah sakit.*
(They **take turns** to go to the hospital.)

Kalau saudara bersara, siapa akan ***menggantikan*** *saudara?*
(When you retire, who is going **to replace** you?)

Kami masih menunggu ***pengganti*** *guru bahasa yang bersara itu.*
(We are still awaiting the **replacement** for the language teacher who retired.)

(b) ***guna: berguna, menggunakan, kegunaan, penggunaan, pengguna***

e.g. *Apa* ***guna*** *kita pergi ke sana?*
(What is **the use** of our going there?)

Dia datang ke bandar ***guna*** *mencari rezeki.*
(He came to the city **in order** to look for a livelihood.)

Semua kotak yang tidak ***berguna*** *hendaklah dibakar.*
(All the boxes which are not **useful** should be burnt.)

Dia ***menggunakan*** *kamus untuk mencari makna perkataan-perkataan yang sukar.*
(He **uses** a dictionary to look for the meaning of difficult words.)

Paip-paip air telah dipasang untuk ***kegunaan*** *orang ramai.*
(Water pipes have been installed for the **benefit** of the public.)

Penggunaan *kata ini tidak sesuai dengan ayat ini.*
(The **use** of this word does not fit in with the sentence.)

Pengguna-pengguna *yang ditipu oleh penjual boleh membuat pengaduan.*
(**Consumers** who have been cheated by salesmen can lodge a complaint.)

(c) ***harga: berharga, menghargai, penghargaan***

e.g. ***Harga*** *rumah mahal sekarang.*
(The **prices** of houses are high nowadays.)

Sebuah kereta baru ***berharga*** *tiga puluh ribu dolar.*
(A new car **costs** thirty thousand dollars.)

Barang itu tidak ***berharga****.*
(The article **has** no **value**.)

Penerbit-penerbit belum tahu ***menghargai*** *karya pengarang-pengarang tempatan.*
(Publishers have not learnt [literally do not know how] **to value** the works of local writers.)

Karya penulis-penulis tempatan tidak mendapat ***penghargaan*** *masyarakat.*
(Local writers' works do not get society's **appreciation**.)

(d) ***hati: sehati, berhati, berhati-hati, memperhatikan, perhatian, pemerhati, pemerhatian***

e.g. *Rupanya cantik tetapi* ***hati****nya buruk.*
(Her look is beautiful but her **intention** [literally 'heart'] is bad.)

Dia beroleh seorang isteri yang ***sehati*** *dengannya.*
(He gets a wife who **shares** his **sentiments** [literally 'is of the same heart as his'].)

Gadis itu ***berhati*** *halus.*
(The girl **has a** sensitive heart.)

Dia membuat kerjanya ***dengan berhati-hati***.
(He does his job **carefully**.)

Budak lelaki itu tidak ***memperhatikan*** *nasihat ibunya.*
(The boy does not **pay attention** to his mother's advice.)

Mereka memberikan sepunuh ***perhatian*** *pada pelajaran mereka.*
(They give full **attention** to their studies.)

Sarjana itu adalah seorang ***pemerhati*** *politik yang tajam.*
(The scholar is a sharp political observer.)

Setelah diperbuat ***pemerhatian*** *kami dapati keadaan mentalnya baik.*
(After an **observation** had been made, we found his mental condition to be good.)

(e) ***hubung: berhubung, berhubungan, menghubungi, menghubungkan, hubungan, perhubungan, penghubungan, penghubung***

e.g. ***Berhubung*** *dengan kurangnya ahli yang hadir, mesyuarat ditangguhkan.*
(**Due to** the small number of members present, the meeting was postponed.)

Kejadian itu ***berhubungan*** *dengan masalah disiplin di sekolah.*
(The incident is **connected** with the problem of discipline in school.)

Polis telah ***menghubungi*** *lelaki itu petang semalam.*
(The police **contacted** the man yesterday afternoon.)

*Ada jalan keretapi yang **menghubungkan** kedua buah bandar itu.*
(There is a railway line **connecting** the two towns.)

*Saya tidak ada **hubungan** dengan lelaki itu.*
(I have no **relationship** with that man.)

***Perhubungan** diplomatik antara India dan China genting.*
(The diplomatic **relationship** between India and China is tense.)

***Penghubungan** sebarang bentuk sistem pegangkutan awam di antara dua buah negeri akan mengambil masa yang panjang.*
(The **connection** of any form of public transport systems between two countries will take a long time.)

*Orang yang menjadi **penghubung** sulit dalam peristiwa itu tidak dapat dikesan.*
(The person who acted as the secret **communicator** in the incident cannot be traced.)

LESSON 18

18A. Conversation

Pakaian Kebangsaan
(National Dress)

Janet: *Saudari Rani, bagaimana pendapat saudari? Perlukah kita mencipta pakaian kebangsaan?*
(Miss Rani, what is your opinion? Should we create a national dress?)

Rani: *Tidak, saya tidak fikir kita perlukan pakaian kebangsaan.*
(No, I do not think we need a national dress.)

Janet: *Mengapa saudari berkata begitu?*
(Why do you say so?)

Rani: *Kita sudah mempunyai pakaian berbagai bangsa. Orang-orang Cina ada* ***cheongsam****nya; orang-orang India ada* ***sari****nya; dan orang-orang Melayu mempunyai baju kurung dan kebayanya. Untuk apa kita perlu mengadakan pakaian kebangsaan?*
(We already have ethnic dresses. The Chinese have their **cheongsam**; the Indians have their **sari**; and the Malays have their **baju kurung** and **kebaya**. Why should we have a national dress?)

Janet: *Pakaian kebangsaan itu menunjukkan kita berasal dari satu bangsa yang sama, bangsa Singapura.*
(The national dress shows that we belong to one nation, the Singaporeans.)

Rani: *Saya tidak setuju. Walaupun kita memakai pakaian yang berlainan, mengamalkan kebudayaan yang berbeza, kita masih dapat merasakan unsur-unsur persamaan. Kita adalah warganegara sebuah negara yang merdeka, iaitu Singapura.*

(I do not agree. Though we dress differently, and have different cultures, we can still have a sense of common values. We are the nationals of an independent country, that is Singapore.)

Janet: *Ada benarnya juga pendapat saudari itu. Mulai sekarang, saya akan lebih banyak memakai* ***cheongsam*** *atau baju kebaya.*

(There is truth in your opinion. From now onwards, I will wear a **cheongsam** or **baju kebaya** more often.)

Rani: *Saya pun akan lebih banyak memakai baju kurung. Biarlah pakaian kebangsaan yang direka itu dipakai oleh peserta-peserta Peraduan Ratu Cantik Singapura.*

(I will also wear a **baju kurung** more often. Let the national dress created be worn by the participants of the Singapore Beauty Queen Contest.)

18B. Structure

Read the following sentences carefully.

SUBJECT	PREDICATE
Saya I	*memanggil lelaki tua itu Pak Long.* call the old man Pak Long.
Dia He	*anggap lelaki itu bodoh.* considers the man to be stupid.
Ahmad Ahmad	*fikir peristiwa itu penting.* thinks that the incident is important.
Dia He	*menyuruh lelaki itu pergi dari sini.* asks the man to go away from here.
Doktor The doctor	*menasihati ayah supaya berhenti menghisap rokok.* advises father to stop smoking.

Exercise 1. Substitute the word in the model sentence with the one given.

e.g.	*Dia* ***mendesak*** *murid-muridnya supaya melanjutkan pelajaran mereka.* (He **urges** his pupils to further their studies.)
mendorong (to exhort)	*Dia* ***mendorong*** *murid-muridnya supaya melanjutkan pelajaran mereka.* (He **exhorts** his pupils to further their studies.)

menasihatkan (to advise)	*Dia* ***menasihatkan*** *murid-muridnya supaya melanjutkan pelajaran mereka.* (He **advises** his pupils to further their studies.)
menggesa (to spur)	*Dia* ***mengesa*** *murid-muridnya supaya melanjutkan pelajaran mereka.* (He **spurs** his pupils to further their studies.)
menggalakkan (to encourage)	*Dia* ***menggalakkan*** *murid-muridnya supaya melanjutkan pelajaran mereka.* (He **encourages** his pupils to further their studies.)

1. *memujuk* (to persuade)
2. *mencadangkan* (to suggest to)
3. *mencabar* (to challenge)
4. *merangsang* (to stimulate)
5. *memerintahkan* (to order)
6. *memaksa* (to force)
7. *menyuruh* (to tell)
8. *meminta* (to ask)
9. *menganjurkan* (to recommend)
10. *mengusulkan* (to suggest)

Exercise 2. Answer the following questions. Use the words given.

e.g.

Question	*Answer*
Saudara memanggil ***siapa*** *Pak Long?* - *lelaki tua itu*	*Saya memanggil* ***lelaki tua itu*** *Pak Long.* (I call the old man Pak Long.)

(Whom did you call Pak Long?
- the old man)

Saudara menganggap ***siapa*** *masih kebudak-budakan?*
- *pemuda itu*
(Whom did you regard as childish?
- the young man)

Saya menganggap ***pemuda itu*** *masih kebudak-budakan.*
(I regard the young man as childish.)

1. *Saudara memanggil* ***siapa*** *abang? - tamu itu*
(Whom do you call *abang* [literally 'elder brother'; used here as a title to refer to an older person]? - the guest)

2. *Dia menamai* ***siapa*** *Naziha? - anak lelakinya*
(Whom does he name Naziha? - his son)

3. *Saudara menggelar* ***siapa*** *Si Manis? - gadis itu*
(Whom do you call The Sweet One? - the girl)

4. *Ahmad memanggil* ***siapa*** *Tuan Besar? - ketua pejabatnya*
(Whom does Ahmad call The Big Boss? - his office chief)

5. *Ahli-ahli jawatankuasa telah memilih* ***siapa*** *sebagai pengerusi? - Encik Adnan.*
(Whom have the commitee members chosen as Chairman? - Mr. Adnan)

6. *Saudara mencadangkan* ***siapa*** *menjadi setiausaha? - Encik Rusli*
(Whom do you suggest as secretary? - Mr. Rusli)

7. *Parti itu telah menerima* ***siapa*** *sebagai calon? - guru agama itu*
(Whom has the party accepted as a candidate? - the religious teacher)

8. *Majikan itu telah melantik* ***siapa*** *sebagai pengawas kilang?* - *Ramli*

(Whom did the employer appoint as a factory supervisor? - Ramli)

9. *Orang-orang kampung memandang **siapa** sebagai ketua mereka? - Wan Derus*
   (Whom does the villagers regard as their chief? - Wan Derus)

10. *Lelaki itu menganggap **siapa** sebagai wira? - dirinya*
   (Whom does the man regard as a hero? - himself)

Exercise 3. Answer the following questions. Use the words given.

e.g.

Question	*Answer*
***Bagaimana anggapannya tentang** lelaki itu?* - *anggap* __________ *bodoh* (What is his opinion of the man? - to think __________ stupid)	*Dia **anggap** lelaki itu **bodoh**.* (He thinks the man is stupid.)
***Bagaimana fikiran Ahmad tentang** peristiwa itu?* - *fikir* __________ *mustahak* (What is Ahmad's view of the incident? - to view __________ important)	*Ahmad **fikir** peristiwa itu mustahak.* (Ahmad views the incident as important.)

1. ***Bagaimana fikirannya terhadap** orang itu? - fikir __________ malas*
   (What is his opinion of the person? - to think __________ lazy)

2. ***Bagaimana dugaan perempuan itu tentang*** *suaminya?*
- duga __________ *marah*
(What is the woman's anticipation towards her husband? - to anticipate __________ angry)

3. ***Apa yang dia agak tentang*** *lelaki itu? agak* __________ *kecewa*
(What does he guess about the man? - to guess __________ disappointed)

4. ***Bagaimana kiranya tentang*** *lelaki itu? - kira* __________ *jahat*
(What is his opinion of the man? - to think __________ bad)

5. ***Bagaimana rasa Ahmad tentang*** *lelaki itu? - rasa* __________ *salah*
(How does Ahmad feel about the man? - to feel __________ guilty)

6. ***Bagaimana sangkaannya tentang*** *lelaki itu? - sangka* __________ *bongkak*
(What is his anticipation towards the man? - to think __________ arrogant)

7. ***Bagaimana pandangannya tentang*** *lelaki itu? - percaya* __________ *jujur*
(What is his view of the man? - to trust __________ honest)

8. ***Bagaimana pandangannya tentang*** *kerja guru? - pandang* __________ *senang*
(What is his view of a teacher's job? - to view __________ easy)

9. ***Bagaimana anggapannya tentang*** *perkara itu? - anggap* __________ *mudah*
(How is his opinion of the matter? - to consider __________ easy)

10. ***Bagaimana fikiran Ahmad tentang*** *hal itu? - fikir*
__________ *penting*
(What is Ahmad's opinion of the matter? - to think
__________ important)

Exercise 4. Answer the following questions. Use the words given.

e.g.

Question	*Answer*
Dia menyuruh lelaki itu ***buat apa****?* *- pergi dari sini* (What did he tell the man to do? - to go away from here)	*Dia menyuruh lelaki itu* ***pergi dari sini****.* (He told the man to go away from here.)
Ahmad mangajak temannya ***buat apa****?* *- pergi ke kantin* (What did Ahmad ask his friend to do [with him]?) - to go to the canteen)	*Ahmad mengajak temannya* ***pergi ke kantin****.* (Ahmad asked his friend to go to the canteen [with him].)

1. *Hasnah memaksa teman-temannya* ***buat apa****? - datang ke majlis harijadinya.*
   (What did Hasnah force her friends to do? - to come to her birthday party)

2. *Dia meminta sahabat-sahabatnya* ***buat apa****? - datang ke majlis perkahwinannya*
   (What did he request his friends to do? - to come to his wedding party)

3. *Dia menyuruh teman sekerjanya* ***buat apa****? - datang ke rumahnya*
   (What did he ask his colleague to do? - to come to his house)

4. *Dia mempelawa sahabatnya* ***buat apa****? - memohon jawatan kosong itu*
   (What did he invite his friend to do? - to apply for the vacant post)

5. *Dia menyilakan abang sepupunya* ***buat apa****? - minum air teh itu*
   (What did he invite his cousin to do? - to drink the tea)

6. *Dia menyarankan saudara* ***buat apa****? - belajar ke luar negeri*
   (What did he suggest that you do? - to study abroad)

7. *Dia menganjurkan saudara* ***buat apa****? - mogok makan*
   (What did he suggest that you do? - to go on a hunger strike)

8. *Dia mencadangkan kita* ***buat apa****? - membahas perkara itu dahulu*
   (What did he suggest that we do? - to discuss the matter first)

9. *Dia memaksa saudara* ***buat apa****? - mendengar nasihatnya*
   (What did he force you to do? - to listen to his advice)

10. *Dia mendesak saudara* ***buat apa****? - melanjutkan cerita itu*
    (What did he urge you to do? - to continue the story)

18C. Grammar

(b) Complex Sentences

There are several ways of combining sentences. Sentence combination by the use of subordinate conjunctions (see Lesson 12) will produce complex sentences. The clause without any preceding conjunction is called the independent or main clause while the clause with preceding subordinate conjunction is called the dependent clause.

	TYPE OF SENTENCE	EXAMPLE
1	Simple sentence	*Mereka datang.* They came. *Saya tidak ada di rumah.* I was not at home.
	Complex sentence	*Apabila mereka datang, saya tidak ada di rumah.* When they came, I was not at home.
	(a) Independent clause (b) Dependent clause	*saya tidak ada di rumah* *apabila mereka datang*
2	Simple sentence	*Dia kaya.* He is rich. *Dia tidak sombong.* He is not arrogant.
	Complex sentence	*Walaupun dia kaya, dia tidak sombong.* Although he is rich, he is not arrogant.
	(a) Independent clause (b) Dependent clause	*dia tidak sombong* ***walaupun** dia kaya*

Exercis 5. Underline the dependent clauses in the following sentences.

e.g.

Tatkala loceng berbunyi, murid-murid masuk ke dalam bilik-bilik darjah.
(When the bell rings, the pupils enter the classrooms.)

***Tatkala loceng berbunyi**, murid-murid masuk ke dalam bilik-bilik darjah.*

Jikalau dia tidak datang, saya tidak mahu pergi.
(If he does not come, I do not want to go.)

***Jikalau dia tidak datang**, saya tidak mahu pergi.*

1. *Sementara ibu memasak, saya membasuh pinggan mangkuk.*
   (While mother is cooking, I wash the dishes.)
2. *Baiklah kita tunggu di sini sehingga dia datang.*
   (It is best that we wait here until he comes.)
3. *Dia selalu dimarahi ibunya sebab dia malas.*
   (He is always scolded by his mother because he is lazy.)
4. *Kalau tidak ada halangan, saya akan datang ke rumah saudara petang ini.*
   (If there is no obstacle, I will come to your house this afternoon.)
5. *Seandainya engkau tidak bersalah, mengapa engkau ditangkap?*
   (If you were not guilty, why were you arrested?)
6. *Meskipun kamus itu mahal, saya akan membelinya juga.*
   (Even though the dictionary is expensive, I will still buy it.)
7. *Sungguhpun dia sakit, dia pergi ke sekolah juga.*
   (Even though he is ill, he still goes to school.)

8. *Semasa budak lelaki itu melintas jalan, dia dilanggar kereta.*
(While the boy was crossing the road, he was knocked down by a car.)

9. *Kita mesti bekerja keras jikalau kita hendakkan kemajuan.*
(We must work hard if we wish to make progress.)

10. *Sejak umurnya tujuh tahun, dia tidak pernah meninggalkan sembahyangnya.*
(Since he was seven, he has never neglected his prayers.)

Exercise 6. Combine the following sentences. Use the subordinate conjunctions given in Lesson 12.

e.g.

Ayahnya meninggal dunia. *Dia masih kecil.* (His father passed away. He was still small.)	***Ketika*** *dia masih kecil,* *ayahnya meninggal dunia.* (When he was still small, his father passed away.)
Dia baru sampai. *Mesyuarat selesai.* (He had just arrived. The meeting ended.)	*Dia baru sampai* ***apabila*** *mesyuarat selesai.* (He had only arrived when the meeting ended.)

1. *Sikapnya berubah. Dia menjadi wakil rakyat.*
(His attitude changes. He becomes a people's representative.)

2. *Saya tidak salah. Lelaki itu memang ayahnya.*
(I am not mistaken. The man is really his father.)

3. *Lelaki tua itu masih bekerja. Dia uzur.*
(The old man is still working. He is sick.)

4. *Permainan tidak dapat dijalankan. Hari hujan.*
(The game cannot be held. It is raining.)

5. *Mulut lelaki itu manis. Hatinya jahat.*
(The man's words [literally 'mouth'] are sweet. His intention [literally 'heart'] is bad.)

6. *Bayi itu menangis. Perutnya lapar.*
(The baby is crying. He [literally 'his stomach'] is hungry.)

7. *Belajarlah sungguh-sungguh. Kamu naik darjah.*
(Study seriously. You will be promoted to the next level.)

8. *Lelaki itu kaya. Dia kedekut.*
(The man is rich. He is stingy.)

9. *Saya tidak bekerja hari ini. Badan saya kurang sihat.*
(I am not working today. I am [literally 'my body is'] not well.)

10. *Kita mesti berjalan cepat. Kita akan lekas sampai.*
(We must walk quickly. We will arrive early.)

18D. Word Formation

jadi, jalan, kasih, kata, kenal

(a) ***jadi: menjadi, menjadi-jadi, menjadikan, terjadi, kejadian***

e.g. *Ibunya sakit,* ***jadi*** *terpaksalah dia pulang.*
(Her mother is ill; **so** she has to go home.)

Akhirnya, ***jadi*** *juga pekerjaan itu.*
(At last, the work **is successfully carried out**.)

Nasi sudah ***menjadi*** *bubur.*
(Rice has **become** porridge.)

Rompakan bersenjata ***menjadi-jadi*** *di bandar itu.*
(Armed robbery is on the increase in the city.)

Ahmad ***menjadikan*** *anak lelakinya pengurus syarikat itu.*

(Ahmad **made/appointed** his son as the company's manager.)

Kebakaran itu ***terjadi*** *kerana kerosakan elektrik.*
(The fire **happened** because of an electrical fault.)

Polis telah menyiasat ***kejadian*** *itu.*
(Police investigated the **incident**.)

(b) ***jalan: sejalan, berjalan, berjalan-jalan, menjalankan, menjalani, terjalan, perjalanan***

e.g. *Dia mencari* ***jalan*** *untuk menyelesaikan masalah itu.*
(He is finding a **means** of solving the problem.)

Minatnya memang ***sejalan*** *dengan minat saya*
(His interest is **parallel** [of the same direction] to mine.)

Persidangan itu ***berjalan*** *dengan lancar.*
(The meeting **goes on** smoothly.)

Ali pergi ***berjalan-jalan*** *ke Melaka.*
(Ali **went on a leisure trip** to Malacca.)

Tiap-tiap hari, dia ***menjalankan*** *kerjanya sebagai seorang pegawai eksekutif.*
(Every day, he **carries out** his work as an executive officer.)

Dia telah ***menjalani*** *satu pembedahan.*
(He has **undergon**e an operation.)

Dia keletihan dan tidak ***terjalan*** *lagi.*
(He is exhausted and is **not able to walk** any further.)

Ibunya meninggal dunia dalam ***perjalanan*** *ke Mekah.*
(Her mother passed away on **the way** to Mecca.)

(*c*) ***kasih: berkasihan, mengasihi, kasihan, mengasihani, kekasih, pengasih***

e.g. *Dia amat **kasih** kepada anak itu.*
(He **loves** the child very much.)

*Walaupun telah lama berpisah, mereka tetap **berkasihan**.*
(Though long separated, they still **love each other**.)

*Dia sangat **mengasihi** sabahatnya itu.*
(He **loves** his friend very much.)

*Dia **kasihan** melihat nasib budak lelaki itu.*
(He **pities** the fate of the boy.)

*Apa gunanya **mengasihani** orang yang tidak tahu mengenang jasa.*
(What is the use of **pitying** a person who is ungrateful.)

*Dia selalu menulis kepada **kekasih**nya.*
(He always writes to his **beloved**.)

*Dia mencari **pengasih** untuk mendapatkan cinta gadis itu.*
(He looks for a **love potion** to win over the girl's love.)

*Mak Timah ialah seorang ibu yang **pengasih**.*
(Mak Timah is a **loving** mother.)

(*d*) ***kata: katakan, sekata, berkata, mengata-ngatai, mengatakan, memperkatakan, perkataan, terkata***

e.g. *Dia **kata** dia hendak ke Bangkok minggu ini.*
(He **says** that he is going to Bangkok this week.)

***Katakan**lah dia kaya raya, saya pasti dia akan menjadi sombong.*

(**Let us assume** [literally 'let us say'] that he is rich, I am certain that he will be arrogant.)

*Dalam semua hal mereka selalu seia-**sekata**.*
(They always **agree** in all matters.)

*Budak lelaki itu **berkata** perlahan-lahan.*
(The boy **speaks** slowly.)

*Dia selalu **mengata-ngatai** kawan-kawannya.*
(He often **speaks badly** of his friends.)

*Dia **mengatakan** hal itu kepada teman-temannya.*
(He **mentioned** the matter to his friends.)

*Sepanjang hari mereka **memperkatakan** hal itu.*
(The whole day, they **talk about** the matter.)

***Perkataan** bahasa Melayu dapat dieja berpandukan bunyinya.*
(**Words** in Malay can be spelt according to its sounds.)

*Mak Mah sungguh terharu hingga tidak **terkata** niat di hatinya.*
(Mak Mah is greatly affected; till her intention is not **expressible**.)

(e) ***kenal: berkenalan, berkenal-kenalan, mengenal, mengenali, memperkenalkan, perkenalan, terkenal, kenalan, pengenalan, pengenal***

e.g. *Saya tidak **kenal** lelaki itu.*
(I do not **know** the man.)

*Kami sudah lama **berkenalan**.*
(We have **known each other** for a long time.)

*Dia datang untuk **berkenal-kenalan** dengan kita.*
(He came to **acquaint himself** with us.)

Apabila dia menyamarkan diri tidak seorang pun ***mengenal****nya.*
(When he disguises himself, no one **recognizes** him.)

Dia sudah lama ***mengenali*** *pemuda itu.*
(He has **known** the young man for a long time.)

Dia ***memperkenalkan*** *sahabatnya kepada saya.*
(He **introduces** his friend to me.)

Sejak ***perkenalan*** *malam tadi, saya tidak berjumpa dengan dia lagi.*
(Since the **introduction** last night, I have not met him again.)

Malaysia ***terkenal*** *dengan getah dan bijih timahnya.*
(Malaysia is **well-known** for its rubber and tin ore.)

Yusuf banyak ***kenalan****nya di Jakarta.*
(Yusuf has many **acquaintances** in Jakarta.)

Kad-kad ***pengenalan*** *yang dicuri itu telah dijumpa.*
(The stolen **identity** cards have been found.)

Botol-botol itu dibubuh label untuk ***pengenalan****.*
(The bottles are attached with labels for **identification**.)

Tanda-tanda ***pengenal*** *terdapat pada setiap mesin-mesin itu.*
(**Identifying** marks are found on each of the machines.)

LESSON 19

19A. Conversation

Belajar Bahasa Melayu
(Learning Malay)

Tan:	*Selamat pagi, Encik Hassan.* (Good morning, Mr. Hassan.)
Hassan:	*Selamat pagi, Encik Tan. Encik Tan sudah pandai cakap bahasa Melayu?* (Good morning, Mr. Tan. Can you already speak Malay, Mr. Tan?)
Tan:	*Tidaklah. Saya baru belajar bahasa Melayu.* (No. I am just starting to learn Malay.)
Hassan:	*Sudah berapa lama Encik Tan belajar bahasa Melayu?* (How long have you been learning Malay?)
Tan:	*Sudah hampir setahun saya belajar bahasa Melayu.* (I have been learning Malay for nearly a year.)
Hassan:	*Bagaimana Encik Tan belajar bahasa Melayu?* (How do you learn Malay?)
Tan:	*Saya belajar bahasa Melayu dengan seorang guru perempuan.* (I am learning Malay from a lady teacher.)
Hassan:	*Bagaimana guru perempuan Encik Tan itu?* (How is your lady teacher?)
Tan:	*Orangnya boleh tahan. Pengajarannya cukup baik juga.* (She [literally 'her person'] is all right. Her teaching is good too.)

Hassan: *Saya harap Encik Tan akan fasih dalam bahasa Melayu tidak lama lagi.*
(I hope you will soon be fluent in Malay.)

Tan: *Saya harap pun begitu.*
(I hope so.)

19B. Structure

Read the following sentences carefully.

SUBJECT	PREDICATE
Dia He	*gembira mendengar berita itu.* is happy to hear the news.
Dia He	*takut menemui lelaki itu.* is afraid to meet the man.
Dia He	*lupa membawa kad pengenalannya.* forgets to bring his identity card.
Dia He	*ingin bertemu dengan pengarang itu.* wishes to meet the writer.
Bayi itu The baby	*duduk menangis.* sits crying.

Exercise 1. Substitute the words or phrase in the model sentence with the one given.

e.g. *Dia* ***berusaha*** *mencapai cita-citanya.*
(He endeavours to achieve his ambition.)

berikhtiar (to attempt)	*Dia* ***berikhtiar*** *mencapai cita-citanya.* (He attempts to achieve his ambition.)
berazam (is determined)	*Dia* ***berazam*** *mencapai cita-citanya.* (He is determined to achieve his ambition.)
melanjutkan pelajarannya ke universiti (to further his study at the university)	*Dia berazam* ***melanjutkan pelajarannya ke universiti.*** (He is determined to further his studies at the university.)
bercadang (to plan)	*Dia* ***bercadang melanjutkan pelajaran ke universiti.*** (He plans to further his studies at the universtiy.)

1. *berjaya* (has succeeded)
2. *bermaksud* (to mean)
3. *membuka perniagaan sendiri* (to start his own business)
4. *bertujuan* (to intend)
5. *melancong ke Bali* (go on a tour to Bali)
6. *berniat* (to contemplate)
7. *berkira-kira* (to consider)
8. *berkhayal* (to have in mind)
9. *memberi derma kepada fakir miskin* (to give a donation to the poor)
10. *berupaya* (to be able)

Exercise 2. Answer the following questions. Use the words given.

e.g.

Question	*Answer*
Mengapa *dia gembira?* *- mendengar berita itu* (Why is he happy? - to hear the news)	*Dia gembira* ***mendengar berita itu****.* (He is happy to hear the news.)
Mengapa *dia takut?* *- menemui lelaki garang itu* (Why is he afraid? - to meet the fierce man)	*Dia takut* ***menemui lelaki garang*** *itu.* (He is afraid to meet the fierce man.)

1. ***Mengapa*** *dia berdukacita? - mendapat khabar kematian tunangnya.*
   (Why is he sad? - to recieve the news of the death of his fiancee)

2. ***Mengapa*** *perempuan itu gelisah? - menunggu kepulangan anaknya*
   (Why is the woman anxious? - to wait for the return of his child)

3. ***Mengapa*** *seluruh dunia terkejut? - mendengar berita pembunuhan pemimpin itu*
   (Why is the whole world shocked? - to hear the news of the killing of the leader)

4. ***Mengapa*** *dia bosan? - mendengar kisah yang sama berulang kali*
   (Why is he bored? - to listen to the same story over and over again)

5. ***Mengapa*** *dia hairan? - melihat orang buta menganyam bakul*
   (Why is he astonished? - to see a blind man weaving baskets)

6. ***Mengapa*** *dia kagum? - melihat kemajuan negeri itu*
   (Why is he amazed? - to witness the country's progress)

7. ***Mengapa*** *dia kaget? - melihat kezaliman abangnya*
   (Why is he shocked? - to witness his elder brother's cruelty)

8. ***Mengapa*** *dia marah? - menerima laporan itu*
   (Why is he angry? - to receive the report)

9. ***Mengapa*** *semua orang sukacita? - melihat mereka berjaya dalam hidup*
   (Why are all the people happy? - to see that they are successful in life)

10. ***Mengapa*** *dia jengkel? - melihat kelakuan gadis itu*
    (Why is he irritated? - to see the girl's behaviour)

Exercise 3. Answer the following questions. Use the words given.

e.g.

Question	*Answer*
Dia lupa membawa ***apa****?* - *membawa kad pengenalannya* (What did he forget to bring? - to bring his identity card)	*Dia lupa* ***membawa kad pengenalannya****.* (He forgot to bring his identity card.)
Dia tahu ***apa****?* - *mencari kesalahan orang lain* (What does he know? - to find faults in others)	*Dia tahu* ***mencari kesalahan orang lain.*** (He knows [how to] find faults in others.)

1. *Dia mengaku* ***apa****? - mencuri wang lelaki itu*
   (What did he admit to? - stealing the man's money)

2. *Dia belajar* ***apa****? - menyanyi*
   (What is he learning? - to sing)

3. *Dia setuju **membuat apa**? - menolong kita*
(What does he agree to do? - to help us)

4. *Dia berjanji **membuat apa**? - datang ke rumah saya*
(What does he promise to do? - to come to my house)

5. *Dia menolak **apa**? - jemputan untuk menghadiri pertemuan itu*
(What does he decline? - the invitation to attend the meeting)

6. *Dia mencuba **apa**? - menangkap bola itu*
(What did he try? - to catch the ball)

7. *Dia gemar **apa**? - membaca buku di perpustakaan*
(What does he like? - to read books in the library)

8. *Dia hendak **buat apa**? - membayar hutang*
(What does he intend to do? - to pay off his debt)

9. *Dia masih ingat **apa**? - mengunci pintu itu*
(What does he still remember? - to lock the door)

10. *Dia ingin **apa**? - bertemu dengan pengarang itu*
(What does he wish? - to meet the writer)

Exercise 4. Answer the following questions. Use the words given.

e.g.

Question	*Answer*
*Sejak **bila** bayi itu menangis?* *- petang tadi* (Since when has the baby been crying? - this afternoon)	*Sejak **petang tadi** bayi itu menangis.* (Since this afternoon the baby has been crying.)
***Bila** para pekerja berhenti bekerja?* *- pada pukul lima petang*	*Para pekerja berhenti bekerja **pada pukul lima petang.***

(When do the workers stop working?
- at five p.m.)

The workers stop working at five p.m.)

1. ***Bila*** *mereka pergi menonton wayang gambar? - sesudah makan*
(When did they go to see the pictures? - after dinner)
2. *Sudah* ***berapa lama*** *dia belajar menyanyi? - enam bulan*
(How long has he been learning to sing? - six months)
3. ***Bila*** *dia akan pulang untuk makan tengah hari? - sekejap lagi*
(When is he coming back for lunch? - soon)
4. ***Bila*** *dia datang meminjam wang? - dua minggu yang lalu*
(When did he come to borrow money? - two weeks ago)
5. *Sejak* **bila** *perempuan itu hidup menderita? - kematian suaminya*
(Since when has the woman lived miserably? - the death of her husband)
6. ***Bila*** *dia mengancam membunuh lawannya? - minggu lepas*
(When did he threaten to kill his opponent? - last week)
7. ***Bila*** *dia masuk kerja? - pada pukul delapan pagi*
(When does he come to work? - at eight in the morning)
8. ***Bila*** *dia keluar makan? - pada pukul satu tengah hari*
(When does he go out to eat? - at one p.m.)
9. ***Bila*** *dia lari menyelamatkan diri? - tatkala bangunan itu roboh*
(When did he run to safety [literally 'save himself']?
- when the building collapsed)
10. ***Bila*** *dia bangun menyambut para tamu? - pada pukul tujuh pagi*
(When did he get up to welcome the guests? - at seven a.m.)

19C. Grammar

(c) Compound Sentences

When two or more simple sentences are joined together by co-ordinating conjunction(s), the sentence formed is called a compound sentence (see Lesson 12). The simple sentences making up a compound sentence are co-ordinate and equal in rank; they are all called main clauses. In other words, compound sentences are made up of main clauses.

	TYPE OF SENTENCE	EXAMPLE
1	Simple sentence	*Dewi menyanyi.* Dewi sings. *Dewi menari.* Dewi dances.
	Compound sentence	*Dewi menyanyi sambil menari.* Dewi sings as [she] dances.
2	Simple sentence	*Ahmad mesti buat kerja itu.* Ahmad must do the job. *Ali mesti buat kerja itu.* Ali must do the job. *Kamu mesti buat kerja itu.* You must do the job.
	Compound sentence	*Ahmad, Ali atau kamu mesti buat kerja itu.* Ahmad, Ali or you must do the job.

Please note that when more than two sentences are joined to form a compound sentence, a comma is often used. There are, however, grammarians who disagree that such a sentence is a compound sentence.

Exercise 5. Combine the following sentences by using co-ordinating conjunctions:

e.g.

Karim rajin. Muthu rajin. (Karim is diligent. Muthu is diligent.)	*Karim* ***dan*** *Muthu rajin.* (Karim and Muthu are diligent.)
Pejabat pos dibuka setiap hari. Pejabat pos tidak dibuka pada hari Ahad. (The post office is open every day. The post office is not open on Sundays.)	*Pejabat pos dibuka setiap hari* ***kecuali*** *pada hari Ahad.* (The post office is open every day but not on Sundays.)

1. *Aminah cantik. Aminah sombong.*
   (Aminah is beautiful. Aminah is arrogant.)
2. *Aminah mesti pergi ke pasar. Fatimah mesti pergi ke pasar.*
   (Aminah must go to the market. Fatimah must go to the market.)
3. *Tuan pengerusi bangun. Tuan pengerusi bercakap.*
   (The chairman stood up. The chairman spoke.)
4. *Badannya belum sihat. Dia pergi juga.*
   (He [literally 'his body'] was not healthy. He still went.)
5. *Dia membaca. Kepalanya sakit.*
   (He reads. His head aches.)
6. *Dia kaya. Dia tidak sombong.*
   (He is rich. He is not arrogant.)

7. *Semua orang pergi. Saya seorang tidak pergi.*
   (Everyone goes. I alone do not go.)

8. *Pemuda itu berjalan. Pemuda itu menyanyi.*
   (The young man walks. The young man sings.)

9. *Kami minum kopi. Kami berbual.*
   (We drink coffee. We chat.)

10. *Saya tidak akan ke majlis itu. Saya tidak diundang ke majlis itu.*
    (I will not go to the party. I am not invited to the party.)

Exercise 6. Convert the following compound sentences into simple sentences.

e.g.

Kakak selalu menolong ibu dan orang gaji di dapur.
(Elder sister is always helping mother and the servant in the kitchen.)

Kakak selalu menolong ibu di dapur. Kakak selalu menolong orang gaji di dapur.
(Elder sister is always helping mother in the kitchen. Elder sister is always helping the servant in the kitchen.)

Malam masih muda tetapi jalan-jalan raya sudah mulai lengang.
(The night is still early but the highways are becoming deserted.)

Malam masih muda. Jalan-jalan raya telah mulai lengang.
(The night is still early. The highways are becoming deserted.)

1. *Saya akan pergi besok atau lusa.*
   (I will go tomorrow or the next day.)

2. *Dia selalu makan dan minum di rumah saya.*
(He always eats and drinks at my house.)

3. *Dia belajar sambil bekerja.*
(He studies while working.)

4. *Fatimah bercakap serta tersenyum.*
(Fatimah speaks and smiles.)

5. *Ahmad membeli sepasang kasut lalu keluar dari kedai itu.*
(Ahmad bought a pair of shoe; then went out of the shop.)

6. *Budak lelaki itu pandai tetapi malas.*
(The boy is clever but lazy.)

7. *Dia tidak akan datang melainkan dijemput.*
(He will not come unless [he is] invited.)

8. *Saudara boleh datang tiap-tiap hari kecuali pada hari Jumaat.*
(You can come every day except on Friday.)

9. *Saya akan naik bas atau keretapi.*
(I will take a bus or train.)

10. *Rumahnya sendiri ada tetapi dia menumpang di rumah orang.*
(He has his own house but he stays at another person's house.)

19D. Word Formation

kerja, laku, nyata, pandang, pinjam

(a) ***kerja: bekerja, mengerjakan, pekerjaan, berpekerjaan, pekerja, sekerja***

e.g. *Tiap-tiap orang hendaklah melakukan* ***kerja*** *masing- masing.*
(Everyone should do his **work**.)

Saudara tidak ***bekerja*** *hari ini?*
(Are you not **working** today?)

Dia ***mengerjakan*** *rancangan itu dengan segera.*
(He **carried out** the plan immediately.)

Pekerjaan *penduduk-penduduk kampung itu ialah menangkap ikan.*
(The **occupation** of the villagers is fishing.)

Semenjak kepulangannya dari London, dia tidak ***berpekerjaan****.*
(Since his return from London, he **has** not had any **job**.)

Tiga orang ***pekerja*** *syarikat itu telah dibuang kerja.*
(Three **workers** of the company have been dismissed.)

Wanita itu ***sekerja*** *dengan saya.*
(That woman has the same occupation as I.)

(b) ***laku: selaku, berlaku, melakukan, kelakuan, berkelakuan, memperlakukan, pelaku***

e.g. *Kain batik sangat* ***laku*** *sekarang.*
(Batik is very **easily sold** now.)

Beliau menjalankan mesyuarat itu ***selaku*** *pengerusi.*
(He conducted the meeting **in his capacity** as chairman.)

Suatu pergaduhan telah ***berlaku*** *malam itu.*
(A fight **broke out** that night.)

Pegawai itu ***melakukan*** *tanggungjawabnya dengan baik.*
(The officer **carried out** his responsibilities well.)

Dia ***melakukan*** *barang-barang di kedainya dengan iklan.*
(He **promotes** the goods in his shop by advertisements.)

Kelakuan *budak lelaki itu kurang baik.*
(The boy's **behaviour** is not [literally 'is less'] good.)

Kamu mesti ***berkelakuan*** *baik di sekolah.*
(You must **behave** properly in school.)

Wanita itu ***memperlakukan*** *anak tirinya sebagai hamba abdi.*
(The woman **treated** her step-son as a slave.)

Pelaku *jenayah itu masih belum dapat ditangkap.*
(The crime **doer** has still not been caught.)

(c) ***nyata: menyatakan, ternyata, kenyataan, pernyataan, penyata***

e.g. *Niat jahatnya sudah* ***nyata*** *sekarang.*
(His bad intention is **clear** now.)

Dia telah ***menyatakan*** *pendapatnya mengenai perkara itu.*
(He **expressed** his opinion about the matter.)

Kebolehan lelaki itu sudah ***ternyata****.*
(The man's ability has been **proven**.)

Akhirnya, aku terpaksa menerima ***kenyataan*** *itu*
(At last, I was forced to accept the **reality**.)

Perdana Menteri akan membuat satu ***kenyataan*** *malam ini.*
(The Prime Minister will make a **statement** tonight.)

Pemerintah masih belum membuat ***pernyataan*** *tentang hal itu.*

(The government has not made any **statement** about the matter.)

Syarikat itu masih belum menyiapkan ***penyata*** *tahunannya.*
(The company has not prepared its annual **report** yet.)

(d) pandang: berpandang-pandangan, memandang, memandangi, terpandang, pandangan, pemandangan

e.g. *Mereka* ***berpandang-pandangan*** *sejurus.*
(They **looked at each other** for a while.)

Dia ***memandang*** *bangunan yang tiga tingkat itu.*
(He **looked** at the three-storey building.)

Saya ***memandang*** *lelaki itu sebagai adik saya sendiri.*
(I **regard** the man as my own younger brother.)

Ismail ***memandangi*** *bapanya bekerja.*
(Ismail **observes** his father working.)

Dia termasuk orang yang ***terpandang*** *di kampung itu.*
(He is one of the **well-known** persons in the village.)

Pandangan*nya terhadap lelaki itu tidak berubah.*
(His **opinion** about the man did not change.)

Di negeri itu banyak ***pemandangan*** *yang cantik.*
(In that country there is a lot of beautiful **scenery**.)

(e) pinjam: meminjam, meminjami, meminjamkan, peminjam, pinjaman

e.g. *Saya* ***pinjam*** *buku itu dari perpustakaan.*
(I **borrowed** the book from the library.)

Dia selalu ***meminjam*** *wang dari saya.*
(He always **borrows** money from me.)

Perpustakaan dapat ***meminjami*** *kami semua buku yang diperlukan.*
(The library can **lend** us all the books needed.)

Dia tidak mahu ***meminjamkan*** *temannya wang.*
(He does not want to **lend** his friend money.)

Peminjam *wang dari bank harus membayar bunga.*
(A **borrower** of money from a bank must pay interest.)

Kata itu adalah kata ***pinjaman.***
(The word is a **loan** word.)

LESSON 20

20A. Conversation

Pentingnya Bahasa Kebangsaan
(The Importance of the National Language)

Hassan: *Mengapa saudara suka belajar bahasa Melayu?*
(Why do you like to study Malay?)

Tan: *Bahasa Melayu adalah bahasa kebangsaan kita. Semua rakyat Singapura mesti tahu bahasa kebangsaannya.*
(Malay is our national language. All Singaporeans should know their national language.)

Hassan: *Apa gunanya kita belajar bahasa kebangsaan? Di Singapura ini kita semua menggunakan bahasa Inggeris.*
(What is the use of studying the national language? In Singapore all of us use English.)

Tan: *Betul. Kita semua menggunakan bahasa Inggeris di Singapura. Tetapi kita mesti ingat bahawa bahasa Melayu yang menjadi bahasa kebangsaan kita itu juga menjadi bahasa kebangsaan orang-orang Indonesia dan Malaysia. Hanya namanya yang berbeza. Di Indonesia ia disebut Bahasa Indonesia dan di Malaysia ia disebut Bahasa Malaysia.*
(It is true. All of us use English in Singapore. But we must remember that the Malay language which is our national language is also the national language of Indonesians and Malaysians. Only its name differs. In Indonesia it is called Bahasa Indonesia and in Malaysia it is called Bahasa Malaysia.)

Hassan: *Jadi, kalau kita tahu bahasa Melayu atau bahasa kebangsaan kita, senanglah kita bergaul dengan orang-orang Malaysia dan Indonesia. Betulkah begitu?*
(So, if we know Malay or our national language, it would be easy for us to associate with Malaysians and Indonesians. Is that so?)

Tan: *Tepat seperti apa yang dikatakan saudara.*
(Just as what you have said.)

Hassan: *Tahniah, Saudara Tan! Saya gembira mendengar orang bukan Melayu seperti saudara juga faham akan pentingnya bahasa Melayu. Belajarlah bersungguh-sungguh. Kalau saudara perlukan bantuan, saya akan menolong saudara dengan suka hati.*
(Congratulations, Mr. Tan! I am glad to hear that a non-Malay like you also understands the importance of Malay. Do study hard. If you need my assistance, I will be very willing help you.)

Tan: *Terima kasih.*
(Thank you.)

20B. Structure

Read the following sentences carefully.

SUBJECT	PREDICATE
Kereta-kereta Jepun Japanese cars	*sudah naik harga.* have gone up in price.
Dia He	*berasa gembira sekarang.* feels happy now.
Lelaki itu The man	*menjadi marah.* became angry.
Sakit lelaki itu The man's illness	*menjadi sembuh.* is cured.
Lelaki itu The man	*kelihatan sedih.* looks sad.

Exercise 1. Substitute the word in the model sentence with the one given.

e.g.	*Lelaki itu kelihatan* ***sedih****.* (The man looks sad.)
bimbang (worried)	*Lelaki itu kelihatan* ***bimbang****.* (The man looks worried.)
penat (tired)	*Lelaki itu kelihatan* ***penat****.* (The man looks tired.)
nampaknya (it seems)	*Lelaki itu* ***nampaknya*** *sedih.* (The man seems to be sad.)
jujur (honest)	*Lelaki itu nampaknya* ***jujur****.* (The man seems to be honest.)

1. *ramah* (friendly)
2. *bengis* (merciless)
3. *gelisah* (restless)
4. *bingung* (perplexed)
5. *rupanya* (it looks)
6. *bahagia* (happy)
7. *kaget* (shocked)
8. *sakit* (sick)
9. *cekap* (efficient)
10. *sombong* (arrogant)

Exercise 2. Answer the following questions. Use the words given.

e.g.

Question	*Answer*
***Apa** sudah naik harga?* *- kereta-kereta Jepun* (What have gone up in price? - Japanese cars)	***Kereta-kereta Jepun** sudah naik harga.* (Japanese cars have gone up in price.)
***Siapa** sudah balik haji?* *- ayah* (Who returned from a pilgrimage? - father)	***Ayah** sudah balik haji.* (Father returned from a pilgrimage.)

1. ***Siapa** naik haji tahun ini? - ramai petani*
   (Who goes on a pilgrimage this year? - many farmers)
2. ***Apa** yang turun harga? - hasil tanaman*
   (What have gone down in price? - agricultural produce)
3. ***Siapa** sudah habis modal? - pensyarah itu*
   (Who has run out of ideas? - the lecturer)
4. ***Siapa** yang hilang nyawa? - ramai penumpang*
   (Who lost [their] lives? - many passengers)

5. ***Siapa*** *jatuh miskin? - usahawan muda itu*
(Who became bankrupt? - the young industrialist)

6. ***Apa*** *yang dapat melukai orang - senjata*
(What can hurt people? - the weapon)

7. ***Apa*** *yang tidak masuk akal? - perkara itu*
(What is illogical? - the matter)

8. ***Siapa*** *yang tidak tahu bahasa? - budak itu*
(Who has no manners? - the child)

9. ***Siapa*** *yang putus harapan? - pemuda itu*
(Who has lost [his] hope? - the young man)

10. ***Apa yang*** *tinggal sedikit? - wangnya*
(What remains a little? - his money)

Exercise 3. Answer the following questions. Use the words given.

e.g.

Question	*Answer*
Bagaimana *dia sekarang?* *- berasa gembira* (How is he now? - to feel happy)	*Dia* ***berasa gembira*** *sekarang.* (He feels happy now.)
Bagaimana *rasa makanan itu?* *- terasa masin* (How does the food taste? - tastes salty)	*Makanan itu* ***terasa masin****.* (The food tastes salty.)

1. ***Bagaimana*** *dia sekarang? - merasa lega*
(How is he now? - feeling relieved)

2. ***Bagaimana*** *rasa makanan itu? - terasa manis*
(How does the food taste? - tastes sweet)

3. ***Bagaimana*** *dia sekarang? - merasa sedih*
(How is he now? - feeling sad)

4. ***Bagaimana*** *rasa masakan itu? - terasa pedas*
(How does the food taste? - tastes spicy)

5. ***Bagaimana*** *dia rasa sekarang? - masih merasa takut*
(How does he feel now? - still feels frightened)

6. ***Bagaimana*** *rasa badannya sekarang? - merasa sakit*
(How does he [literally 'his body'] feel now? - feels sick)

7. ***Bagaimana*** *dia sekarang? - merasa tenteram*
(How does he feel now? - feels peaceful)

8. ***Bagaimana*** *kakinya sekarang? - berasa kebas*
(How is his foot now? - feels numb)

9. ***Bagaimana*** *dia sekarang? - merasa selamat*
(How does he feel now? - feels safe)

10. ***Bagaimana*** *dia sekarang? - berasa lapar*
(How does he feel now? - feels hungry)

Exercise 4. Answer the following questions. Use the words given.

e.g.

Question	*Answer*
Apa yang terjadi dengan *lelaki itu?* - *menjadi marah* (What happened to the man? - became angry)	*Lelaki itu menjadi marah.* (The man became angry.)
Bagaimana penyakit *lelaki itu?* - *menjadi sembuh* (How is the man's illness? - is cured)	*Penyakit lelaki itu menjadi sembuh.* The man's illness is cured.)

1. ***Apa yang terjadi dengan*** *lelaki itu? - menjadi buta*
   (What happened to the man? - became blind)

2. ***Apa yang terjadi dengan*** *penjudi itu? - menjadi gila*
   (What happened to the gambler? - became mad)

3. ***Apa yang terjadi dengan*** *mimpinya? - menjadi kenyataan*
   (What happened to his dream? - became a reality)

4. ***Apa yang terjadi dengan*** *penulis itu? - menjadi terkenal*
   (What happened to the writer? - became famous)

5. ***Apa yang terjadi dengan*** *makanan itu? - menjadi basi*
   (What happened to the food? - became stale)

6. ***Apa yang terjadi dengan*** *bandar itu? - menjadi lengang*
   (What happened to the town? - became deserted)

7. ***Bagaimana*** *suasana pertemuan itu? - menjadi tegang*
   (How is the atmosphere of the meeting? - becomes tense)

8. ***Apa yang terjadi dengan*** *Ahmad? - menjadi pengerusi jawatankuasa*
   (What happened to Ahmad? - became chairman of the committee)

9. ***Apa yang terjadi dengan*** *budak miskin itu? - menjadi kaya raya*
   (What happened to the poor child? - became very rich)

10. ***Apa yang terjadi dengan*** *gadis itu? - menjadi ratu kebaya*
    (What happened to the girl? - became a kebaya queen)

20C. Grammar

Sentence Type

Sentences in Malay can be functionally classified into four groups.

(a) Statements or Narrative Sentences

e.g. *Dia guru.*
(He is a teacher.)

Dia suka makan durian.
(He likes to eat durian.)

Hujan lebat pagi ini.
(The rain was heavy this morning.)

Ibu di rumah.
(Mother is at home.)

(b) Commands or Imperative Sentences

e.g. *Pergi!*
(Go away!)

Keluar dari sini!
(Get out of here!)

Tolong bawa buku itu ke sini.
(Please bring the book here.)

Sila datang ke rumah saya.
(Please come to my house.)

(c) Exclamations or Exclamatory Sentences

e.g. *Aduh! Sakitnya kaki saya!*
(Ouch! My foot hurts!)

Wah! Cantiknya baju awak itu!
(Wow! How beautiful is your dress!)

Horei! Kita sudah menang!
(Hurray! We won!)

Cis! Berani engkau kata begitu!
(Oh! How dare you say so!)

(d) Questions or Interrogative Sentences

e.g. *Dia gurukah?*
(Is he a teacher?)

Siapa nama lelaki itu?
(What is the name of the man?)

Bila saudara tiba?
(When did you arrive?)

Sudahkah dia berangkat?
(Has he left?)

Statement or narrative sentences do not need further explanation. All the sentences given in boxes under sections B of this book are narrative sentences. Imperative sentences are transformed from narrative sentences by deleting the subject or by replacing it with words like *sila*, *tolong* or *cuba*. For example, the imperative sentences given under group (b) above are transformed from:

Saudara pergi.
(You go.)

Saudara keluar dari sini.
(You get out of here.)

Saudara bawa buku itu ke sini.
(You bring the book here.)

Saudara datang ke rumah saya.
(You come to my house.)

Notice that the subject *saudara* (you) has been omitted to derive the sentences given under group (b).

Exclamatory sentences begin with exclamatory words which are associated with the speaker's feeling.

e.g.

Exclamatory word	*Feeling associated with*
Aduh! (Ouch!)	sadness, pain
Wah! (Wow)!	happiness, surprise
Cih! (Oh!)	scorn
Amboi! (Wow!)	admiration

Alangkah (What/How a ...) is also used.

e.g. ***Alangkah*** *besarnya rumah itu!*
(What a big house!)

Alangkah *pandai budak itu!*
(How clever the child is!)

Interrogative sentences have also been extensively illustrated in Sections B of this book. In this and the last lesson, we will summarize what has been stated so far. There are several ways of forming questions or interrogative sentences in Malay. These are:

(a) by using intonation
(b) by using the particle ***-kah***
(c) by using question words
(d) by using the question tag; ***bukan***

(a) By using intonation

e.g.

Statement	*Question*
Dia pergi. (He goes.)	*Dia pergi?* (He goes?)

Dia cantik. (She is beautiful)	*Dia cantik?* (She is beautiful?)
Dia sahabat saya. (He is my friend.)	*Dia sahabat saya?* (He is my friend?)
Ahmad di sekolah. (Ahmad is at school.)	*Ahmad di sekolah?* (Ahmad is at school?)

(b) By using the particle ***-kah***

e.g. *Dia **pergikah**?*
(Did he go?)

*Dia **cantikkah**?*
(Is she beautiful?)

*Dia sahabat **sayakah**?*
(Is he my friend?)

*Ahmad **di sekolahkah**?*
(Is Ahmad at school?)

The question particle ***-kah*** can also be placed with the predicate at the beginning of the question. For example, the above questions may also be framed as follows:

***Pergikah** dia?*

***Cantikkah** dia?*

*Sahabat **sayakah** dia?*

***Di sekolahkah** Ahmad?*

Yet another way of asking this kind of yes/no question is by using *adakah* (does/did) at the beginning of the sentence.

e.g. ***Adakah** dia pergi?*
(Did he go?)

***Adakah** dia cantik?*
(Is she beautiful?)

Adakah *dia sahabat saya?*
(Is he my friend?)

Adakah *Ahmad di sekolah?*
(Is Ahmad at school?)

(c) By using question words

Most of the question words used to form questions are either interrogative pronouns (see Lesson 5) like *apa* (what), *siapa* (who, whom), *yang mana* (which), *berapa* (how many/much/...) or interrogative adverbs see Lesson 10) like *bagaimana* (how), *bila* (when), *di mana* (where) and *mengapa* (why).

e.g. ***Apa*** *dia buat?*
(What did he do?)

Siapa *lelaki itu?*
(Who is that man?)

Siapa *dia pukul?*
(Whom did he beat?)

Berapa *orang anak saudara?*
(How many children have you?)

Yang mana *rumah saudara?*
(Which one is your house?)

Bagaimana *saudara pergi kerja?*
(How do you go to work?)

Bila *dia datang?*
(When did he come?)

Mengapa *saudara ketawa?*
(Why did you laugh?)

Di mana *saudara tinggal sekarang?*
(Where do you live now?)

(d) By using the question tag: *bukan*

e.g. *Lelaki itu guru, bukan?*
(The man is a teacher, isn't he?)

Lelaki itu kaya, bukan?
(The man is rich, isn't he?)

Ramli datang, bukan?
(Ramli came, didn't he?)

Saudara ada di rumah, bukan?
(You are at home, aren't you?)

Exercise 5. Fill in the blanks with suitable question words.

e.g.

__________ *dia sakit?* (__________ he sick?)	***Adakah*** *dia sakit?* (Is he sick?)
__________ *penceramah itu tidak datang?* (__________ the speaker not come?)	***Mengapa*** *penceramah itu tidak datang?* (Why did the speaker not come?)

1. *Dia belajar bahasa* __________*?*
(__________ language is he learning?)
2. __________ *dia suka membaca buku Melayu?*
(__________ he like to read Malay books?)
3. __________ *orang anak lelaki itu?*
(__________ are the man's children?)
4. __________ *memandang kita hina?*
(__________ looks down on us?)
5. *Budak itu anak* __________*?*
(The child was __________?)

6. *Saudara membeli kamus itu __________?*
   (You bought the dictionary at __________ place?)

7. __________ *keadaan orang tua saudara?*
   (__________ are your parents?)

8. __________ *saudara tidak kerja hari ini?*
   (__________ are you not working today?)

9. __________ *saudara berangkat ke Jakarta?*
   (__________ are you departing for Jakarta?)

10. __________ *lelaki itu datang?*
    (__________ did the man come from?)

Exercise 6. Form at least two questions from the following sentences.

e.g.

Sentence	*Question*
Ramlah hendak bertolak sekarang. (Ramlah wishes to leave now.)	***Siapa*** *hendak bertolak sekarang?* (Who wishes to leave now?)
	Bila Ramlah hendak bertolak? (When is Ramlah going to leave?)
Lelaki tua itu berjalan sangat lambat. (The old man walks very slowly.)	***Siapa*** *berjalan sangat lambat?* (Who walks very slowly?)
	Bagaimana *lelaki tua itu berjalan?* (How does the old man walk?)

1. *Lelaki itu datang dari Malaysia.*
   (The man came from Malaysia.)
2. *Murid itu suka menulis dengan dakwat merah.*
   (The pupil likes to write with red ink.)
3. *Aminah pergi ke pasar dengan ibunya.*
   (Aminah goes to the market with her mother.)
4. *Cikgu Ali tinggal di Bedok.*
   (Teacher Ali lives in Bedok.)
5. *Adik selalu membaca buku pada waktu malam.*
   (Younger brother always reads book at night.)
6. *Dia hendak melanjutkan pelajarannya di luar negeri.*
   (He wishes to continue his studies abroad.)
7. *Rumah saya jauh dari bandar.*
   (My house is far from the city.)
8. *Minggu lepas kami berkelah di tepi laut.*
   (Last week we picnicked by the seaside.)
9. *Lelaki tua itu suka makan durian.*
   (The old man likes to eat durian.)
10. *Saya kenal lelaki itu.*
    (I know the man.)

20D. Word Formation

salah, satu, temu, tinggal, tolak

(a) ***salah: bersalah, bersalahan, menyalahi, menyalahkan, tersalah, kesalahan, pesalah***

e.g. *Kira-kira kamu ini* ***salah****, buat semula.*
(Your sum is **incorrect**, do it again.)

*Jikalau saya **bersalah**, saya minta maaf.*
(If I am **in the wrong**, I apologize.)

*Menghukum seseorang tanpa bukti adalah **bersalahan** dengan pendirian saya.*
(To punish a person without proof **contradicts** my principle.)

*Saya tidak dapat **menyalahi** pendiriannya.*
(I cannot **oppose** his opinion.)

*Saya tidak mahu **menyalahkan** sesiapa.*
(I do not want **to wrong/blame** anyone.)

*Jikalau ada apa-apa yang **tersalah**, saya pohonkan maaf.*
(If there is any **mistake**, I ask for forgiveness.)

*Lelaki itu sudah mengaku **kesalahannya**.*
(The man has confessed his **crimes**.)

***Pesalah-pesalah** itu akan dihukum.*
(The **convicts** will be punished.)

(b) ***satu: satu-satu, bersatu, menyatukan, satuan, kesatuan, persatuan, penyatuan***

e.g. *Timbang barang-barang ini **satu-satu**.*
(Weigh these items **one by one**.)

*Kita mesti **bersatu** untuk menjaga keamanan dalam kampung.*
(We must **unite** in order to maintain peace in the village.)

*Kita patut berusaha **menyatukan** semua kaum di dalam negeri.*
(We must try **to unite** all the races in the country.)

*Ringgit merupakan **satuan** wang di Malaysia.*
(The Ringgit is a currency **unit** in Malaysia.)

Manusia sukar memelihara ***kesatuan*** *bahasa.*
(It is difficult for human being to maintain linguistic **unity**.)

Ahmad ialah seorang ahli ***Persatuan*** *Bahasa Melayu.*
(Ahmad is a member of the Malay Language **Society**.)

Ahli-ahli bahasa sedang berusaha mencapai ***penyatuan*** *bahasa Melayu dan Indonesia.*
(Linguists are striving to accomplish the **unification** of Malay and Indonesian.)

(c) ***temu: bertemu, menemui, menemukan, mempertemukan, pertemuan, penemuan***

e.g. *Dia* ***bertemu*** *dengan pemuda itu minggu lalu.*
(He **met** the young man last week.)

Dia pulang ke kampung ***menemui*** *kaum keluarganya.*
(He went back to the village **to visit** his family.)

Tuhan sahajalah yang boleh ***menemukan*** *kami.*
(Only God can **make us meet** again.)

Jikalau perlu saya akan ***mempertemukan*** *saudara dengan pegawai itu.*
(If it is necessary, I will **bring** you **to meet** the officer.)

Dia masih ingat ***pertemuannya*** *dengan pegawai itu.*
(He can still remember his **meeting** with the officer.)

Beliau telah membuat beberapa ***penemuan*** *dalam bidang kimia.*
(He made several **discoveries** in chemistry.)

(d) ***tinggal: meninggal, meninggalkan, tertinggal, ketinggalan, peninggalan, sepeninggalan***

e.g. *Kamu* ***tinggal*** *di sini; saya hendak keluar sekejap.*
(You **remain** here; I want to go out for a while.)

Ayahnya ***meninggal*** *di tanah suci.*
(His father **passed away** in the holy land.)

Dia ***meninggalkan*** *anak lelakinya di rumah.*
(He **left** his son at home.)

Dalam perlumbaan itu Rosnah ***tertinggal*** *di belakang.*
(In the race, Rosnah **is left** behind.)

Kunci saya ***ketinggalan*** *di rumah.*
(My keys **were left** at home.)

Kami ***ketinggalan*** *bas.*
(We **missed** the bus.)

Harta ***peninggalan*** *ayahnya tidaklah banyak.*
(The property **left behind** by his father was not much.)

Sepeninggalan *ibunya rumahnya menjadi kucar-kacir.*
(**After the death** of his mother, the house was in a mess.)

(e) ***tolak: bertolak, menolak, menolakkan, penolakan, tolakan***

e.g. *Dia* ***bertolak*** *petang ini.*
(He will **depart** this afternoon.)

Orang-orang kampung datang ***menolak*** *motokar saya.*
(The villagers came **to push** my car.)

Saya ***menolak*** *permintaan lelaki itu.*
(I **reject** the man's request.)

Ketua itu ***menolakkan*** *kesilapan itu kepada bawahannya.*
(The chief **pushes** the mistake onto his subordinates.)

Dia merasa malu kerana ***penolakan*** *itu.*
(He feels ashamed because of the **rejection**.)

Orang itu memberikan perempuan itu ***tolakan*** *yang kuat.*
(That person gave the woman a hard **push**.)

PART II

LESSON 1

Kehidupan Di Rumah Pangsa
(Living In A Flat)

A. Sentence Patterns

1. *Pada abad kedua puluh ini lebih separuh daripada rakyat*
   In the twentieth century, more than half of the people of

   Singapura tinggal di rumah-rumah pangsa.
   Singapore live in flats.

2. *Kebanyakan daripada mereka dapat menyesuaikan diri*
   Most of them can adapt themselves

   dengan kehidupan di rumah pangsa.
   to life in the flats.

3. *Penghuni rumah pangsa sekarang ini tidak lagi menghadapi*
   Flat dwellers now do not face any

   masalah.
   problems.

4. *Penghuni rumah pangsa mengadakan majlis perkahwinan.*
   The flat dwellers hold a wedding party.

5. *Mereka boleh menggunakan kolong rumah pangsa untuk*
   They can use the void-deck of the flats for

   tujuan itu.
   that purpose.

6. *Mereka juga boleh menggunakan kolong itu untuk*
   They can also use the void-deck to

beribadat.
perform religious duties.

7. *Mereka mengadakan sembahyang tarawih dalam*
They say special prayers in

bulan puasa.
the fasting month.

8. *Adalah menjadi dasar pemerintah.*
This is the government's policy.

9. *Pemerintah menyediakan kawasan untuk membina*
The government sets aside an area to build

rumah ibadat bagi semua golongan agama.
a religious place for all the religious groups.

10. *Pemerintah membina rumah-rumah ibadat.*
The government builds houses of worship.

11. *Di tiap-tiap kawasan perumahan telah didirikan masjid,*
In every housing estate there are built mosques,

gereja dan kuil untuk rakyat yang berlainan agama
churches and temples for people of different religions

membuat ibadat masing-masing.
to perform their religious duties.

12. *Padang permainan, tempat-tempat riadah*
Playgrounds, recreational centres,

kompleks sukan dan kompleks renang telah diadakan
sport complexes and swimming complexes have been built

khusus untuk kegunaaan penghuni rumah pangsa
especially for the use of the flat dwellers

dan penduduk sekitarnya.
and the residents around it.

13. *Tempat-tempat ini amat mustahak untuk mengadakan*
These places are very important for organizing

kegiatan bagi mengisi masa lapang.
activities for leisure time.

14. *Di samping itu, timbul masalah baru bagi*
Besides, new problems arise for

penghuni rumah pangsa.
the flat dwellers.

15. *Di antaranya ialah kejadian jenayah seperti rompakan dan*
Among them are criminal acts like robbery and

merosakan harta benda.
vandalism.

16. *Kejadian seperti ini sangat menakutkan mereka.*
Happenings like this greatly frightened them.

17. *Suatu lagi masalah yang timbul ialah*
Another problem which has risen is

masalah kemasyarakatan.
social problem.

18. *Ada di antara penghuni rumah pangsa yang*
Some of the flat dwellers are

mementingkan diri sendiri.
selfish.
(literally 'There are dwellers who give priority to self-interest.')

19. *Ada penghuni rumah pangsa yang kurang bertimbang rasa*
Some flat dwellers are less considerate

sesama jiran.
of (their) neighbours.
(literally 'There are dwellers who are less considerate.')

20. *Sikap ini bertentangan dengan cita-cita kita.*
This attitude runs against our ideals.

21. *Kita hendak membentuk sebuah masyarakat yang*
We wish to form a society which is

bersatu-padu dan rukun damai.
united and harmonious.

B. Comprehension

Pada abad yang kedua puluh ini, lebih separuh daripada rakyat Singapura tinggal di rumah-rumah pangsa. Kebanyakan daripada mereka telah dapat menyesuaikan diri dengan kehidupan di rumah pangsa itu.

Penghuni-penghuni rumah pangsa sekarang ini tidak lagi menghadapi masalah jika hendak mengadakan majlis perkahwinan. Mereka boleh menggunakan kolong rumah pangsa untuk tujuan itu. Mereka juga menggunakan kolong itu untuk beribadat seperti mengadakan sembahyang tarawih dalam bulan puasa. Adalah menjadi dasar pemerintah menyediakan kawasan untuk membina rumah-rumah ibadat bagi semua golongan agama. Sebagaimana yang kita lihat, di tiap-tiap kawasan perumahan telah didirikan masjid-masjid, gereja-gereja atau kuil-kuil untuk rakyat yang berlainan agama membuat ibadat masing-masing.

Padang permainan, tempat-tempat riadah, kompleks sukan dan kompleks renang juga telah diadakan khusus untuk kegunaan penghuni-penghuni rumah pangsa dan penduduk sekitarnya. Tempat-tempat ini amatlah mustahak untuk mengadakan kegiatan-kegiatan bagi mengisi masa lapang mereka.

Di samping itu, timbul pula masalah baru bagi penghuni-penghuni rumah pangsa. Di antaranya ialah kejadian jenayah seperti rompakan dan merosakkan harta benda. Kejadian-kejadian seperti ini sangatlah menakutkan mereka.

Suatu lagi masalah yang timbul ialah masalah kemasyarakatan. Ada di antara penghuni-penghuni rumah pangsa yang mementingkan diri sendiri dan kurang bertimbang rasa sesama jiran. Sikap seperti ini adalah bertentangan dengan cita-cita kita hendak membentuk sebuah masyarakat yang bersatu-padu dan rukun damai.

Jawab soalan-soalan di bawah ini:

(*a*) Berapa ramaikah rakyat Singapura yang tinggal di rumah pangsa?
(*b*) Apakah kemudahan-kemudahan yang disediakan untuk penghuni rumah pangsa?
(*c*) Nyatakan masalah baru yang dihadapi oleh penghuni rumah pangsa.
(*d*) Masyarakat yang bagaimanakah yang kita kehendaki?

LESSON 2

Cita-Cita Setinggi Langit
(Ambition Is As High As The Sky)

A. Sentence Patterns

1. *Sekali peristiwa Sarah dan kawan-kawannya ditanyai*
   Once Sarah and her friends were asked

   oleh gurunya.
   by her teacher.

2. *Kamu suka jadi apa?*
   What would you like to be?

3. *Apa jawatan yang kamu sukai?*
   What post would you like?

4. *Kamu kelak menjadi orang dewasa.*
   [When] you become an adult later.

5. *Kawan-kawannya menjawab dengan serkap jarang sahaja.*
   Her friends answered casually.

6. *Saya mahu menjadi kerani Pejabat Tanah.*
   I want to be a clerk in the Land Office.

7. *Saya dapat menolong ayah saya meringankan cukai.*
   I can help my father to reduce the tax.

8. *Saya mahu jadi menteri.*
   I want to be a minister.

9. *Saya mahu menjadi posman.*
I want to become a postman.

10. *Ayah bersara.*
Father retires.

11. *Ada pelajar-pelajar yang menjawab dengan tersipu-sipu.*
There are pupils who answer bashfully.

12. *Saya mahu jadi guru untuk mendidik*
I want to be a teacher to teach

anak bangsa.
children of the nation.

13. *Saya mahu jadi pahlawan negara.*
I want to be a national hero.

14. *Sarah menjawab dengan tegas.*
Sarah answered firmly.

15. *Saya mahu jadi pengarang besar.*
I want to be a great writer.

16. *Saya akan memimpin manusia melalui*
I will guide the human race through

karangan-karangan saya.
my writings.

17. *Semua kawannya tertawa mendengar*
All her friends laughed hearing

jawapan Sarah yang tegas.
Sarah's firm reply.

18. *Nafsu besar, tenaga kurang.*
Desire is strong, energy is lacking.

19. *Kata seorang di antara pelajar-pelajar.*
Says one of the pupils.

20. *Sarah seorang perempuan yang tidak pernah mendapat*
Sarah is a girl who has never occupied

tempat pertama.
the first position.

21. *Seorang perempuan hendak memimpin manusia.*
A woman wishes to guide mankind.

22. *Darjah itu menjadi riuh-rendah dengan gelak mengejek-ejek*
The class became noisy with laughter teasing

Sarah.
Sarah

23. *Sarah sampuk dengan tenang dan sabar.*
Sarah butted in with calm and patience.

24. *Mudah-mudahan sangkaan itu tidak benar.*
Hopefully the suspicion is not true.

25. *Kawan-kawannya menyeru: 'Hidup Intan, Hidup Intan'.*
Her friends shouted: 'Live Diamond, Live Diamond'.

26. *Kawan-kawan memuja Sarah kerana cita-citanya.*
Her friends praised Sarah for her ambition.

27. *Darjah itu jadi makin riuh sehingga seolah-olah tidak*
The class became noisy as if it cannot be

dapat dikawal oleh gurunya.
controlled by the teacher.

28. *Guru besar masuk ke dalam darjah itu.*
The headmaster went into the classroom.

29. *Guru besar bertanya kepada guru darjah.*
The headmaster asked the class teacher.

30. *Apa yang telah terjadi?*
What has happened?

31. *Apa yang menyebabkan riuh-rendah itu?*
What is the cause of the noise?

32. *Guru darjah menerangkan segala hal yang terjadi.*
The class teacher explained everything that took place.

B. Comprehension

The following passage is taken from 'Sarah Pengarang Kecil' (Sarah, The Small Writer) a novel for young people by Mas or Muhammad Ariff Ahmad, a well-known Malay writer and linguist in Singapore.

Sekali peristiwa Sarah dan kawan-kawannya telah ditanyai oleh gurunya, 'Kamu suka jadi apa, apa jawatan yang kamu sukai, bila kamu kelak menjadi orang dewasa?'

Kawan-kawannya ada yang menjawab serkap jarang sahaja:

'.... mahu jadi kerani Pejabat Tanah supaya dapat menolong ayah meringankan cukai tanah.'

'.... mahu jadi menteri.'

'.... mahu jadi posmen bila ayah bersara.'

Bahkan ada pula yang tersipu-sipu menjawab:

'Saya mahu jadi guru untuk mendidik anak bangsa.'

'Saya mahu jadi pahlawan negara,' dan lain-lain.

Tetapi Sarah, dengan tegas menjawab, 'Saya mahu jadi pengarang besar yang akan memimpin manusia dengan fikiran, hati serta nyawa saya melalui karangan-karangan saya.'

Semua kawannya tertawa mendengar jawapan Sarah yang begitu tegas.

'Nafsu besar tenaga kurang,' kata seorang di antara pelajar-pelajar itu.

'Seorang perempuan yang tidak pernah mendapat nombor satu hendak memimpin manusia,' sorak kawannya yang seorang pula. Darjah itu menjadi riuh-rendah dengan gelak mengejek-ejek Sarah.

'Mudah-mudahan semua sangkaan itu tidak benar,' sampuk Sarah dengan tenang dan sabar.

'Hidup Intan, Hidup Intan!' seru kawan-kawannya yang memuja-muja Sarah dan cita-citanya. Darjah itu jadi makin riuh hingga seolah-olah tidak terkawal lagi oleh gurunya. Maka guru besar pun masuk ke dalam darjah itu dan bertanya kepada guru darjah apa yang telah terjadi menyebabkan riuh-rendah itu. Guru darjah itu menerangkan segala hal yang terjadi.

Jawab soalan-soalan di bawah:

(*a*) Siapakah pengarang 'Sarah Pengarang Kecil'?
(*b*) Apakah cita-cita Sarah?
(*c*) Mengapakah cita-citanya itu dikatakan setinggi langit?
(*d*) Mengapakah darjah itu menjadi riuh-rendah?

LESSON 3

Keluarga Bahagia
(A Happy Family)

A. Sentence Patterns

1. *Keluarga Encik Murad tinggal di sebuah*
   Mr. Murad's family lives in a

   kawasan kediaman swasta di Katong.
   private housing estate in Katong.

2. *Mereka tinggal di sebuah rumah banglo.*
   They live in a bungalow.

3. *Rumah itu telah dipusakai oleh Encik Murad daripada*
   The house was inherited by Mr. Murad from

   arwah ayahnya.
   his late father.

4. *Keluarga Encik Murad terdiri daripada lima orang.*
   Mr. Murad's family consists of five persons.

5. *Encik Murad bekerja sebagai peguam.*
   Mr. Murad works as a lawyer.

6. *Dia* ***membuka*** *sebuah firma guaman dengan*
   He set up a law firm with
   (literally 'open')

   seorang sahabatnya.
   one of his friends.

7. *Encik Murad sihat orangnya.*
Mr. Murad is a healthy person.

8. *Dia tampan.*
He is handsome.

9. *Dia* ***berbadan tegap***.
He is physically well-built. (literally 'has a well-built body')

10. *Dia selalu beriadah selepas kerja.*
He always exercises after work.

11. *Encik Murad sentiasa sibuk dengan pekerjaannya.*
Mr. Murad is always busy with his work.

12. *Dia selalu mengambil berat tentang*
He always cares about

kebahagiaan keluarganya.
his family's happiness.

13. *Dia sentiasa berkumpul dan berbual dengan*
He always gets together and chats with

keluarganya.
his family.

14. *Dia sering mengawasi kemajuan pelajaran*
He often monitors the educational progress of

anak-anaknya.
his children.

15. *Di samping itu dia memberikan didikan agama yang cukup*
Besides that he gives sufficient religious instruction

kepada anak-anaknya.
to his children.

16. *Encik Murad memanggil seorang guru agama ke*
Mr. Murad calls a religious teacher to

rumahnya.
his house.

17. *Guru agama itu memberikan didikan agama kepada*
The religious teacher gives religious teaching to

anak-anaknya.
his children.

18. *Siti Aisyah adalah isteri yang taat.*
Siti Aisyah is a loyal wife.

19. *Dia* ***baik hati*** *dan penyayang.*
She is kind and compassionate.

20. *Dia tidak bekerja.*
She is not working.

21. *Dia sentiasa sibuk dengan urusan rumahtangga.*
She is always busy with household matters.

22. *Sebagai suri rumahtangga, dia bertanggungjawab atas*
As a housewife, she is responsible for

kebahagiaan keluarganya.
her family's happiness.

23. *Rumahnya sentiasa kemas.*
Her house is always tidy.

24. *Dia sudah selesai* ***menguruskan keadaan rumah****.*
She has finished her chores.
(literally 'manage [the condition of] the house')

25. *Siti Aisyah berehat di* ***bilik tamu***.
Siti Aisyah is resting in the sitting room.
(literally 'guest-room')

26. *Siti Aisyah membaca suratkhabar atau majalah.*
Siti Aisyah reads newspapers or magazines.

27. *Yazid anak sulung Encik Murad.*
Yazid is Mr. Murad's elder son.

28. *Yazid sedang menuntut*
Yazid is studying
di universiti dalam jurusan kejuruteraan.
engineering at the university.
(literally 'Yazid is studying in the university in the field of engineering.')

29. *Sekarang dia ialah mahasiswa tahun pertama.*
Now he is a first year undergraduate.

30. *Pada pendapat Yazid kerja kejuruteraan amat penting*
In Yazid's opinion engineering work is vital

kepada negara.
to the country.

31. *Siti Fatimah ialah anak Encik Murad yang tengah.*
Siti Fatimah is Mr. Murad's mid child.

32. *Siti Fatimah sedang menuntut dalam menengah empat.*
Siti Fatimah is studying in secondary four.

33. *Dia bercita-cita hendak melanjutkan pelajarannya*
She is ambitious to further her study

hingga ke universiti.
at the university.
(literally 'up to')

34. *Dia bercita-cita hendak menjadi guru bahasa Inggeris*
She is ambitious to be an English language teacher

di sekolah menengah setelah tamat.
in a secondary school after graduation.

35. *Siti Khadijah anak Encik Murad yang bongsu.*
Siti Khadijah is Mr. Murad's youngest child.

36. *Siti Khadijah sedang belajar di kelas menengah satu.*
Siti Khadijah is studying in secondary one.

37. *Dia bercita-cita hendak menjadi doktor.*
Her ambition is to become a doctor.

38. *Dia dewasa kelak.*
She grows up later.

B. Comprehension

Keluarga Encik Murad tinggal di sebuah kawasan kediaman swasta di Katong. Mereka tinggal di sebuah rumah banglo. Rumah itu telah dipusakai oleh Encik Murad daripada arwah ayahnya. Keluarga Encik Murad terdiri daripada lima orang: Encik Murad, isterinya, Siti Aisyah, seorang anak laki-laki dan dua orang anak perempuan.

Encik Murad bekerja sebagai peguam. Dia membuka sebuah firma guaman dengan seorang sahabatnya. Encik Murad sihat orangnya, berbadan tegap dan tampan. Dia selalu beriadah selepas bekerja. Walaupun Encik Murad sentiasa sibuk dengan pekerjaannya, dia selalu mengambil berat tentang kebahagiaan keluarganya. Setelah makan malam, dia sentiasa berkumpul dan berbual-bual dengan keluarganya. Dia seringkali mengawasi kemajuan palajaran anak-anaknya. Di samping itu, dia juga memberikan didikan agama yang cukup kepada anak-anaknya.

Encik Murad memanggil seorang guru agama ke rumahnya untuk memberikan didikan agama kepada anak-anaknya.

Siti Aisyah, isteri Encik Murad, adalah isteri yang taat, baik hati dan penyayang. Dia tidak bekerja tetapi sentiasa sibuk dengan urusan rumahtangganya. Sebagai suri rumahtangga, dia bertanggungjawab di atas kebahgiaan keluarganya. Rumahnya sentiasa bersih dan kemas. Setelah selesai menguruskan keadaan rumahnya, Siti Aisyah berehat di bilik tamu sambil membaca suratkhabar atau majalah.

Yazid, anak sulung Encik Murad, sedang menuntut di universiti dalam jurusan kejuruteraan. Sekarang dia ialah mahasiswa tahun pertama. Pada pendapat Yazid, kerja-kerja kejuruteraan amatlah penting kepada negara ini. Siti Fatimah, iaitu anak Encik Murad yang tengah, sedang menuntut dalam menengah empat. Dia bercita-cita hendak melanjutkan pelajarannya hingga ke universiti dan bercita-cita hendak menjadi guru bahasa Inggeris di sekolah menengah setelah tamat. Siti Khadijah, anak Encik Murad yang bongsu pula sedang belajar di kelas menengah satu. Dia bercita-cita hendak menjadi doktor apabila dewasa kelak.

Jawab soalan-soalan di bawah:

(*a*) Di manakah keluarga Encik Murad tinggal?

(*b*) Terangkan bagaimanakah cara Encik Murad memainkan peranannya sebagai ketua keluarga.

(*c*) Apakah tanggungjawab suri rumahtangga seperti Siti Aisyah?

(*d*) Terangkan apakah cita-cita anak-anak Encik Murad?

LESSON 4

Asal Usul Nama Singapura
(The Origin of the Name 'Singapura')

A. Sentence Patterns

1. *Menurut keterangan dalam buku*
   According to the explanation in the book (entitled)

   'Sejarah Melayu' Sang Nila Utama berkahwin dengan
   The 'Malay Annals' Sang Nila Utama married

   Wan Seri Beni.
   Wan Seri Beni.

2. *Wan Seri Beni puteri Raja Bintan.*
   Wan Seri Beni was the princess of Raja Bintan.

3. *Ia belayar ke Singapura.*
   He sailed to Singapore.

4. *Maksudnya ialah membuat negeri di situ bersama-sama*
   His intention was to form a country there together

   dengan pengiring-pengiringnya.
   with his followers.

5. *Pada masa itu Singapura disebut Temasek.*
   At that time, Singapore was called Temasek.

6. *Perahu yang dinaiki oleh Sang Nila Utama* ***sampai ke***
   The boat boarded by Sang Nila Utama reached

   tengah laut.
   the open sea.

(literally 'reached the middle of the sea')

7. *Ribut turun dengan hebatnya.*
A gale came down heavily.

8. *Kemudian perahu itu di**masuki** air.*
Then the boat was flooded with water.
(literally 'enter')

9. *Perahu itu membahayakan jiwa para penumpangnya.*
The boat is endangering the lives of its passengers.

10. *Perahu itu hampir tenggelam.*
The boat nearly sank.

11. *Segala **harta** di dalam perahu itu, termasuk mahkota*
All the treasures in the boat, including the crown

dibuang ke dalam laut.
were thrown into the sea.
(literally 'property', 'assets')

12. *Barulah perahu itu ter**hindar** daripada bahaya.*
Only then was the boat saved from danger.
(literally 'avoid')

13. *Baginda mendarat di Temasek.*
His Majesty landed at Temasek.

14. *Baginda dengan pengiring-pengiringnya bermain di*
His Majesty with his followers played on

padang kuala itu.
the field at the river mouth.

15. *Tiba-tiba baginda melihat seekor binatang.*
Suddenly His Majesty saw an animal.

16. *Warna tubuhnya merah.*
The colour of its body was red.

17. *Kepalanya hitam.*
Its head was black.

18. *Dadanya putih.*
Its chest was white.

19. *Sikapnya terlalu pantas dan perkasa.*
Its demeanour was very swift and gallant.

20. *Badannya besar sedikit daripada kambing* ***randuk****.*
Its body was slightly bigger than a billy-goat.
(meaning 'bearded old billy-goat')

21. *Itulah 'singa' namaya.*
That is what is called a'lion'.

22. *Ada binatang* ***gagah*** *di situ.*
There was a powerful animal there.

23. *Tempat itu dianggap baik oleh Sang Nila Utama.*
The place was considered auspicious by Sang Nila Utama.

24. *Di situ di**buat**nya sebuah negeri dengan nama*
There he built a country with the name

'Singapura'.
'Singapura'.
(literally 'make')

25. *Tidak ada* ***keterangan*** *dalam buku 'Sejarah Melayu'*
There were no details in the book of 'Malay Annals'

tentang tarikh pembinaan negeri.
on the date of the country's founding.
(literally 'explanation')

26. *Menurut perhitungan para pakar sejarah, peristiwa itu*
According to the calculations of historians, the incident

terjadi pada kurun yang ke-13.
took place in the 13th century.

B. Comprehension

Menurut keterangan dalam buku 'Sejarah Melayu', Sang Nila Utama, cucu Raja Suran, setelah berkahwin dengan Wan Seri Beni, puteri raja Bintan, ia pun belayar ke Singapura. Maksudnya ialah membuat negeri di situ bersama-sama dengan pengiring-pengiringnya. Pada masa itu Singapura disebut Temasek.

Konon khabarnya, demi perahu yang dinaiki oleh Sang Nila Utama itu sampai ke tengah laut, ribut pun turunlah dengan hebatnya. Kemudian perahu itu dimasuki air dan membahayakan jiwa para penumpangnya. Maka perahu itu hampir tenggelam. Hanya sesudah segala harta di dalam perahu itu, termasuk mahkota, dibuang ke dalam laut, barulah perahu itu terhindar daripada bahaya tenggelam.

Setelah mendarat di Temasek, baginda dengan pengiring-pengiringnya bermain di padang kuala itu. Tiba-tiba baginda melihat seekor binatang yang maha tangkas lakunya. Warna tubuhnya merah, kepalanya hitam dan dadanya putih. Sikapnya terlalu pantas dan perkasa. Badannya besar sedikit daripada kambing randuk. Itulah 'singa' namanya.

Oleh kerana ada binatang gagah di situ, maka tempat itu dianggap baik oleh Sang Nila Utama. Di situlah dibuatnya sebuah negeri dengan nama 'Singapura', ertinya 'Kota Singa'.

Tentang tarikh pembinaan negeri itu, dalam buku 'Sejarah Melayu' itu tidak ada keterangannya tetapi menurut perhitungan para pakar sejarah, peristiwa itu tentunya tidak mungkin terjadi sebelum kurun yang ke-13.

Jawab soalan-soalan di bawah:

(*a*) Siapakah Sang Nila Utama dan mengapakah dia membuang mahkotanya ke dalam laut?

(*b*) Apakah tujuan Sang Nila Utama datang ke Temasek?

(*c*) Apakah yang dilihat oleh Sang Nila Utama di pulau itu?

(*d*) Bilakah agaknya peristiwa Temasek dibuka menjadi Singapura oleh Sang Nila Utama berlaku?

LESSON 5

Comprehension:

Harun Aminurrashid

Harun Aminurrashid ialah pengarang Singapura yang sangat terkenal dan menghasilkan banyak tulisan.

Nama sebenarnya Harun Bin Mohd. Amin. Ia dilahirkan di Singapura pada tahun 1907. Ia menjadi guru semasa berumur 14 tahun dan menjalani latihan perguruan di Maktab Perguruan Sultan Idris, Tanjung Malim dari tahun 1924 hingga tahun 1927. Dia juga mengajar di Maktab tersebut. Pada tahun 1939, ia dihantar ke Brunei untuk menjadi Penguasa Pelajaran Melayu hingga selesai Perang Dunia Kedua. Ia balik ke Singapura pada tahun 1946 dan mengundurkan diri dari pekerjaannya sebagai guru untuk berkecimpung sepenuh masa dalam bidang penerbitan dan kesusasteraan. Novel pertamanya diterbitkan dalam tahun 1930 dan diberi nama 'Melur Kuala Lumpur'. Novel ini menceritakan tentang percintaan yang suci, tetapi ia tidak mendapat sambutan yang menggalakkan. Mungkin oleh kerana itulah Harun berhenti menulis novel selama 16 tahun.

Harun menulis banyak rencana dalam majalah dan akhbar dan menulis novel semula bila ia tinggal tetap di Singapura. Dia menerbitkan lebih daripada dua puluh buah novel baik tentang masyarakat Borneo Utara mahupun yang berlatarbelakang sejarah. Di antara novel-novel Harun, yang paling banyak diperkata orang ialah yang bersifat 'sejarah', terutama novelnya yang dihasilkan pada tahun 1958 yang berjudul 'Panglima Awang'. Novel tersebut menceritakan tentang seorang pemuda Melayu sebagai kawan Magellan yang pertama-tama belayar mengelilingi dunia selepas Melaka jatuh ke tangan orang Portugis. Oleh kerana novel tersebut berjaya, pada tahun 1961 ia menulis sambungannya yang bernama 'Anak Panglima Awang'. Kemudian ia menerbitkan tiga buah novel yang berlatarbelakang sejarah juga iaitu 'Wan Derus', 'Gugur Di Lembah Kinabalu' dan 'Tun Mandak'. Selain daripada karya-karya pengarang yang muncul setelah perang, buah tangan Harun lebih menonjolkan keMelayuannya. Di samping menulis novel, ia juga menulis cerpen dan sebuah antologi cerpennya diberi nama '12 Cerita Pendek'.

Vocabulary

mengundurkan diri	-	to retire
berkecimpung	-	to splash (in the water), to be active in
rencana	-	article
berlatarbelakang	-	to have as background
menonjolkan	-	to show, to present

Jawab soalan-soalan berikut:

(*a*) Apakah taraf pendidikan Harun Aminurrashid? Apakah pekerjaannya yang pertama?

(*b*) Apakah yang dilakukannya setelah ia meninggalkan Maktab Perguruan di Semenanjung Malaysia?

(*c*) Sebutkan nama novel Harun yang pertama. Bilakah novel itu diterbitkan dan apakah isinya? Terangkan secara ringkas tentang novel Harun yang pertama.

(*d*) Apakah yang dilakukan oleh Harun setelah ia kembali ke Singapura?

LESSON 6

Comprehension

Lawatan Ke Rumah Panjang

Sarawak terkenal dengan rumah panjang. Sejak dahulu lagi rumah panjang menjadi daya penarik para pelancong. Kehidupan di rumah panjang juga sering menarik orang dari negara lain untuk melihat suasana kehidupan rumah panjang dari dekat. Baru-baru ini serombongan wartawan dari Singapura telah melawat sebuah rumah panjang di Kampung Mongkos, Serian, kira-kira 100 km dari bandar Kuching. Di bawah ini adalah laporan tentang sambutan yang diberikan kepada rombongan Singapura.

Upacara sambutan yang diberikan ialah seperti berikut: Setiap pelawat mesti mencecahkan kaki di dulang yang berisi air sebaik masuk di rumah itu. Setiap pelawat dihidangkan minuman tuak. Kalau tidak minum juga boleh tetapi hendaklah memberikan alasan yang munasabah. Ramai pelawat cuma meletakkan hujung cawan itu di bibir sahaja, tetapi tidak meminumnya.

Kemudian para pelawat dimestikan bersalaman dengan setiap penghuni yang sedang beratur di sepanjang bangsal itu. Setiap penghuni yang sudi dijabat tangan mereka oleh para pelawat, menurut mereka, akan dilimpahi 'tuah'.

Sebelum para pelawat bersalaman dengan para penghuni tadi, ketua agama di rumah panjang akan mengelilingkan ayam putih di kalangan para pelawat. Ini seolah-olah mendoakan 'selamat' kepada mereka.

Vocabulary

daya penarik	-	attraction
suasana	-	atmosphere
mencecahkan	-	to touch some thing lightly
dulang	-	a tray
munasabah	-	reasonable
dilimpah tuah	-	to be overflowed by luck
selamatan	-	ritual ceremony
kelamin	-	family

Jawab soalan-soalan berikut:

(*a*) Di manakah letaknya rumah panjang yang dilawati rombongan Singapura itu?

(*b*) Apakah yang mesti dilakukan oleh seorang pelawat apabila ia memasuki rumah panjang?

(*c*) Mengapakah ketua agama mengelilingkan ayam putih di kalangan para pelawat?

(*d*) Bagaimanakah '*selamatan*' itu diadakan?

(*e*) Apakah sebabnya kehidupan di rumah panjang sentiasa tenang?

LESSON 7

Comprehension

Perbualan Tentang Buku Yang Telah Dibaca

Tempat	:	Di pekarangan sebuah perpustakaan
Masa	:	Pagi Sabtu, jam 8.15 pagi
Pelakon	:	Anita Jamilah

Anita	:	*Eh! Jamilah. Apa awak buat di sini?*
Jamilah	:	*(Terkejut) Eh, Anita. Tidak sangka kita boleh bertemu di sini. Saya hendak memulangkan buku-buku yang saya pinjam dari perpustakaan ini. Awak pula buat apa di sini?*
Anita	:	*(Gembira) Saya pun hendak memulangkan buku-buku yang saya pinjam.*
Jamilah	:	*Kita datang terlalu awal.*
Anita	:	*Tidak mengapalah, Milah. Lebih baik tercepat daripada terlambat.*
Jamilah	:	*Buku apakah yang awak pinjam itu?*
Anita	:	*Saya meminjam tiga buah buku tetapi hanya dua buah buku sahaja yang sempat saya baca. Sebuah buku lagi saya belum baca. Yang sebuah ini sangat menarik.*
Jamilah	:	*Apakah nama buku yang menarik itu?*
Anita	:	*Buku 'Sejarah Melayu'.*

Jamilah	:	*'Sejarah Melayu'?*
Anita	:	*Mengapakah awak hairan?*
Jamilah	:	*Saya telah membaca buku itu. Ia ditulis dalam bentuk bahasa lama yang membosankan. Sebab itu saya hairan apabila awak mengatakan yang buku itu menarik.*
Anita	:	*Kalau dipandang dari segi bahasa, buku itu memang tidak menarik tetapi dari segi isinya, banyak memberikan pengetahuan kepada kita.*
Jamilah	:	*Saya fikir isinya juga banyak yang tidak munasabah. Tidak masuk di akal.*
Anita	:	*Itu pendapat awak sahaja tetapi pendapat saya berlainan. Saya kira buku 'Sejarah Melayu' itu sangat berguna dan patut dibaca oleh setiap orang terutama orang Melayu sendiri.*
Jamilah	:	*Mengapakah awak kata begitu?*
Anita	:	*Dengan membaca 'Sejarah Melayu', kita akan mengetahui tentang asal usul bangsa kita serta keagungannya pada suatu ketika dahulu.*
Jamilah	:	*Percayakah awak bahawa orang Melayu berasal daripada keturunan Iskandar Zulkarnain, seperti yang tercatat dalam buku 'Sejarah Melayu' itu?*
Anita	:	*Sama ada percaya atau tidak, itu tidaklah penting. Yang penting nenek moyang kita percaya bahawa orang Melayu itu berasal daripada Iskandar Zulkarnain.*
Jamilah	:	*Tetapi, mengapakah nama Iskandar Zulkarnain itu dihubungkan dengan asal keturunan raja Melayu?*
Anita	:	*Oh! Itu mudah difahami. Pada zaman Hindu dahulu hanya dewa atau jelmaan dewa sahaja yang boleh menjadi raja. Bagi orang Melayu yang sudah memeluk agama Islam, tidak boleh*

mempercayai hal ini. Maka dicari seorang tokoh yang setanding dengan dewa atau titisan dewa. Pilihan itu jatuh pada Iskandar Zulkarnain. Iskandar ialah penakluk dunia yang sangat mengagumkan. Namanya juga disebut di dalam Al-Quran. Orang Islam percaya Iskandar ialah nabi yang menyebarkan agama Islam. Tambahan pula orang Melayu yakin bahawa Iskandar pernah mendarat di Pulau Andalas yang tidak lain adalah Sumatera.

Jamilah : *Wah! Awak pandai sekali. Awak bercakap seperti pensyarah universiti.*

Anita : *Oh! Tidak, saya hanya tahu sedikit sahaja.*

Jamilah : *(Tiba-tiba) Eh! Nampaknya pintu perpustakaan sudah pun dibuka. Marilah kita masuk sekarang. Orang pun sudah ramai di situ.*

Anita : *Marilah!*

Vocabulary

kenamaan - famous
memulangkan - to return
pengetahuan - knowledge
keturunan - descendant
jelmaan - incarnation
titisan - incarnation

Jawab soalan-soalan berikut:

(*a*) Di manakah dan bilakah perbualan di atas berlaku?
(*b*) Apakah yang dibualkan oleh kedua orang pelajar itu?
(*c*) Apakah nama buku yang dikatakan membosankan oleh Jamilah?
(*d*) Apakah pula pendapat Anita tentang buku itu?
(*e*) Siapakah Iskandar Zulkarnain?

LESSON 8

Comprehension

Salah Pimpin

Keris Mas adalah nama pena Kamaludin Muhammad, seorang pengarang Malaysia yang kenamaan. Cerpennya yang bertajuk 'Salah Pimpin' ini mengisahkan tentang seorang isteri di kampung yang mencuba meniru kehidupan orang bandar setelah mengikuti sebuah kursus di Kuala Lumpur. Di bawah ini adalah petikan daripada cerpen itu:

Waktu Halimah mencadangkan supaya mereka memakai dapur minyak tanah dahulu, Agus bersetuju sebab dia kasihan melihat isteri yang comel itu hari-hari berlumur arang menggosok punggung periuk dan kuali. Dia belum lagi merasa waktu itu bahawa perubahan dari dapur tungku ke dapur minyak tanah itu hanya permulaan sahaja daripada berbagai-bagai perubahan yang akan dibawa oleh Halimah sebagai hasil daripada kursusnya di Kuala Lumpur. Sebelum dapur itu dibeli, dia mengurangkan dahulu kira-kira belanja kedai kopi dan belanja rokoknya.

Petang itu dia pulang dan disambut oleh isterinya dan tiga orang cik-cik puan yang baru datang dari bandar. Sepuluh minit kemudian ramah-tamah itu bertukar menjadi ribut taufan. Halimah rupanya telah mengadukan peristiwa dapur oven minyak tanah itu kepada rakan-rakannya. Cik-cik puan itu rupanya sudah bermurah hati berpakat tiga orang hendak membelikannya untuk Halimah.

'Janganlah cik-cik puan bersusah payah kerana kami,' kata Agus.

'Susah payah apa pula. Oven itu bukan mahal benar harganya.'

'Tapi cik-cik puan bukan tidak tahu oven macam itu bukan mustahak sangat untuk rumahtangga macam ini.'

Halimah tiba-tiba berubah air mukanya. Dia hendak berkata. Cik puan sudah mendahuluinya.

'Encik Agus, maafkan saya berkata. Kami berniat baik. Kami, termasuk isteri Encik Agus ini, ialah ketua-ketua yang hendak memajukan pergaulan hidup kaum wanita kita. Wanita-wanita kampung tidak patut dibiarkan menderita sahaja, berlumur arang dan bertangas asap di ceruk dapur.'

'Maafkan saya, cik puan. Nampak pada saya hal yang kita perkatakan ini mengenai rumahtangga saya. Ia tidak ada kena-mengenanya dengan kemajuan wanita.'

'Jangan marah, Encik Agus. Kami tidak sedikit pun hendak mencampuri hal-hal rumahtangga orang.'

'Saya tidak keberatan cik-cik puan semua hendak memajukan kaum wanita. Yang saya tidak suka orang membelikan isteri saya barang-barang keperluan rumahtangga saya seperti oven, entah apa bendanya itu.'

Cik puan itu ketiga-tiganya serta Halimah sendiri sama serentak hendak berkata tetapi Agus meneruskan, 'Jangan cik-cik puan tidak tahu, cara cik puan ini bukan memimpin namanya tetapi meruntuhkan. Berapa banyak dapur oven yang sanggup cik puan belikan, berapa banyakkah segala macam flour dan powder dapat cik puan adakan untuk wanita-wanita dari rumah-rumah yang miskin seperti rumah saya ini?'

'Itu bukan urusan kami. Kami takkan hendak menjaga tiap-tiap ceruk dapur sekalian ahli kami.'

'Kalau begitu tolonglah jangan bersusah payah mencampuri ceruk dapur rumahtangga saya. Saya nanti menyelesaikan soal oven yang wonderful itu dengan isteri saya sendiri.'

Halimah menutup muka dengan tangannya. Ia bangun lalu lari ke dalam meninggalkan tetamu-tetamunya. Tetamu-tetamu yang terhormat itu pun serentak bangun dan turun dengan tidak meminta diri lagi.

(Dikutip dan disesuaikan daripada
Cerpen-cerpen ASEAN, terbitan
Dewan Bahasa dan Pustaka)

Jawab soalan-soalan di bawah:

(*a*) Apakah yang terjadi setelah Halimah mengikuti kursus di Kuala Lumpur?

(*b*) Dari manakah datangnya tetamu-tetamu Halimah? Apakah yang mereka hendak belikan untuk Halimah?

(*c*) Apakah tujuan kunjungan tetamu-tetamu Halimah?

(*d*) Mengapakah Agus mengatakan bahawa rakan-rakan Halimah bukan memimpin malainkan meruntuhkan?

(*e*) Apakah yang terjadi setelah Agus bertengkar dengan rakan-rakan Halimah?

LESSON 9

Comprehension

Ekonomi Asean

Ekonomi Asean yang serba dinamik itu bagaimanapun tidak terlepas daripada berbagai masalah khususnya akibat kemelesetan ekonomi dunia dan inflasi yang terburuk dalam masa tiga dasawarsa. Jadi, untuk menyesuaikan struktur ekonomi rantau ini dengan perubahan ekonomi dunia, kelima-lima buah negara Asean kini menumpukan perhatian mereka kepada usaha meningkatkan lagi kecekapan sektor perusahaan masing-masing.

Menurut para pemerhati ekonomi, usaha-usaha kini sedang dilaksanakan ke arah membaiki lagi mutu persaingan untuk membolehkan jentera ekonomi mereka bergerak sesuai dengan pertumbuhan ekonomi dunia. Ini bermakna ia bergantung kepada kejayaan meluaskan eksport hasil pengilangan.

Bank Dunia berpendapat, walaupun eksport barangan seperti minyak, getah, bijih timah dan balak akan bertambah baik daripada bahan-bahan lain, perdagangan dunia bagi bahan-bahan mentah tidak akan berkembang dalam tahun lapan puluhan. Sebaliknya masa depan sektor pengilangan dijangka bertambah baik. Eksport bahan-bahan pengilangan Asean telah meningkat purata dua puluh satu peratus setahun dalam tempoh satu dekad.

Adalah diharapkan agar kelima-lima negara anggota Asean akan dapat mengekalkan pertumbuhan pesat dalam tahun lapan puluhan ini dengan mempelbagaikan hasil keluaran dan pasaran serta mengurangkan persaingan di kalangan mereka.

Inilah yang menjadi tema penyesuaian struktur ekonomi yang dilancarkan di Filipina dan Thailand dengan pinjaman-pinjaman yang diberikan oleh Bank Dunia yang bernilai berjuta-

juta dolar dan berjanji akan memberikan bantuan lanjut untuk melaksanakan perubahan-perubahan itu. Negara-negara Asean tidak menghadapi masalah untuk mendapatkan pinjaman daripada Bank Dunia. Apa yang diharapkan ialah kerjasama yang berterusan antara sektor swasta dengan pemerintah dan kerajaan Asean hendaklah dikekalkan.

Negara-negara Asia Tenggara dan Timur akan mendapat faedah daripada usaha China untuk memodenkan ekonominya. Negara itu akan memerlukan bahan-bahan mentah yang terdapat di negara-negara jiran. Negara-negara Asean boleh membekalkan bahan-bahan mentahnya kepada China. Perdagangan Asean akan bertambah baik lagi jika negara-negara rantau ini meluaskan lagi perdagangan bersama dengan merendahkan sekatan-sekatan tarif.

Sekatan-sekatan yang lebih rendah akan memberikan sumbangan yang penting kepada usaha untuk menambahkan kecekapan dan kemampuan perusahaan-perusahaan dalam negeri. Sekatan-sekatan itu juga menyediakan pengkhususan yang lebih besar daripada firma-firma individu. Ini akan menambahkan peluang bagi menyaingi para pengeluar dari luar rantau ini dalam merebut pasaran.

(Dipetik dari Berita Harian,
24.2.83. Disesuaikan)

Jawab soalan-soalan di bawah:

(*a*) Mengapakah ekonomi Asean tidak terlepas daripada masalah?

(*b*) Apakah usaha-usaha yang ditumpukan oleh negara-negara Asean?

(*c*) Pada pendapat Bank Dunia, eksport barangan apa yang tidak akan bertambah baik?

(*d*) Apakah yang diharapkan oleh negara-negara anggota Asean?

(*e*) Apakah faedah yang didapati oleh negera-negara Asean daripada usaha China untuk memodenkan ekonominya?

LESSON 10

Comprehension

Bahasa Melayu Dan Bahasa Indonesia

Adalah menjadi pengetahuan umum bahawa bahasa Indonesia itu berasal daripada bahasa Melayu. Sebelum dijadikan bahasa kebangsaan di negara tetangga kita, bahasa Melayu merupakan ***lingua franca****, iaitu bahasa perantaraan untuk pelbagai suku bangsa dan orang asing yang hidup di kepulauan Nusantara ini. Ketika rakyat Indonesia yang berbilang suku memperjuangkan kemerdekaannya, mereka memerlukan bahasa yang boleh mempersatukan suku-suku yang berlainan itu, dan* ***lingua franca*** *itulah yang dipilih menjadi bahasa persatuan, bukan bahasa Jawa atau Sunda yang merupakan bahasa-bahasa suku besar di Indonesia. Ini disebabkan bahasa Jawa dan Sunda tidak digunakan oleh suku-suku lain dan sangat sukar untuk dikuasai.*

Bahasa Melayu dinamakan bahasa Indonesia pada tahun 1928 ketika pemuda-pemuda Indonesia mengadakan kongres di Jakarta. Dalam kongres itu para pemuda Indonesia bersumpah mempunyai bangsa, negara dan bahasa yang satu, iaitu Indonesia. Sejak tahun itu, penggunaan bahasa Indonesia menjadi lebih luas dan setelah Indonesia merdeka, bahasa Indonesia dijadikan bahasa pengantar dari sekolah rendah sampai ke universiti.

Walaupun bahasa Melayu dan bahasa Indonesia bahasa serumpun, namun perkembangan sejarah yang berlainan, ciri-ciri kedua bahasa itu pun ada sedikit perbezaan. Indonesia yang pernah dijajah oleh Belanda banyak dipengaruhi oleh bahasa Belanda sedangkan Malaysia yang dijajah oleh Inggeris pula dipengaruhi oleh bahasa Inggeris. Setelah kedua-dua buah negara *mencapai kemerdekaan, pemerintah negara masing-masing telah berusaha menyeragamkan, jikalau bukan menyatukan, bahasa Indonesia dan bahasa Melayu. Mula-mula yang diseragamkannya adalah dalam hal ejaan. Pada waktu itu, pernah terdapat satu ejaan yang bernama Ejaan Malindo (singkatan daripada Malaya Indonesia), akan tetapi persetujuannya baru tercapai pada tahun 1972. Ejaan yang dipakai oleh kedua-dua buah negara itu di Malaysia dinamakan '**Ejaan Baru**' sedangkan di Indonesia namanya ialah '**Ejaan Yang Disempurnakan**'. Kedua-dua jenis ejaan itu hampir serupa tetapi tidak sama. Banyak istilah dieja menurut kebiasaan masing-masing yang mencerminkan perkembangan sejarahnya yang berbeza: misalnya '**televisyen**' adalah ejaan Malaysia sedangkan '**televisi**' adalah ejaan Indonesia; di Malaysia dieja '**universiti**' sementara di Indonesia dieja '**universitas**'.*

*Di samping ejaan, ada juga terdapat perbezaan dalam erti perkataan. Misalnya, perkataan '**jemput**' di Indonesia bererti '**sambut**' sedangkan di Malaysia dan Singapura perkataan itu bererti '**mengundang**'. Di bawah ini adalah sebuah lelucon mengenai '**jemput**':*

Seorang Indonesia baru bertemu dengan seorang Melayu. Pada suatu hari, orang Melayu itu menjemput orang Indonesia makan malam di rumahnya. Orang Indonesia itu menerima jemputan tersebut dengan senang hati. Akan tetapi pada malam itu orang Indoneisa itu tidak kunjung muncul, kerana dia mengira bahawa temannya itu akan datang menjemputnya' (menyambutnya). Ia sedang menanti-nantikan kedatangan temannya.

*Selain daripada itu, banyak lagi perkataan yang berbeza ertinya. Misalnya '**sulit**' dalam bahasa Indonesia bererti '**sukar**' sedangkan dalam bahasa Melayu perkataan itu bererti '**rahsia**'; '**mata-mata**' dalam bahasa Indonesia bererti '**agen rahsia**' tetapi dalam bahasa Melayu bererti '**polis**'. Istilah '**polis**' di Indonesia tidak digunakan, yang dipakai ialah perkataan '**polisi**', yang ertinya lain lagi dalam bahasa Melayu.*

Jawab soalan-soalan berikut:

(*a*) Daripada manakah asal bahasa Indonesia?

(*b*) Apakah ertinya *lingua franca*? Bahasa apa yang dijadikan *lingua franca* di kepulauan Nusantara pada zaman dahulu?

(*c*) Mengapakah pemimpin Indonesia memilih bahasa Melayu sebagai bahasa persatuan? Mengapakah bukan bahasa Jawa atau Sunda yang diambil?

(*d*) Mengapakah bahasa Melayu dan bahasa Indonesia berbeza? Sebutkan pengaruh mereka yang berbeza.

(*e*) Dapatkah kamu memberikan lima patah perkataan Melayu yang ertinya berbeza dalam bahasa Indonesia.

APPENDIX 1

Bahasa Melayu and Bahasa Indonesia

It is common knowledge that Indonesian (Bahasa Indonesia) originated in Malay (Bahasa Melayu). Long before it was called Bahasa Indonesia, Malay had been used as the *lingua franca* among various ethnic groups in the Malay archipelago. During the struggle for independence, the Indonesian nationalists required a language which could be used as a means of communication as well as a symbol of unity, so they decided to use the Malay language, which was the language of a minority group in Sumatra. They consciously avoided choosing Javanese, the language of a major ethnic group in Central and East Java, because of the limitation of its usage and other political considerations. In fact, the choice of Malay as the language of nationalists was fortunate because it successfully defused the language issue.

In October 1928, the representatives of Indonesian youth organizations held a congress in Jakarta at which they took a pledge 'of one motherland, one nation and one unifying language'. Since then Bahasa Melayu has been renamed Bahasa Indonesia and has begun to be popularized by Indonesian nationalists. The language was further promoted during the Japanese occupation. After Indonesia's independence, Bahasa Indonesia was used as the language of instruction from primary to tertiary education levels.

As bahasa Indonesia originated in Malay, it is not surprising that, the two languages have a lot of similarities. The Indonesian language used in Sumatra is particularly close to the Malay language. One can argue that their similarity is much greater than the Indonesian language used in Java where Jakarta, the capital of Indonesia, is located. When we speak of 'standard' Bahasa Indonesia, we in fact, refer to the language used in Jakarta and Java.

Bahasa Indonesia in Java is not identical with the Malay language. This is due to several factors: Indonesia and Malaysia are two political entities and they have different colonial experiences and socio-political structures. Besides, Indonesian ethnic composition is different from that of Malaysia and this is also reflected in their respective languages. One obvious difference was in their spelling. In Indonesian before 1972 the spelling system followed Dutch: *djalan*, *tjatat*, *achir*, *ajah*, *tanja*; while in Malay, the spelling followed English: *jalan*, *chatat*, *akhir*, *ayah*, *tanya*.

There have been efforts in both countries to standardize the languages. During the Sukarno era, for instance, a spelling system called Malindo (Malaya-Indonesia) was prosposed, but it did not materialise. The efforts continued and eventually an agreement was reached in 1972. The new spelling was used by both sides with some exceptions. In Malaysia, the spelling system is called 'Ejaan Baru' (new spelling) and in Indonesia, it is called 'Ejaan Yang Telah Disempurnakan' (perfected spelling). Nevertheless, there are still some minor differences where Malaysia and Indonesia have agreed to disagree; for examples, the Malaysian spelling literature is *sastera*, whereas Indonesia has *sastra*. For the transcription of project, Malaysia has *projek*, Indonesia *proyek*.

But it should be noted that both sides have tried to make their language closer to the other by using each other's vocabulary. '*Dewan Bahasa*' in Kuala Lumpur and '*Tempo*' in Jakarta are two examples where both Indonesian and Malaysian vocabularies are constantly used. For instance, 'encourage' in Malay is *menggalakkan*, in Bahasa Indonesia it is either *menganjurkan* or *mendorong*, which does not convey the real meaning of 'encourage'. In the last few years, Indonesian newspapers/ magazines adopted *menggalakkan* and it has now become an Indonesian term. Another example: 'relaxed' in Indonesian is *santai*, while in Malay there is no single word which can convey that meaning. In recent years, *santai* has also been adopted in Malaysia. Other new Indonesian words adopted in Malaysia include *kendala* (constraint), *tuntas* (exhaustive). For more examples, please refer to the appendix.

Generally speaking, there are a few areas where the differences still exist. One area is related to loan-words, especially from Western languages. While Malaya (Malaysia) was colonized by the British, Indonesia was ruled by the Dutch. Not surprisingly the Malay language was influenced by English while Bahasa Indonesia was influenced by Dutch. For examples:

televesion	(M) *televisyen*	(I) *televisi; tv (teve)*
station	(M) *stesen*	(I) *stasiun*
university	(M) *universiti*	(I) *universitas*
party	(M) *parti*	(I) *partai*

Not only loan-words are influenced by their colonial experiences, even some usages have also had the imprint of either Dutch or English. For instance, in mathematics, '2.2' (two point two) is '2,2' (*dua koma dua*) in Indonesian but '2.2' (*dua titik dua*) in Malay. But '2.2' in Indonesian is in fact '22' (twenty-two), while '2,2' in Malay does not make any sense.

In telling the time, Indonesian is also different from Malay. For instance, 'half past two' is *jam dua setengah* in Malay but *jam setengah tiga* in Bahasa Indonesia.

It should be noted that there are words which have more than one meaning: One meaning is more popularly known in Malaysia but the other meaning is more frequently used in Indonesia. For example, *banci* means 'census' and 'transvestite'. In Malaysia *banci* is more frequently used to mean 'census'. When the Malays refer to 'transvestite', *pondan* is used. In Indonesia, *banci* is frequently used to mean 'transvestite'. For 'census', *sensus* or *cacah jiwa* is used.

One more example: *senang* means 'easy', 'free' (time) or 'happy'. In Malaysia, the first two meanings are frequently used while in Indonesia, the third meaning is most common. In Malay, *Saya akan datang kalau saya senang* means 'I will come if I am free'; but in Bahasa Indonesia, it means 'I will come if I am happy'. Indeed, readers should be wary of this type of polysemy words.

Differences were often a result of different ethnic composition. For instance, Bahasa Indonesia used in Jakarta and Java tends to have been influenced by Javanese. A common word 'can' in Bahasa Indonesia is *bisa* while in Malay, *boleh* is used. Although *boleh* in Bahasa Indonesia also means 'can', more frequently the word is used to mean 'permitted'. For instance, *Dia tidak bisa datang*, means 'He cannot come'; but *Dia tidak boleh datang* in Indonesian means 'He is not allowed to come'.

There are other words which are more commonly used in Indonesia rather than in Malaysia. 'To talk' is *bicara* in Indonesian but in Malay, *cakap* is often used. *Bicara* in Malay is often associated with a court case. 'To turn' is *putar* in Bahasa Indonesia but in Malay, the word *pusing* is often used. In Indonesia, *pusing* is often associated with headache.

It is also interesting to note that Islamic culture has a greater impact in West Malaysia than in Indonesia, especially Java. Malays by definition are Muslim, but not all Indonesians are Muslim. Understandably, more Arabic loan-words are in use in Malaysia than Java/Indonesia. For instance, *mengharamkan* (to ban), *maktab* (college), *tuala* (towel) and *arnab* (rabbit) are more often used in Malaysia than in Indonesia.

Indonesia is also different from Malaysia in terms of their political structure. Indonesia is a republic while Malaysia is a constitutional monarchy. When referring to the Indonesian government, the term *pemerintah* is used. For example, *Pemerintah Indonesia*. When referred to Malaysian government, the term *Kerajaan* is used. But it is wrong to say *Kerajaan Indonesia* when referring to the Indonesian government.

In the Appendix 2 we have included an English-Indonesian-Malay vocabulary. Needless to say, the list can only serve as a guide. A word listed under Indonesian may also occur in the Malay vocabulary. Likewise, a word listed as Malay may occur in the Indonesian usage, but is used especially in Sumatra.

English-Indonesian-Malay Vocabulary

English	Indonesian	Malay
able	***dapat***	*boleh*
absent from	***bolos***	*ponteng*
accident	***kecelakaan***	*kemalangan*
achievement	***prestasi***	*pencapaian/prestasi*
accord	***akur***	*setuju*
action	***aksi***	*tindakan*
actor	***aktor***	*pelakon*
administration	***administrasi***	*pentadbiran*
advertisement	***advertensi***	*iklan*
advise	***advis***	*nasihat*
advocate	***pengacara***	*peguam bela*
afternoon	***sore***	*petang*
agent	***agen***	*wakil*
airplane	***pesawat udara***	*kapal terbang*
allocation	***jatah/catu***	*peruntukan*
announcer	***pewarta/penyiar***	*juruhebah*
appeal	***menghimbau***	*merayu*
appoint	***mengangkat***	*melantik*
archive	***arsip***	*arkib*
arithmetic	***ilmu hitungan***	*ilmu hisab/kira-kira*
attorney	***pengacara***	*wakil mutlak*
aunt	***bibi***	*emak saudara*
bachelor	***jejaka***	*bujang*
bag	***tas***	*beg*
beautician	***ahli kecantikan***	*jurusolek*
bell	***lonceng***	*loceng*
bicycle	***sepeda***	*basikal*
big	***gede***	*besar*
birthday	***hari ulang tahun***	*hari jadi*
boast	***bual***	*cakap besar*

boss	***bas***	*majikan*
broom	***sapu***	*penyapu*
brush	***sikat***	*berus*
budget	***anggaran (belanja)***	*belanjawan*
building	***gedung***	*bangunan*
bus	***bis***	*bas*
busy	***repot***	*sibuk*
can	***bisa***	*dapat*
capable	***cekatan***	*cekap*
car	***mobil***	*kereta*
card	***kartu***	*kad*
cash	***kontan***	*tunai*
census	***cacah jiwa/sensus***	*banci*
chairman	***ketua***	*pengerusi*
champion	***juara***	*johan*
chase	***buru***	*kejar*
chauffeur	***supir***	*pemandu/drebar*
cinema	***bioskop***	*pawagam/panggung wayang gambar*
clerk	***jurutulis***	*kerani*
clown	***badut***	*pelawak*
coat	***jas***	*kot*
cobbler	***tukang sepatu***	*tukang kasut*
collapse	***ambruk***	*runtuh/roboh*
collide	***menubruk***	*melanggar*
comb	***sisir***	*sikat*
committee	***panitia***	*jawatankuasa*
company	***maskapai***	*syarikat*
condolence	***belasungkawa***	*takziah*
confiscate	***menyita/beslah***	*merampas*
constraint	***kendala***	*sekatan*
continuity	***kesinambungan***	*persambungan*
cook	***koki***	*tukang masak*
court	***pengadilan***	*mahkamah*
criminal	***pidana***	*jenayah*
cup	***cangkir***	*cawan*
cupboard	***lemari***	*almari*
customs	***doane***	*kastam*
date	***tanggal***	*haribulan/tarikh*
decade	***dasawarsa/dekade***	*dekad*

defination	***pembatasan***	*definisi/takrif*
delegation	***delegasi***	*utusan*
delicious	***enak***	*sedap*
difficult	***sukar/sulit***	*susah*
direction	***jurusan***	*arah*
director	***direktor***	*pengarah*
dirty	***jorok***	*kotor*
disturbance	***musibah***	*bencana*
disturbance	***ribut***	*gaduh*
dizzy	***pusing***	*pening*
drive, to	***mengendari/mengemudi/ menyetir***	*memandu*
driver	***pengemudi/pengendara/ sopir***	*pemandu*
drug	***narkotik***	*dadah*
duck	***bebek***	*itik*
duty	***bea***	*cukai*
ear	***kuping***	*telinga*
easy	***gampang***	*mudah*
editor	***redaktur***	*pengarang*
education	***pendidikan***	*pelajaran*
effort	***prihatin***	*usaha*
electricity	***listrik***	*elektrik*
engine	***mesin/motor***	*enjin/jentera*
engineer	***insinyur***	*jurutera*
envelope	***ampelop***	*sampul/sarung surat*
established	***mapan***	*mantap*
eternal	***lestari/langggeng***	*kekal/abadi*
examination	***ujian***	*peperiksaan*
excuse me	***permisi***	*maafkan*
exhaustive	***tuntas***	*lengkap*
expense	***ongkos/biaya***	*belanja*
expert	***ahli***	*pakar*
factory	***pabrik***	*kilang*
facilities	***fasilitas***	*kemudahan*
feast	***selamatan/jamuan***	*kenduri*
fetch	***jemput***	*mengambil*
field	***lapangan***	*padang*
firm	***tandas***	*tegas*
flanky	***blak-blakan***	*terus-terang*

flood	***banjir***	*bah*
football	***sepakbola***	*bola sepak*
form	***formulir***	*borang*
free (of time)	***senggang***	*senang*
free	***gratis***	*percuma*
fuss	***heboh***	*kecoh*
gap	***kesenjangan***	*jurang*
garage	***garasi***	*tempat kereta*
geography	***ilmu bumi***	*ilmu alam*
gifts	***kado***	*hadiah*
government	***pemerintah***	*kerajaan*
grandfather	***kakek***	*datuk*
gratis	***gratis***	*percuma/cuma-cuma*
guarantee	***garansi***	*tanggungan/jaminan*
hall	***ruangan***	*dewan*
handsome	***ganteng***	*kacak/lawa*
happy	***senang***	*suka*
hero	***pahlawan***	*wira*
holiday	***libur***	*cuti*
ice	***es***	*air batu*
idea	***ide***	*gagasan*
image	***citra***	*gambaran*
impact	***dampak***	*pengaruh/kesan*
important	***penting***	*mustahak*
information	***keterangan***	*taklimat*
injunction	***wejangan***	*pesan*
ink	***tinta/mangsi***	*dawat*
initiative	***prakarsa***	*langkah pertama*
insight	***wawasan***	*pandangan*
inspector	***inspektor***	*merinyu*
instalment	***cicilan***	*ansuran*
interpreter	***penterjemah***	*jurubahasa*
interview	***wawancara***	*temuduga*
invite	***mengundang***	*menjemput*
lane	***gang***	*lorong*
laundry	***binatu***	*dobi*
law	***hukum***	*undang-undang*
lawyer	***pengacara***	*peguam*
leave	***perlop/cuti***	*cuti*
lecturer	***dosen***	*pensyarah*

license	***rebewes/s.t.m.****	*lesen*
list (of price)	***tarif***	*daftar harga*
livestook	***ternak***	*ternakan*
lottery	***undian/loteri***	*loteri*
luggage	***bagasi***	*bagasi*
mad	***edan***	*gila*
man	***pria/cowok***	*lelaki/laki-laki*
maid	***babu***	*orang gaji/amah*
main (reason)	***pokok***	*utama*
many (people)	***banyak (orang)***	*ramai (orang)*
mark (exam)	***angka***	*markah*
mass	***masal***	*orang banyak*
mathematics	***ilmu pasti***	*ilmu hisab*
mattress	***kasur***	*tilam*
meeting	***rapat***	*pertemuan*
member	***anggota***	*ahli*
millionaire	***milliuner***	*hartawan*
movie	***bioskop***	*wayang gambar*
must	***harus***	*mesti*
need, to	***membutuhkan***	*memerlukan*
neighbour	***tetangga***	*jiran*
newspaper	***koran/suratkhabar***	*suratkhabar/akhbar*
noisy	***ramai***	*bising*
nurse	***perawat***	*jururawat*
office	***kantor***	*pejabat*
officer (army)	***opsir***	*perwira*
officer	***pejabat/pegawai***	*pegawai/kakitangan*
organisation	***organisasi***	*pertubuhan/badan*
pail	***ember***	*baldi*
park, to	***parkir***	*meletak*
patient	***pasien***	*pesakit*
pharmacist	***apoteker***	*ahli ubat*
permission	***izin***	*kebenaran*
photo	***potret***	*gambar*
physic	***ilmu alam***	*fizik*
picnic	***bertemasya***	*berkelah*
plan	***rencana***	*rancangan*
plate (of rice)	***piring***	*pinggan*
pocket	***kantung/saku***	*kocek*
police	***polisi***	*mata-mata/polis*

policy	***garis haruan/ kebijaksanaan***	*polisi*
policy (insurance)	***polis***	*polisi*
position	***jabatan***	*kedudukan/jawatan*
prestige	***gengsi/kehormatan***	*martabat*
private	***partikelir***	*swasta*
problem	***soal***	*masalah*
programme	***acara***	*rancangan*
pronunciation	***ucapan***	*sebutan/lafaz*
prosecutor	***jaksa***	*pendakwa*
psychologist	***psikolog***	*ahli jiwa*
question (exam)	***pertanyaan***	*soalan*
queue, to	***antre***	*beratur*
rate (of exchange)	***kurs***	*kadar*
refrigerator	***lemari es/kulkas***	*peti sejuk*
relative	***sanak-saudara***	*saudara-mara*
relax	***santai***	*senang-lenang*
repairs	***reparasi***	*perbaikan*
rest	***istirahat***	*rehat*
return (home)	***pulang***	*balik*
river	***kali***	*sungai*
room	***kamar***	*bilik*
rubber	***karet***	*getah*
ruler	***garisan/mistar/ penggaris***	*pembaris*
rumours	***desas-desus/khabar angin***	*khabar angin*
saleable	***laris***	*laku*
salty	***asin***	*masin*
say	***bilang***	*kata*
science	***ilmu***	*sains*
scout	***pandu/pramuka***	*pengakap*
secret	***rahsia***	*sulit/rahasia*
secretary	***sekretaris***	*setiausaha*
security	***keamanan***	*keselamatan*
seed	***bibit***	*benih*
serve, to	***meladeni***	*melayani*
sentence	***kalimat***	*ayat*
service	***dinas***	*jabatan/perkhidmatan*
share	***andil***	*saham*

shoes	***sepatu***	*kasut*
shop	***toko***	*kedai*
skill	***ketrampilan***	*kemahiran*
slave	***budak***	*hamba*
snatch	***jambret***	*merampas*
spectacles	***kacamata***	*cermin mata*
speech	***pidato***	*ucapan*
spokesman	***jurubicara***	*jurucakap*
spoon	***senduk***	*sudu*
sport	***olahraga***	*sukan*
squeeze	***peras***	*perah*
stab, to	***bacok***	*tikam*
stamp	***perangko***	*setem*
statement	***pernyataan***	*kenyataan*
startled	***kaget***	*terkejut*
station	***stasiun***	*stesen*
statue	***patung***	*arca/patung*
steer	***stir***	*kemudi*
stenographer	***penulis steno***	*jurutrengkas*
stir, to	***mengaduk***	*mengacau*
stubborn	***bandel***	*degil*
subscriber	***pelanggan***	*langganan*
suddenly	***mendadak***	*tiba-tiba*
suggestion	***saran***	*usul*
suitcase	***koper***	*kopor*
supervisor	***pengawas***	*penyelia*
suppress	***breidel***	*menindas*
talk	***omong***	*cakap*
tax	***pajak***	*cukai*
team (football)	***kesebelasan***	*pasukan*
thief	***maling/pencuri***	*pencuri*
thumb	***jempol***	*ibu jari*
ticket	***karcis***	*tiket*
tin	***tong/kaleng***	*tin*
tired	***capek***	*penat*
toilet	***w.c. (we se)/kakus/ kamar kecil***	*tandas/bilik air*
tourist	***wisatawan/turis***	*pelancong*
towel	***handuk***	*tuala*
trader	***pedagang***	*peniaga*

train	***sepur***	*keretapi*
train, to	***gembleng***	*melatih*
tranvestite	***banci***	*pondan*
tree	***pohon***	*pokok*
trousers	***celana***	*seluar*
turn	***belok/putar***	*pusing*
typewriter	***mesin tulis***	*mesin taip*
typist	***juru/tukang tik***	*jurutaip*
ugly	***jelek***	*hodoh*
uncle	***paman***	*pakcik*
valid	***sahih/sah***	*sah/benar*
visitor	***pengunjung***	*pelawat*
vocabulary	***kosakata***	*perbendaharaan kata*
vote, to	***memilih***	*mengundi*
wait	***tunggu***	*menanti*
wanderer	***perantau***	*pengembara*
watch	***arlogi***	*jam tangan*
weighter	***penimbang***	*timbangan*
when	***kapan***	*bila*
window	***jendela***	*tingkap*
without	***sonder***	*tanpa*
woman	***wanita***	*perempuan*
worker	***karyawan***	*pekerja/buruh*
workshop	***lokakarya***	*bengkel*
yesterday	***kemarin***	*semalam/kelmarin*
zero	***nul***	*kosong/sifar*

---

* surat tanda mengemudi

KEY TO THE EXERCISES

PART I

LESSON 1

Exercise 1

1. Orang laki-laki itu askar.
2. Orang laki-laki itu kelasi.
3. Orang laki-laki itu mata-mata.
4. Orang laki-laki itu ustaz.
5. Orang laki-laki itu mahasiswa.
6. Orang laki-laki itu siswazah.
7. Orang laki-laki itu majikan.
8. Orang laki-laki itu peragawan.
9. Orang laki-laki itu pramugara.
10. Orang laki-laki itu sarjana.

Exercise 2

1. Encik Atan seorang jurucakap.
2. Dia seorang juruhebah.
3. Dia seorang jurutera.
4. Puan Fatimah seorang jurutaip.
5. Dia seorang jurutrengkas.
6. Osman seorang tukang kebun.
7. Dia seorang tukang jahit.
8. Puan Khadijah seorang pemegang wang tunai/kasir.
9. Dia seorang tukang cetak.
10. Ah Lam seorang tukang emas.

Exercise 3

1. Ya, dia seorang tukang kasut.
2. Ya, dia seorang buruh.
3. Ya, dia seorang penjaja.
4. Ya, dia seorang nelayan.
5. Ya, dia seorang nakhoda.
6. Ya, dia seorang pegawai bahasa.
7. Ya, dia seorang pegawai kerajaan.
8. Ya, dia seorang pegawai tinggi.
9. Ya, dia seorang pelakon.
10. Ya, dia seorang pemandu.

Exercise 4

1. Bukan, dia bukan seorang ahli biasa.
2. Bukan, Yusof bukan seorang ahli bersekutu.
3. Bukan, Datuk Tan bukan seorang ahli kehormat.
4. Bukan, dia bukan seorang ahli tetap.
5. Bukan, Ahmad bukan seorang ahli sejarah.
6. Bukan, dia bukan seorang ahli bedah.
7. Bukan, Talib bukan seorang ahli ubat.
8. Bukan, dia bukan seorang ahli jiwa.
9. Bukan, Encik Lim bukan seorang ahli negara.
10. Bukan, Samy bukan seorang ahli sains.

Exercise 5

1. teman
2. Budak
3. Barang
4. duit
5. dolar
6. orang

7. wang
8. roti
9. murid
10. pegawai

Exercise 6

1. pagi, Pantai Cantik
2. orang
3. baju
4. Adik, ombak
5. Adik, pasir, pantai
6. laki-laki, pasir
7. orang, ular
8. orang, rumah sakit

Exercise 7

1. Penumpang
2. Peniaga
3. penjual
4. Penari
5. pemarah
6. petani
7. penyapu
8. penimbang
9. pembaris
10. pembengis

Exercise 8

1. ucapan
2. harapan
3. makanan
4. Pakaian
5. minuman
6. tapisan
7. manisan
8. lapangan
9. Harian
10. Mingguan

LESSON 2

Exercise 1

1. Ya, ini kunci.
2. Ya, itu kerusi.
3. Ya, ini meja.
4. Ya, itu bangku.
5. Ya, ini kipas.
6. Ya, itu kertas.
7. Ya, ini pembaris.
8. Ya, itu papan hitam.
9. Ya, ini pemadam.
10. Ya, itu dakwat.

Exercise 2

1. Bukan, ini bukan piring.
2. Bukan, itu bukan dapur.
3. Bukan, ini bukan cangkir.
4. Bukan, itu bukan jam tangan.
5. Bukan, ini bukan cermin.
6. Bukan, itu bukan sikat.
7. Bukan, ini bukan pisau.
8. Bukan, itu bukan suratkhabar.
9. Bukan, ini bukan perpustakaan.
10. Bukan, itu bukan asrama.

Exercise 3

1. Ya, orang laki-laki itu adalah sahabat saya.
2. Ya, perempuan itu adalah ibu saya.
3. Ya, gadis itu adalah adik perempuan saya.
4. Ya, wanita itu adalah seorang doktor.
5. Ya, orang laki-laki tua itu adalah datuk saya.
6. Ya, perempuan tua itu adalah nenek saya.
7. Ya, pemuda itu ialah seorang jurutera.

8. Ya, perempuan muda itu adalah seorang jururawat.
9. Ya, orang itu adalah jiran saya.
10. Ya, rumah itu adalah rumah saya.

Exercise 4

1. Ahmad pesertakah?
2. John seorang pelancongkah?
3. Cik Fatimah setiausahakah?
4. Cik Timah seorang jurusolekkah?
5. Tuan Talib seorang tabibkah?
6. Encik Tan doktor gigikah?
7. Ahmad ahli bombakah?
8. Dr. Lee seorang menterikah?
9. Dr. Yusuf duta besarkah?
10. Abdullah ketua kampungkah?

Exercise 5

1. Melayu
2. sekolah
3. kaya
4. kosong
5. kulit
6. laki-laki
7. Inggeris
8. baru
9. perempuan
10. hitam

Exercise 6

1. Orang laki-laki itu bapa saudara saya.
2. Anjing itu menggigit seorang budak lelaki.
3. Penulis itu guru kita.
4. Hujan telah reda.
5. Budak lelaki itu sentiasa menangis.
6. Ikan itu bermain-main.
7. Buku itu buku saya.
8. Ali pandai.
9. Pemandu itu abang saya.
10. Orang itu hendaklah berhati-hati.

Exercise 7

1. pemberian
2. Pendengaran
3. Pengakuan
4. Pembahagian
5. Pembangunan
6. Pembayaran
7. Pembetulan
8. Pembesaran
9. Pendapatan
10. perbezaan

Exercise 8

1. Perbuatan
2. Pekerjaan
3. Pertahanan
4. Pertandingan
5. Persaingan
6. Perjalanan
7. Perubahan
8. Pertanyaan
9. Perbualan
10. perkahwinan

Exercise 9

1. kebaikan
2. kesihatan
3. kepentingan
4. Kedaulatan
5. kerajinan
6. kemakmuran

7. kebenaran
8. kebebasan
9. Kedudukan
10. Kehidupan

LESSON 3

Exercise 1

1. Pemuda itu nakal.
2. Pemuda itu sedih.
3. Pemuda itu gembira.
4. Pemuda itu cerdas.
5. Pemuda itu degil.
6. Pemuda itu lokek.
7. Pemuda itu jujur.
8. Pemuda itu sihat.
9. Pemuda itu sibuk.
10. Pemuda itu sombong.

Exercise 2

1. Pakaian itu murah.
2. Kemeja itu mahal.
3. Seluar itu panjang.
4. Jalan itu lebar.
5. Lorong itu sempit.

Exercise 3

1. Ya, bangunan itu tinggi.
2. Ya, rumah ini rendah.
3. Ya, air itu jernih.
4. Ya, lampu itu terang.
5. Ya, murid itu tekun.
6. Ya, sungai itu dalam.
7. Ya, taman itu indah.
8. Ya, bunga itu wangi.
9. Ya, tempat itu gelap.
10. Ya, meja itu berat.

Exercise 4

1. Pekerja itu cekapkah?
2. Ketua itu bengiskah?
3. Perempuan itu hodohkah?
4. Tasik itu tohorkah?
5. Orang itu kejamkah?
6. Tukang itu pandaikah?
7. Emak Yusuf bimbangkah?
8. Pekerja asing itu malangkah?
9. Masakan itu pedaskah?
10. Minuman itu panaskah?

Exercise 5

1. baru
2. baru
3. gemuk
4. gemuk
5. lama
6. lama
7. berat
8. berat
9. kuat
10. kuat

Exercise 6

1. kedekut
2. bijak
3. gelisah
4. sopan
5. kasar
6. penting
7. pedas
8. mudah
9. sukar
10. sukar

Exercise 7

1. secantik
2. sekuat

3. setinggi
4. sebodoh
5. sebaik
6. terdekat
7. teristimewa
8. terkenal
9. tersayang
10. terpencil

Exercise 8

1. pemalu
2. pendiam
3. pengasih
4. peramah
5. berbahaya
6. berguna
7. bergembira
8. berterima kasih
9. bersemangat
10. bertimbang rasa

LESSON 4

Exercise 1

1. Dia sudah lari.
2. Dia sudah masuk.
3. Dia akan sampai.
4. Dia akan pergi.
5. Dia telah pindah.
6. Dia sedang makan.
7. Dia sudah kahwin.
8. Dia belum bangun.
9. Dia sedang ketawa.
10. Dia belum mandi.

Exercise 2

1. Ya, dia gagal.
2. Ya, lelaki itu menang.
3. Ya, dia belum sembuh.
4. Ya, pencuri itu telah lepas.
5. Ya, dia lupa.
6. Ya, dia kalah.
7. Ya, pelajar itu sudah tamat.
8. Ya, dia masih belum siap.
9. Ya, harga beras sudah turun.
10. Ya, harga rumah sudah naik.

Exercise 3

1. Kedai itu masih belum tutupkah?
2. Burung terbangkah?
3. Rantai itu sudah putuskah?
4. Cawan itu sudah pecahkah?
5. Pokok itu sudah tumbuhkah?
6. Daun gugurkah?
7. Bangunan itu robohkah?
8. Gigi nenek tanggalkah?
9. Harga barang-barang naikkah?
10. Perniagaan mundurkah?

Exercise 4

1. Dia kerja hari ini.
2. Dia sakit kelmarin.
3. Dia akan sembuh lusa.
4. Dia jatuh minggu lepas.
5. Dia akan pulang minggu depan.
6. Dia akan terbang ke Jakarta esok.
7. Dia singgah di rumah saya malam tadi.
8. Anak saya lahir setahun kemudian.
9. Saya lalu di depan kedai itu tiap-tiap hari.
10. Lampu padam jam enam.

Exercise 5

1. Dia
2. Mereka
3. Kami

4. Mereka
5. Dia
6. Dia
7. Dia
8. Mereka
9. Mereka
10. Mereka

Exercise 6

1. Awak
2. Saya
3. awak
4. saya
5. awak
6. saya
7. Pak
8. kita
9. saya
10. Encik

Exercise 7

1. melamar
2. memasak
3. meniaga
4. menyanyuk
5. meraba
6. membahas
7. memekik
8. mendapat
9. mencabar
10. menampal

Exercise 8

1. menganggur
2. mengerti
3. mengingat
4. mengorak
5. mengurus
6. menggigit
7. mengirim
8. mengesyor
9. manyamar
10. menyajak

LESSON 5

Exercise 1

1. Saudara boleh bantu orang itu.
2. Saudara boleh turut orang itu.
3. Saudara boleh tuduh orang itu.
4. Saudara boleh bawa orang itu.
5. Saudara boleh tahan orang itu.
6. Saudara boleh tentang orang itu.
7. Saudara boleh tampung orang itu.
8. Saudara boleh tegur orang itu.
9. Saudara boleh periksa orang itu.
10. Saudara boleh tanggung orang itu.

Exercise 2

1. Ya, dia hukum orang jahat itu.
2. Ya, dia jemput guru itu.
3. Ya, dia tumbuk orang laki-laki itu.
4. Ya, dia sebat orang salah itu.
5. Ya, dia puji budak laki-laki itu.
6. Ya, dia sindir sahabat kita.
7. Ya, polis kejar lelaki itu.
8. Ya, polis kenal lelaki itu.
9. Ya, polis tembak orang jahat itu.
10. Ya, dia larang semua parti politik.

Exercise 3

1. Tidak, kawan kita tidak minta buku itu.
2. Tidak, anak itu tidak berus gigi.

3. Tidak, anak itu tidak cuci muka.
4. Tidak, anak itu tidak sisir rambut.
5. Tidak, perempuan itu tidak basuh pakaian.
6. Tidak, pekerja itu tidak simpan wang.
7. Tidak, dia sudah tidak pegang jawatan itu.
8. Tidak, dia sudah tidak pasang lampu.
9. Tidak, Salimah sudah tidak tukar baju.
10. Tidak, Ayah tidak minum kopi.

Exercise 4

1. Ibu sedang atur bungakah?
2. Tukang kayu sedang bakar kayukah?
3. Perempuan itu sedang cuci pakaiankah?
4. Penjaja itu buang sampahkah?
5. Ibu sudah buka peti itukah?
6. Kakak belum bungkus nasikah?
7. Abang sedang cari dompetkah?
8. Ayah usir anjing itukah?
9. Lelaki miskin itu sudah gadai rumahnyakah?
10. Lelaki kaya itu sudah beli rumah barukah?

Exercise 5

1. siapa
2. apa
3. siapa
4. apa
5. Siapa
6. Apa
7. apa
8 Siapa
9. siapa
10. Siapa

Exercise 6

1. Berapa
2. Yang mana
3. Yang mana
4. Berapa
5. Berapa
6. Yang mana
7. Yang mana
8. Yang mana
9. Berapa
10. Berapa

Exercise 7

1. Dia memarang kayu itu.
2. Nelayan itu menjaring ikan.
3. Adik memberus giginya.
4. Gadis itu menudung mukanya.
5. Abang suka memancing ikan.
6. Makcik saya sedang menyayur.
7. Lelaki itu suka merokok.
8. Kami menepi.
9. Kami menyeberang jalan itu.
10. Salmiah menggambar di bawah pohon.

Exercise 8

1. Padi menguning.
2. Asap menebal.
3. Harapannya menipis.
4. Luka itu mendalam.
5. Bulan sudah merendah.
6. Perbincangan menghangat.
7. Lembaga itu membesar.
8. Pokok itu meninggi dari sehari ke sehari.
9. Perhubungan kita merenggang.
10. Kedua pihak merapat.

LESSON 6

Exercise 1

1. Saya di masjid hari ini.
2. Saya di gereja hari ini.
3. Saya di kedutaan hari ini.
4. Saya di kedutaan pagi ini.
5. Saya di madrasah pagi ini.
6. Saya di makmal pagi ini.
7. Saya di makmal bahasa pagi ini.
8. Saya di makmal bahasa malam tadi.
9. Saya di panggung wayang malam tadi.
10. Saya di pusat bahasa malam tadi.

Exercise 2

1. Ya, Cikgu Ali ke sekolah.
2. Ya, kakak ke pasar.
3. Ya, buah-buahan itu di dalam keranjang.
4. Ya, surat itu di dalam laci.
5. Ya, surat itu daripada abangnya.
6. Ya, pelancong itu dari Indonesia.
7. Ya, kamus Melayu itu di atas meja.
8. Ya, Pejabat Pos Besar itu di hadapan rumah saya.
9. Ya, balai polis itu di belakang rumah saya.
10. Ya, ibu pejabat syarikat di sebelah rumah saya.

Exercise 3

1. Nelayan itu masih di lautkah?
2. Sarjana itu dari negeri Belandakah?
3. Pesakit itu tidak ke pejabatnyakah?
4. Bungkusan ini untuk kamukah?
5. Para tamu masih di lapangan terbangkah?
6. Kertas itu di atas mejakah?
7. Gambar ayah di dindingkah?
8. Cawan di dapurkah?
9. Bunga di kebunkah?
10. Kasut di dalam bilik tidurkah?

Exercise 4

1. Perpustakaan Kebangsaan di Stamford Road.
2. Kebun Bunga di sana.
3. Kawan-kawan Ali di sini.
4. Rumah Sakit Universiti Nasional di Kent Ridge.
5. Lelaki itu ke kota.
6. Wartawan-wartawan itu dri Bangkok.
7. Pensel kamu di atas meja.
8. Kawan saya di panggung wayang semalam.
9. Tamu itu dari London.
10. Danau Toba di Sumatera.

Exercise 5

1. akan
2. telah
3. sudah
4. hendak
5. sedang
6. akan
7. harus
8. mahu
9. akan
10. mungkin

Exercise 6

1. memekik
2. membaca

3. memeriksa
4. menonton
5. menjerit
6. meninjau
7. berbincang
8. menyoal
9. berlari
10. bertiup

Exercise 7

1. Kain itu berwarna biru.
2. Buku bacaan itu bergambar.
3. Rumah itu tidak berlampu.
4. Guru itu berilmu.
5. Budak lelaki itu tidak berakal.
6. Negeri itu tiada beraja.
7. Lukisan itu tidak bermutu.
8. Ayah saya tidak berwang.
9. Surat itu tidak beralamat.
10. Lelaki itu berduit.

Exercise 8

1. Budak lelaki itu tidak berkasut ke sekolah.
2. Almari itu tidak bercermin.
3. Lelaki itu suka berpidato.
4. Kakak saya suka berbaju cantik.
5. Kami berkereta ke Kuala Lumpur.
6. Lelaki itu bercermin mata hitam.
7. Sarjana itu suka berceramah.
8. Abang sedia berkuli.
9. Musim hujan ramai nelayan berladang.
10. Sudah dua tahun dia berkedai.

LESSON 7

Exercise 1

1. Saya tahu saudara bertengkar dengan orang laki-laki itu.
2. Saya tahu saudara bergaul dengan orang laki-laki itu.
3. Saya tahu saudara berbaik dengan orang laki-laki itu.
4. Saya tahu saudara berjumpa dengan orang laki-laki itu.
5. Saya tahu saudara bertanding dengan orang laki-laki itu.
6. Saya tahu saudara bermusuh dengan orang laki-laki itu.
7. Saya tahu saudara bersahabat dengan orang laki-laki itu.
8. Saya tahu saudara bersalam dengan orang laki-laki itu.
9. Saya tahu saudara berbincang dengan orang laki-laki itu.
10. Saya tahu saudara bertumbuk dengan orang laki-laki itu.

Exercise 2

1. Adik sedang berkhayalkah?
2. Orang itu sudah berkuasakah?
3. Orang itu sedang bermimpikah?
4. Perempuan itu sedang bernyanyikah?
5. Budak lelaki itu belum berpuasakah?
6. Mereka belum bergerakkah?
7. Mereka masih berundingkah?
8. Mereka bersalahkah?
9. Mereka akan berpestakah?
10. Orang itu beragama Islamkah?

Exercise 3

1. Ya, mereka sedang berkumpul di padang sekolah.

2. Ya, mereka sedang bermuafakat di pejabat.
3. Ya, mereka berniaga di Johor.
4. Ya, saya berehat di rumah.
5. Ya, saya bersembahyang di masjid.
6. Ya, dia berada di Ipoh.
7. Ya, perempuan itu bersolek di dalam bilik.
8. Ya, rombongan itu akan berangkat ke Kuantan.
9. Ya, orang itu sedang bercukur di bilik.
10. Ya, perajurit sedang bertahan di kubu.

Exercise 4

1. Guru itu berdiri di depan darjah.
2. Bas itu berhenti di depan perpustakaan.
3. Murid-murid berhimpun di padang sekolah.
4. Tamu kita bermalam di hotel.
5. Kereta itu berlalu di belakang rumah saya.
6. Perahu itu belayar ke Sumatera.
7. Mereka berkelah di Port Dickson.
8. Peristiwa itu berlaku di hadapan mata kita.
9. Ali bersembunyi di balik pokok.
10. Amin berlatih di Jepun.

Exercise 5

1. Surat itu sudah ditulis Saleh.
2. Fatimah selalu dipuji guru.
3. Pensel itu sedang dipegang Laila.
4. Wangnya sudah dicuri pencuri.
5. Pakaian dibasuh Siti Salina.
6. Bilik darjah sedang disapu Halimah.
7. Suratkhabar belum dibaca Cikgu Ali.
8. Temannya sedang dinanti Ali.
9. Baju sedang dijahit ibu.
10. Orang itu ditolong Ahmad.

Exercise 6

1. Saya memanjat pokok kelapa itu.
2. Saya sudah mendengar berita itu.
3. Saya sudah memakan nasi itu.
4. Aku sudah menulis karangan itu.
5. Kamu sudah menerima surat itu.
6. Engkau sudah membawa kamus itu.
7. Saya sudah meminjam penselmu.
8. Engkau memukul budak itu.
9. Aku sudah minum kopi itu.
10. Kamu sudah menangkap ayam itu.

Exercise 7

1. berlindung
2. bercerita
3. bertaubat
4. berdandan
5. berpusing
6. bersuara
7. bernafas
8. berganjak
9. beratur
10. berkunjung

Exercise 8

1. berakhir
2. berangin

3. berbau
4. berbuah
5. berbeza
6. berbintang
7. berambut
8. berbunga
9. bergambar
10. beralamat

LESSON 8

Exercise 1

1. Saya mengantuk di rumah sahabat malam tadi.
2. Saya memekik di rumah sahabat malam tadi.
3. Saya membohong di rumah sahabat malam tadi.
4. Saya membisu di rumah sahabat malam tadi.
5. Saya mengeluh di rumah sahabat malam tadi.
6. Saya menangis di rumah sahabat malam tadi.
7. Saya mengarut di rumah sahabat malam tadi.
8. Saya merungut di rumah sahabat malam tadi.
9. Saya menguap di rumah sahabat malam tadi.
10. Saya menyanyi di rumah sahabat malam tadi.

Exercise 2

1. Ya, penyakit itu sudah menjangkit.
2. Ya, bom itu belum meledak.
3. Ya, angin sedang membadai.
4. Ya, hujan sudah mereda.
5. Ya, fajar sedang menyingsing.
6. Ya, air sedang mendidih.
7. Ya, kaki budak lelaki itu sedang membengkak.
8. Ya, anjing itu sedang menyalak.
9. Ya, lembu jantan itu sedang mengganas.
10. Ya, perang sudah meletus.

Exercise 3

1. Suka mengajikah budak lelaki itu?
2. Sudahkah dia mengalah?
3. Sukakah adik memancing?
4. Selalukah perempuan itu merajuk?
5. Sukakah perempuan itu membazir?
6. Sudah menghilangkah pencuri itu?
7. Bolehkah mereka mengundi?
8. Bolehkah mereka mengundur?
9. Sedang menganggurkah orang itu?
10. Selalukah rakyat negeri itu memberontak?

Exercise 4

1. Bola itu melambung ke atas air.
2. Air memancar dari paip.
3. Semut-semut sedang merayap di lantai.
4. Pekerja itu sudah menetap di Singapura.
5. Kassim sedang menuntut di universiti.
6. Ali menoleh ke arah belakang.
7. Lelaki itu menyelundup ke negeri kita.
8. Bom itu meledak di tengah bandar.
9. Air hujan menitis dari bumbung bocor.
10. Budak lelaki itu melangkah ke depan.

Exercise 5

1. batang
2. helai
3. bidang
4. orang
5. keping
6. ekor
7. buah
8. biji
9. helai
10. biji

Exercise 6

1. Semua
2. sebahagian
3. sedikit
4. Ramai
5. banyak
6. Ramai
7. Seluruh
8. Ramai
9. sedikit
10. satu

Exercise 7

1. Budak lelaki itu terjatuh.
2. Lelaki itu terminum racun.
3. Ali ternampak pencuri itu.
4. Dia terbaca berita itu.
5. Halimah terambil buku kawannya.
6. Dia tersepak kayu itu.
7. Polis itu tertembak kawannya.
8. Dia teringat hendak pulang ke kampung.
9. Saya terjaga pada pukul lima.
10. Dia tertidur dikelas.

Exercise 8

1. Soalan itu tidak terjawab oleh Ali.
2. Tulisan itu tidak terbaca oleh guru.
3. Hutang itu tidak terbayar oleh negara.
4. Kuman tidak terlihat oleh mata kasar.
5. Suara itu tidak terdengar oleh kita.
6. Pencuri itu tertangkap.
7. Buku-bukunya tersusun di atas meja.
8. Wangnya tersimpan dengan baik.
9. Pintu terkunci.
10. Pelita belum terpasang.

LESSON 9

Exercise 1

1. Kita mencium orang itu.
2. Kita mendakap orang itu.
3. Kita mendera orang itu.
4. Kita mengejek orang itu.
5. Kita menelefon orang itu.
6. Kita mengejar orang itu.
7. Kita memfitnah orang itu.
8. Kita menggaji orang itu.
9. Kita menggambar orang itu.
10. Kita mengganggu orang itu.

Exercise 2

1. Tidak, jururawat tidak merawat orang sakit itu.
2. Tidak, guru itu tidak membimbing muridnya.
3. Tidak, perempuan itu tidak mengasuh anaknya.
4. Tidak, saya tidak mengacau

gadis itu.

5. Tidak, saya tidak menguji budak itu.
6. Tidak, penyamun tidak menyamun orang itu.
7. Tidak, polis tidak menembak orang itu.
8. Tidak, penguam itu tidak memanggil saksinya.
9. Tidak, hakim tidak mencela peguam itu.
10. Tidak, dia tidak menculik saudagar itu.

Exercise 3

1. Sudahkah Ali menjemput orang itu?
2. Dapatkah Amin membayar orang itu?
3. Mahukah orang kampung membelasah pencuri itu?
4. Mahukah doktor membedah pesakit itu?
5. Dapatkah kita mengepung penjahat itu?
6. Sudahkah dia menghalau pengemis itu?
7. Mahukah dia menyapa orang itu?
8. Mahukah perempuan itu memeluk anaknya?
9. Sudahkah ibu tiri menyeksa anak tirinya?
10. Dapatkah mereka menuduh orang itu?

Exercise 4

1. Dia menyindir orang itu pagi tadi.
2. Doktor menyuntik budak itu tahun lalu.
3. Dia mengajar budak itu tiap-tiap hari.
4. Dia menegur orang itu kelmarin.
5. Dia mencemuh orang itu kelmarin dulu.
6. Dia akan mencerca orang itu semalam.
7. Kerajaan akan melantik orang itu minggu depan.
8. Anjing menggigit orang itu minggu lalu.
9. Yusuf menggertak orang itu kelmarin.
10. Kerajaan akan mengganjar orang itu tahun depan.

Exercise 5

1. Ali tidur.
2. Yusuf sedang bersiar-siar.
3. Bayi itu menangis.
4. Saya akan belayar.
5. Lelaki itu bercakap.
6. Dia sudah menerima surat itu.
7. Dia meninggalkan tempat itu.
8. Murid-murid belajar.
9. Dia membaca surat itu.
10. Mereka berbual.

Exercise 6

1. amat
2. benar
3. betul
4. sangat
5. kurang
6. cukup
7. sekali
8. terlalu
9. terlampau
10. hampir

Exercise 7

1. Dia sudah datang.
2. Mereka berdiri.
3. Dia merenung muka adiknya.
4. Lelaki itu berjalan.
5. Pelajar itu belajar.
6. Perempuan itu menangis.
7. Semua permohonan hendaklah sampai.
8. Mereka akan sampai.
9. Mereka duduk.
10. Kita pergi.

Exercise 8

1. Barangkali
2. Semestinya
3. Seharusnya
4. Sesungguhnya
5. Sebetulnya
6. Sememangnya
7. Sewajarnya
8. Agaknya
9. Rupanya
10. Nampaknya

LESSON 10

Exercise 1

1. Kita akan mendengar soal itu.
2. Kita akan mengupas soal itu.
3. Kita akan mengusut soal itu.
4. Kita akan menyebut soal itu.
5. Kita akan menyebut hal itu.
6. Kita akan menyiasat hal itu.
7. Kita akan menyelidik hal itu.
8. Kita akan meneliti hal itu.
9. Kita akan menimbang hal itu.
10. Kita akan meninjau hal itu.

Exercise 2

1. Pemandu itu sedang memandu kereta.
2. Para penonton sedang menonton sandiwara.
3. Pengawai itu sedang mengawal keselamatan.
4. Pelawat itu sedang melawat sekolah.
5. Perompak itu sedang merompak sebuah kedai.
6. Peminta sedekah itu sedang meminta sedekah.
7. Penjaga itu sedang menjaga rumah.
8. Penjual itu sedang menjual buku.
9. Pengumpul itu sedang mengumpul setem.
10. Penderma itu sedang menderma wang.

Exercise 3

1. Peladang itu sedang menganyam tikar.
2. Orang itu sedang mengasah pisau.
3. Petani itu sedang membajak sawah.
4. Ibu sedang membancuh susu.
5. Kakak sedang membasuh kain.
6. Ahmad sedang memberus giginya.
7. Kerajaan sedang membina perpustakaan baru.
8. Budak lelaki itu sedang membongkar lacinya.
9. Mak Limah sedang mencencang daging.
10. Budak itu sedang mencubit tangan adiknya.

Exercise 4

1. Mahukah dia menghantar anaknya ke sekolah?
2. Bolehkah dia memakai kasut kulit?
3. Bolehkah dia menyanyi lagu Melayu?
4. Mahukah dia menanam modal di sini?
5. Mahukah dia mengulas buku itu?
6. Bolehkah dia menolak cadangan itu?
7. Bolehkah dia mengukir bunga-bungaan?
8. Mahukah dia mengkaji masalah itu?
9. Bolehkah dia menyadur cerita itu?
10. Bolehkah dia menyandang jawatan itu?

Exercise 5

1. Bagaimana dia berlari?
2. Bagaimana Ahmad memandu keretanya?
3. Bila mereka akan menjalankan kerja itu?
4. Bila para tamu sampai?
5. Di mana rumahnya?
6. Di mana mereka berkelah?
7. Mengapa dia tinggal di rumah?
8. Mengapa dia mengantuk?
9. Mengapa dia tidak datang?
10. Mengapa Kamil tidak membeli barang itu?

Exercise 6

1. Dengan siapa Ahmad selalu berkelahi?
2. Dengan siapa Azman tinggal di rumah?
3. Dengan apa Dewi makan nasi?
4. Dengan apa dia membelah kayu?
5. Untuk apa dia pergi ke bandar?
6. Untuk siapa dia mencari duit?
7. Untuk apa dia menelefon kawannya?
8. Untuk siapa lelaki itu datang ke mari?
9. Dengan apa dia pergi ke sekolah?
10. Dengan apa dia memotong daging?

Exercise 7

1. Dia telah dapat menjaringkan 4 gol.
2. Budak itu menabungkan wang sakunya.
3. Mereka mengetinkan buah-buah tempatan.
4. Gembala itu mengandangkan lembu-lembunya.
5. Perbuatan pemuda itu mengaibkan jirannya.
6. Dia selalu menasihatkan adik lelakinya.
7. Dia tidak pernah mendendamkan lelaki itu.
8. Saya tidak pernah mengatakan hal itu kepadanya.
9. Asia Tenggara menghasilkan bijih timah yang banyak.
10. Budak-budak semua menuankan Ahmad.

Exercise 8

1. Pengangguranlah yang menyusahkan saya.

2. Jawapan itu menggusarkan Ahmad.
3. Tindakan majikan mengecewakan pekerja.
4. Ubat itu boleh menguatkan badan kita.
5. Kurang tidur boleh menguruskan badan.
6. Orang kampung beramai-ramai melapangkan jalan itu.
7. Senaman boleh mencergaskan badan.
8. Dia cuba mengeraskan tanah itu.
9. Kita boleh mengecilkan api dapur dengan serta-merta.
10. Sukan boleh mencerdaskan tubuh.

LESSON 11

Exercise 1

1. Dia sudah mencetak buku itu.
2. Dia sudah mengutip buku itu.
3. Dia sudah menyemak buku itu.
4. Dia sudah meminjam buku itu.
5. Dia sudah meminjam kereta itu.
6. Dia sudah menyewa kereta itu.
7. Dia sudah menyewa rumah itu.
8. Dia sudah menghuni rumah itu.
9. Dia sudah mengunci rumah itu.
10. Dia sudah mengetuk rumah itu.

Exercise 2

1. Lelaki itu menggaul nasinya dengan kuah.
2. Dia menyumbat mulut botol itu dengan gabus.
3. Dia menetak pokok itu dengan sebilah kapak.
4. Emak menudung hidangan itu dengan tudung saji.
5. Pekedai itu menimbang gula dengan dacing.
6. Dia menimbus lubang itu dengan tanah.
7. Lelaki itu menangkap burung dengan jerat.
8. Kakak menapis air kopi dengan penapis.
9. Lelaki itu menyisir rambut dengan sikat.
10. Emak menyapu lantai dengan penyapu.

Exercise 3

1. Orang itu menderma wang untuk membantu anak-anak yatim.
2. Polis menggeledah rumah itu untuk mencari senjata.
3. Kakak menggubah bunga untuk perhiasan.
4. Kakak menghiris bawang untuk menggoreng telur.
5. Emak menjerang air untuk membuat kopi.
6. Orang itu mengembara untuk mencari rezeki.
7. Kerajaan mengerah para pemuda untuk berkhidmat dalam tentera.
8. Ibu memerah kelapa untuk mengambil santannya.
9. Mereka menyingsing baju untuk bekerja.
10. Emak meramas tepung itu untuk membuat kuih.

Exercise 4

1. Dia memberi wang itu kepada ketuanya.
2. Dia mengucap terima kasih kepada bapa Hasyim.

3. Dia menulis surat itu kepada orang tuanya.
4. Dia meminta bantuan kepada gurunya.
5. Dia melempar bola kepada budak lelaki itu.
6. Dia mengutus surat itu ke Jakarta.
7. Ahmad membawa makanan itu ke rumah sakit.
8. Anak lelaki itu mengikut ibunya ke pasar.
9. Dia mendayung sampannya ke tengah laut.
10. Dia memandang ke bukit itu.

Exercise 5

1. di
2. Pada
3. daripada
4. ke
5. dari
6. kepada
7. dalam
8. dengan
9. untuk
10. kerana

Exercise 6

1. di
2. kepada
3. dari
4. sejak
5. sampai
6. oleh
7. dengan
8. untuk
9. dari
10. kepada

Exercise 7

1. Dia mengeluarkan kotak rokok itu.
2. Dia menurunkan layang-layang itu.
3. Dia memulangkan motokar itu kepada tuannya.
4. Kerajaan mendatangkan guru-guru dari luar negeri.
5. Para doktor tidak dapat menghidupkan orang mati itu.
6. Kuli-kuli sedang menaikkan barang-barang itu ke kapal.
7. Sebuah bom telah meruntuhkan seluruh bandar.
8. Setiap pagi ibu membangunkan saya pada pukul enam.
9. Ribut telah menumbangkan pokok itu.
10. Letupan bom itu telah menghancurkan pertahanan musuh.

Exercise 8

1. Ahmad membawakan ayahnya beg.
2. Ibu mamasakkan ayah nasi.
3. Dia menuliskan kawannya sepucuk surat.
4. Aminah membasuhkan ibunya kain.
5. Osman membelikan isterinya baju.
6. Yusuf membuatkan orang tuanya rumah di kampung.
7. Kakak mengikatkan adik tali kasut.
8. Dia membukakan tamu pintu.
9. Dia menuangkan kawannya secawan kopi.
10. Dia menyimpankan kawannya cincin itu.

LESSON 12

Exercise 1

1. Mereka kasih akan kawan kita.
2. Mereka rindu akan kawan kita.
3. Mereka kenal akan kawan kita.
4. Mereka gusar akan kawan kita.
5. Mereka malu akan kawan kita.
6. Mereka marah akan kawan kita.
7. Mereka percaya akan kawan kita.
8. Mereka patuh akan kawan kita.
9. Mereka cinta akan kawan kita.
10. Mereka suka akan kawan kita.

Exercise 2

1. Peristiwa itu menghebohkan seluruh kampung.
2. Akibatnya sangat memalukan.
3. Pertanyaan itu sungguh memusykilkan.
4. Pekerjaan itu sungguh memenatkan.
5. Layanan kedai itu sangat memuaskan.
6. Syarahan lelaki itu sangat menjemukan.
7. Angin malam di pergunungan sangat menyegarkan.
8. Kemalangan itu sungguh menakutkan.
9. Keadaan orang-orang miskin di bandar sangat menyedihkan.
10. Cuaca hari ini baik.

Exercise 3

1. Tindakan majikan itu mengecewakan para pekerja.
2. Berita itu menggemparkan seluruh dunia.
3. Ugutan perempuan itu membimbangkan hatinya.
4. Pembunuhan itu menggoncangkan dunia.
5. Kepintaran akrobat itu menghairankan para penonton.
6. Sepinggan nasi dapat mengenyangkan saya.
7. Leteran ibunya membingungkan dia.
8. Berita orang minyak menggentarkan orang kampung.
9. Muzik dapat mengharukan perasaan penonton.
10. Bau makanan itu memuakkan kita.

Exercise 4

1. Anak Cik Limah lima orang.
2. Rumah orang kaya itu sepuluh buah.
3. Lembu Pak Haji itu tujuh ekor.
4. Harga buku itu sebelas dolar.
5. Umur murid itu dua belas tahun.
6. Banyak penduduk kota itu satu juta.
7. Adik-beradik saya empat orang.
8. Berat badan lelaki itu empat puluh lima kilogram.
9. Dalam sungai itu dua puluh meter.
10. Tinggi gunung itu seribu meter.

Exercise 5

1. ketika
2. walaupun
3. Apabila
4. sesudah
5. Selama
6. supaya
7. kecuali

8. atau
9. Sejak
10. jikalau

Exercise 6

1. sampai
2. supaya
3. Jikalau
4. Walaupun
5. seperti
6. agar
7. kecuali
8. Sementara
9. sambil
10. melainkan

Exercise 7

1. Dia menandai rumah itu.
2. Dia menasihati temannya.
3. Rosminah sedang menyusui anaknya.
4. Doktor mengubati orang sakit itu.
5. Dia membelanjai adik lelakinya setiap bulan.
6. Kata-katanya mengilhami pengarang itu.
7. Lelaki itu tidak menafkahi isterinya.
8. Aku tak sudi menyedekahi orang pemalas.
9. Dia mengupahi mereka membakar rumah itu.
10. Dia menaungi pelarian itu.

Exercise 8

1. Dia mewakili saudagar itu.
2. Dia yang mengantarai perselisihan itu.
3. Siapa yang mendalangi pemberontakan itu?
4. Dia mengetuai majlis itu.
5. Dia merajai negeri itu.
6. Lampu minyak itu menerangi biliknya.
7. Gadis itu memerahi kukunya.
8. Sebuah kipas menyejuki bilik itu.
9. Setiap malam binatang-binatang liar merosaki tanamannya.
10. Air mata membasahi pipinya.

LESSON 13

Exercise 1

1. Dia akan membahagiakan handai taulan kita.
2. Dia boleh mengejutkan handai taulan kita.
3. Dia akan memencilkan handai taulan kita.
4. Dia akan menguntungkan handai taulan kita.
5. Dia akan menguntungkan rakan sejawat kita.
6. Dia akan menyatukan rakan sejawat kita.
7. Dia boleh mengistimewakan rakan sejawat kita.
8. Dia boleh mendiamkan rakan sejawat kita.
9. Dia akan membahayakan rakan sejawat kita.
10. Dia akan merugikan rakan sejawat kita.

Exercise 2

1. Syarahan itu menjemukan siapa?

2. Dia selalu mengenangkan siapa?
3. Dia jarang mengetawakan siapa?
4. Fatimah sedang memandikan siapa?
5. Ucapannya memarahkan siapa?
6. Dia tidak dapat memaafkan siapa?
7. Racun itu boleh mematikan siapa?
8. Orang itu memburukkan nama siapa?
9. Lelaki itu sudah memberangkan siapa?
10. Ibu itu sedang menidurkan siapa?

Exercise 3

1. Dia sudah menyingkirkan pegawai tadbir dari jawatan.
2. Ramli menundukkan kawannya dalam permainan itu.
3. Dia sudah mencalonkan iparnya untuk jawatan itu.
4. Dia meraikan kakitangannya dalam majlis itu.
5. Dia menjatuhkan lawannya dalam perlawanan tinju.
6. Ahmad menumpangkan anaknya di rumah sahabat.
7. Razak menyelimutkan adiknya dengan selimut.
8. Dia menyedarkan pengawal itu dari lalainya.
9. Dia menjagakan abangnya dari tidurnya.
10. Kerajaan telah memberhentikan guru itu dari jawatan.

Exercise 4

1. Boleh, dia boleh memenjarakan lelaki itu di rumah.
2. Dapat, dia dapat memulaukan orang itu dari masyarakat.
3. Boleh, dia boleh menyelamatkan lelaki itu daripada mati lemas.
4. Dapat, dia dapat menukarkan pegawai itu ke tempat lain.
5. Boleh, dia boleh menurunkan kita di depan masjid.
6. Dapat, pengetua itu dapat mendatangkan guru-guru dari luar.
7. Boleh, seorang gadis boleh mendedahkan mukanya kepada pelanggan.
8. Dapat, dia dapat memasukkan anaknya ke sekolah itu.
9. Boleh, dia boleh menitipkan anaknya kepada jirannya.
10. Boleh, dia boleh menyewakan rumahnya kepada kita.

Exercise 5

1. Latif pemuda Melayu.
2. Umurnya lima belas tahun pada bulan Ogos ini .
3. Dia berbakat di dalam bidang perniagaan.
4. Saudagar kaya itu kedekut.
5. Guru bahasa Melayu kita itu pengarang.
6. Orang berkumpul di kedai Pak Sudin.
7. Ahmad mencuci keretanya setiap hari.
8. Murid-murid duduk di dalam darjah.
9. Budak kecil itu menangis.
10. Lembu ketua kampung makan rumput di padang.

Exercise 6

1. lelaki/perempuan
2. Melayu
3. baru
4. panas/sejuk/hujan
5. Ali
6. lama
7. cerita
8. hitam
9. gemuk
10. gembala

Exercise 7

1. Ramai sungguh orang mendatangi rumahnya.
2. Dia tidak menghadiri majlis perkahwinan sahabatnya.
3. Dia selalu melalui jalan itu.
4. Mereka tidak pernah menyinggahi pelabuhan itu.
5. Jerawat menumbuhi mukanya.
6. Siapa yang menempati rumah itu sekarang?
7. Dia tidak mahu mencampuri orang itu.
8. Perbuatan itu menyalahi undang-undang.
9. Dia menikami lelaki itu.
10. Dia menembaki orang jahat itu.

Exercise 8

1. Sejak itu dia tidak mahu mendiami kampung itu lagi.
2. Dia mendiamkan adiknya yang menangis dengan gula-gula.
3. Perempuan itu sedang menidurkan anaknya.
4. Kemudian dia pergi meniduri katil itu.
5. Setiap pagi, saya menaiki bas itu ke sekolah.
6. Pekedai itu telah menaikkan harga barang-barangnya.
7. Lelaki itu berlari-lari menuruni tangga hotel itu.
8. Pemerintah boleh membuat undang-undang untuk menaikkan atau menurunkan cukai.
9. Apabila dia pulang ke rumah, dia mendapati ibunya sedang tidur.
10. Anak itu berlari-lari mendapatkan ibunya yang pulang dari pasar.

LESSON 14

Exercise 1

1. Kita mesti mengeluarkan wang untuk membeli kereta.
2. Kita mesti mengadakan wang untuk membeli kereta.
3. Kita mesti menyumbangkan wang untuk membeli kereta.
4. Kita mesti mengumpulkan wang untuk membeli kereta.
5. Kita mesti mengumpulkan wang untuk membeli bangunan baru.
6. Kita mesti mengumpulkan wang untuk membeli sebidang tanah.
7. Kita mesti meninggalkan wang untuk membeli sebidang tanah.
8. Kita mesti menyerahkan wang untuk membeli sebidang tanah.
9. Kita mesti menjimatkan wang untuk membeli sebidang tanah.
10. Kita mesti mencarikan wang untuk membeli sebidang tanah.

Exercise 2

1. Dia menjanjikan pertolongan kepada mangsa-mangsa kebakaran.
2. Dia menjelaskan perkara itu kepada para pekerja.
3. Dia mengemukakan pertanyaan itu kepada seorang menteri.
4. Dia mengajukan usul itu kepada ketua pejabatnya.
5. Dia mengucapkan terima kasih kepada sahabat handainya.
6. Fatimah menghidangkan makanan untuk para tamu.
7. Dia menunjukkan cincin itu kepada kekasihnya.
8. Datuk Tan menyampaikan hadiah kepada para pemenang.
9. Lelaki tua itu meninggalkan hartanya kepada anak-anaknya.
10. Dia mengembalikan surat itu kepada pengirimnya.

Exercise 3

1. Bom telah meruntuhkan rumah itu.
2. Guru telah mendirikan persatuan itu.
3. Air bah menghanyutkan pondok itu.
4. Jurujual itu telah menggadaikan rumahnya.
5. Kerajaan mengharamkan perjudian.
6. Kapal selam menenggelamkan kapal itu.
7. Kementerian Pelajaran mengelolakan kursus bahasa itu.
8. Perdana Menteri telah mempengerusikan sidang mingguan itu.
9. Polis telah menyuraikan pertemuan itu.
10. Pemerintah menubuhkan perpustakaan di mana-mana.

Exercise 4

1. Bolehkah dia melaksanakan kewajipannya?
2. Dapatkah Ali menjalankan kerjanya?
3. Bolehkah dia menjayakan usaha itu?
4. Dapatkah dia mengemaskan rumah itu sendiri?
5. Bolehkah anak perempuan itu mengemudikan perusahaan ayahnya?
6. Bolehkah anak itu mengkhatamkan Quran dalam tiga bulan?
7. Bolehkah ubat itu menguatkan badan?
8. Bolehkah hadiah percuma melariskan barang dagangan?
9. Dapatkah dia menyalakan api itu?
10. Dapatkah dia memadamkan api itu?

Exercise 5

1. Ahmad
2. laut, saya
3. mustahak
4. sekolah
5. kaya, miskin
6. kosong
7. semua, sekolah
8. saya
9. Persatuan Bahasa Melayu
10. di dalam kampung

Exercise 6

1. Ramai
2. banyak
3. Segala
4. kencang
5. lebat
6. di dalam air
7. di atas meja
8. cerdik
9. dari Jepun
10. dalam keluarga

LESSON 15

Exercise 1

1. Dia tidak mahu menghabisi rakannya.
2. Dia tidak mahu menyumpahi rakannya.
3. Dia tidak mahu menyertai rakannya.
4. Dia tidak mahu menyekutui rakannya.
5. Dia tidak mahu meramahi rakannya.
6. Dia tidak mahu memusuhi rakannya.
7. Dia tidak mahu menanyai rakannya.
8. Dia tidak mahu menyakiti rakannya.
9. Dia tidak mahu menakuti rakannya.
10. Dia tidak mahu mempercayai rakannya.

Exercise 2

1. Allah selalu melindungi orang yang salih.
2. Jururawat itu sedang mengubati orang sakit.
3. Dia akan mewakili ketua pejabatnya dalam pertemuan itu.
4. Pihak polis telah menghubungi usahawan itu petang semalam.
5. Dia sangat mengasihi sahabatnya.
6. Ramlan mengasihani orang miskin.
7. Rosminah sedang menyusui anaknya.
8. Dia mengesyaki saudara kandungnya sendiri.
9. Orang itu telah mengkhianati bangsanya sendiri.
10. Dia sanggup mengahwini gadis itu.

Exercise 3

1. Tiada orang enggan menikahi gadis kaya itu.
2. Lelaki itu sangat menyayangi isterinya.
3. Kita semua menyegani lelaki itu.
4. Pihak polis masih mencurigai lelaki itu.
5. Ramai budak nakal suka mencampuri orang-orang jahat.
6. Penulis itu selalu mendampingi adiknya ke pekan.
7. Murid-murid sekolah mengerumuni pengarang itu.
8. Ahli bahasa itu pulang menemui kaum keluarganya.
9. Tiada seorang pun dapat menandingi Ahmad dalam permainan itu.
10. Ahli sejarah menanyainya tentang hal itu.

Exercise 4

1. Dia menistai lawannya dengan kata-kata menghina.
2. Dia memberkati anak lelakinya dengan membaca mantera.
3. Hakim mengadili lelaki itu dengan bijaksana.
4. Dia menghadapi lelaki tua itu dengan hati yang berdebar-debar.
5. Dia mempengaruhi pegawai itu dengan wang.
6. Dia menyuapi pegawai itu dengan hadiah.
7. Dia menziarahi ibunya dengan senang hati.
8. Dia menyirami bunga dengan getah paip.
9. Dia melayani pelanggan-pelanggannya dengan ramah.
10. Dia mempercayai lelaki itu dengan sepenuh hati.

Exercise 5

1. Cerita itu panjang.
2. Bubur itu manis.
3. Saudagar itu lokek.
4. Pekerjaan itu susah.
5. Mereka masuk.
6. Dia merenung muka adik.
7. Kamu akan menyesal.
8. Ayah sudah pergi.
9. Saya tidak masuk sekolah.
10. Dia pergi.

Exercise 6

1. Airnya sangat jernih.
2. Udaranya bersih sekali.
3. Budak itu degil betul.
4. Pelabuhan itu besar sekali.
5. Lelaki itu berjalan dahulu.
6. Bayi itu menangis semalamam.
7. Ali datang lambat.
8. Keretapi bergerak cepat.
9. Angin bertiup kencang.
10. Hujan turun lebat.

LESSON 16

Exercise 1

1. Dia sedang menggarami daging itu.
2. Dia sedang menggarami telur rebus itu.
3. Dia sedang menggarami lauk itu.
4. Dia sedang merasai lauk itu.
5. Dia sedang merasai gado-gado itu.
6. Dia sedang merasai soto ayam itu.
7. Dia sedang memanasi soto ayam itu.
8. Dia sedang memanasi sayur-sayur itu.
9. Dia sedang memanasi nasi goreng itu.
10. Dia sedang memanasi minuman itu.

Exercise 2

1. Mereka sedang menikmati pertunjukan itu.
2. Murid-murid sedang menjalani peperiksaan.
3. Lelaki itu sudah mengakui kesalahannya.
4. Kita mesti mengatasi kesukaran kita.
5. Mereka mesti mendalami pengetahuan mereka.

6. Kakak mesti mengemasi rumah hari ini.
7. Anak-anak patut menghargai usaha orang tua mereka.
8. Mereka sudah mengelilingi dunia tahun lepas.
9. Mereka sedang menghalangi pekerjaan kita.
10. Mereka disuruh menjauhi budak-budak nakal.

Exercise 3

1. Emaknya sudah memanasi makanan itu.
2. Semua orang dapat menaiki kereta itu.
3. Saksi sudah memungkiri janjinya.
4. Peguam itu akan menepati janjinya.
5. Inspektor sekolah sudah melawati sekolah baru itu.
6. Pekedai itu sudah mengurangi harga beras.
7. Orang-orang kampung dapat mengharungi sungai itu.
8. Pekerja-pekerja sudah membaiki jalan itu.
9. Abang saya dapat menghabisi kerja itu dalam seminggu.
10. Kakak saya sudah menghiasi bilik itu dengan gambar-gambar.

Exercise 4

1. Dia akan mengetuai rombongan ke Kuala Lumpur minggu depan.
2. Sejak bulan lalu Pak Man sudah memagari kebunnya.
3. Sejak lima tahun yang lalu dia sudah menganggotai syarikat itu.
4. Dia akan mengepalai syarikat itu dalam dua tahun.
5. Sejak dua minggu dia sudah mendiami rumah itu.
6. Razak akan menduduki peperiksaannya minggu ini.
7. Sejak setahun yang lalu dia banyak menghadiri seminar.
8. Sejak tiga bulan yang lalu dia selalu menuruti permintaan anak lelakinya.
9. Pelajar-pelajar akan memasuki universiti pada bulan Julai nanti.
10. Sejak malam tadi Ali sudah mematuhi cakap ibunya.

Exercise 5

1. Majlis perkahwinan itu telah dilakukan.
2. Emaknya mengalas meja.
3. Aliran tenaga elektrik terputus.
4. Firma itu akan mengambil kakitangan baru.
5. Dia berangan menjadi pensyarah.
6. Jemaah haji telah berangkat.
7. Murid-murid beratur.
8. Saya akan ke Jakarta.
9. Dia berpuasa.
10. Bapa balik.

Exercise 6

1. Dia sakit batuk sejak dua tahun dahulu.

2. Saya bersiar-siar di Taman Bunga pada hari Ahad yang lalu.
3. Dia membela anaknya dengan penuh kasih sayang.
4. Haji Ali membentang pendapatnya mengenai perkara itu.
5. Ahli jawatankuasa telah berbincang hingga larut malam.
6. Dia menyanyi dengan nyaring.
7. Dia telah menyatakan pendapatnya dengan panjang lebar dalam mesyuarat itu.
8. Perkara itu mudah saja pada pendapatnya.
9. Dia akan datang pada 10hb. Ogos nanti.
10. Kita mesti menambah harta dengan usaha kita sendiri.

Exercise 2

1. Perempuan itu sedang masak sayur untuk suaminya.
2. Dia sedang memanggil teksi untuk kawannya.
3. Guru itu sudah memesan buku untuk murid-muridnya.
4. Dia memilih sebuah kereta untuk sahabat.
5. Salina sedang membawa kopi untuk anak lelakinya.
6. Dia jarang membeli barang perhiasan untuk isterinya.
7. Dia membeli sebuah buku cerita untuk adik lelakinya.
8. Dia sedang membuat segelas minuman untuk adik lelakinya.
9. Dia sudah mencari pekerjaan untuk sahabatnya.
10. Lelaki itu sedang mengambil buah-buahan untuk anaknya.

LESSON 17

Exercise 1

1. Saya menyerahi Ali payung itu.
2. Saya menyerahi Ali kereta baru.
3. Saya membelikan Ali kereta baru.
4. Saya memesankan Ali kereta baru.
5. Saya menjualkan Ali kereta baru.
6. Saya mendapatkan Ali kereta baru.
7. Saya mendapatkan Ali tugas baru.
8. Saya membebani Ali tugas baru.
9. Saya memberikan Ali tugas baru.
10. Saya memberikan Ali segelas minuman.

Exercise 3

1. Ali membangunkan orang tuanya sebuah rumah batu di kampung.
2. Aminah menghantarkan ayahnya makanan yang lazat setiap hari.
3. Guru menghadiahi murid itu sebatang pena.
4. Lelaki itu membuatkan anak lelakinya layang-layang.
5. Guru itu akan mengajarkan bahasa Melayu kepada kita.
6. Kerani itu memberikan Ahmad dua helai borang kosong.
7. Dia memberikan adik lelakinya sebuah buku cerita.
8. Murid itu menyanyikan teman-temannya sebuah lagu yang merdu.

9. Ali mengikatkan adik lelakinya tali kasut.
10. Saudagar itu mendapatkan Amir satu pekerjaan di bandar.

Exercise 4

1. Dia mengirimi ibunya wang.
2. Dia meminjami lelaki itu keretanya.
3. Guru bahasa menyerahi pelajar itu tugas yang berat.
4. Encik Ali mengajar budak-budak lelaki itu bahasa Melayu.
5. Ibu memberi adik sebungkus biskut.
6. Ali membawakan adik lelakinya buah anggur.
7. Hang Mahmud telah membungkuskan anak lelakinya beberapa gantang beras.
8. Fatimah membelikan adik lelakinya sepasang kasut kulit.
9. Tuhan telah mencurahi kami kurnia dan rahmat-Nya.
10. Suami itu menghantari isterinya surat.

Exercise 5

1. yang dapat menolong saya
2. yang mencuri jam tangan saya
3. yang bertanggungjawab
4. yang terletak di tepi jalan
5. yang saudara pinjamkan kepada saya
6. yang saya letakkan di atas meja
7. yang disimpan di dalam bank
8. yang berumur dua puluh lima tahun
9. yang terlatih
10. yang berhampiran dengan rumahnya

Exercise 6

1. Guru yang terlatih itu sudah meninggal dunia.
2. Saya mengenangkan Encik Rahim yang baik hati.
3. Wang yang disimpan itu tidaklah banyak.
4. Dia hampir-hampir menghabiskan wang yang di bawanya itu.
5. Pelajar-pelajar yang menuntut di sekolah Tun Fatimah akan tiba.
6. Guru kami suka kepada pelajar yang cerdik itu.
7. Suatu peristiwa yang menyayat hati telah terjadi pada hari itu.
8. Saya telah mendengar peristiwa yang menggembirakan itu.
9. Buku-buku yang dipesan itu masih belum sampai.
10. Saya masih belum menerima surat yang dikirimnya itu.

LESSON 18

Exercise 1

1. Dia memujuk murid-muridnya supaya melanjutkan pelajaran mereka.
2. Dia mencadangkan murid-muridnya supaya melanjutkan pelajaran mereka.
3. Dia mencabar murid-muridnya supaya melanjutkan pelajaran mereka.
4. Dia merangsang murid-muridnya supaya melanjutkan pelajaran mereka.

5. Dia memerintahkan murid-muridnya supaya melanjutkan pelajaran mereka.
6. Dia memaksa murid-muridnya supaya melanjutkan pelajaran mereka.
7. Dia menyuruh murid-muridnya supaya melanjutkan pelajaran mereka.
8. Dia meminta murid-muridnya supaya melanjutkan pelajaran mereka.
9. Dia menganjurkan murid-muridnya supaya melanjutkan pelajaran mereka.
10. Dia mengusulkan murid-muridnya supaya melanjutkan pelajaran mereka.

Exercise 2

1. Saya memanggil tamu itu abang.
2. Dia menamai anak lelakinya Naziha.
3. Saya menggelar gadis itu Si Manis.
4. Ahmad memanggil ketua pejabatnya Tuan Besar.
5. Ahli-ahli jawatankuasa telah memilih Encik Adnan sebagai pengerusi.
6. Saya mencadangkan Encik Rusli menjadi setiausaha.
7. Parti itu telah menerima guru agama itu sebagai calon.
8. Majikan itu telah melantik Ramli sebagai pengawas kilang.
9. Orang-orang kampung memandang Wan Derus sebagai ketua mereka.
10. Lelaki itu menganggap dirinya sebagai wira.

Exercise 3

1. Dia fikir orang itu malas.
2. Perempuan itu duga suaminya marah.
3. Dia agak lelaki itu kecewa.
4. Dia kira lelaki itu jahat.
5. Ahmad rasa lelaki itu salah.
6. Dia sangka lelaki itu bongkak.
7. Dia percaya lelaki itu jujur.
8. Dia pandang kerja guru senang.
9. Dia anggap perkara itu mudah.
10. Ahmad fikir hal itu penting.

Exercise 4

1. Hasnah memaksa teman-temannya datang ke majlis harijadinya.
2. Dia meminta sahabat-sahabatnya datang ke majlis perkahwinannya.
3. Dia menyuruh teman sekerjanya datang ke rumahnya.
4. Dia mempelawa sahabatnya memohon jawatan kosong itu.
5. Dia menyilakan abang sepupunya minum air teh itu.
6. Dia menyarankan saya belajar ke luar negeri.
7. Dia menganjurkan saya mogok makan.
8. Dia mencadangkan kita membahas perkara itu dahulu.
9. Dia memaksa saya mendengar nasihatnya.
10. Dia mendesak saya melanjutkan cerita itu.

Exercise 5

1. Sementara ibu memasak
2. Sehingga dia datang
3. Sebab dia malas

4. Kalau tidak ada halangan
5. Seandainya engkau tidak bersalah
6. Meskipun kamus itu mahal
7. Sungguhpun dia sakit
8. Semasa budak lelaki itu melintas jalan
9. Jikalau kita hendakkan kemajuan
10. Sejak umurnya tujuh tahun

Exercise 6

1. Sikapnya berubah sejak dia menjadi wakil rakyat.
2. Kalau saya tidak salah, lelaki itu memang ayahnya.
3. Lelaki tua itu masih bekerja walaupun dia uzur.
4. Permainan tidak dapat dijalankan kalau hari hujan.
5. Mulut lelaki itu manis tetapi hatinya jahat.
6. Bayi itu menangis kerana perutnya lapar.
7. Belajarlah sungguh-sungguh, kamu akan naik darjah.
8. Lelaki itu kaya tetapi dia kedekut.
9. Saya tidak bekerja hari ini kerana badan saya kurang sihat.
10. Kita mesti berjalan cepat supaya kita akan lekas sampai.

LESSON 19

Exercise 1

1. Dia berjaya melanjutkan pelajarannya ke universiti.
2. Dia bermaksud melanjutkan pelajarannya ke universiti.
3. Dia bermaksud membuka perniagaan sendiri.
4. Dia bertujuan membuka perniagaan sendiri.
5. Dia bertujuan melancong ke Bali.
6. Dia berniat melancong ke Bali.
7. Dia berkira-kira melancong ke Bali.
8. Dia berkhayal melancong ke Bali.
9. Dia berkhayal memberi derma kepada fakir miskin.
10. Dia berupaya memberi derma kepada fakir miskin.

Exercise 2

1. Dia berdukacita mendapat khabar kematian tunangannya.
2. Perempuan itu gelisah menunggu kepulangan anaknya.
3. Seluruh dunia terkejut mendengar berita pembunuhan pemimpin itu.
4. Dia bosan mendengar kisah yang sama berulang kali.
5. Dia hairan melihat orang buta menganyam bakul.
6. Dia kagum melihat kemajuan negeri itu.
7. Dia kaget melihat kezaliman abangnya.
8. Dia marah menerima laporan itu.
9. Semua orang sukacita melihat mereka berjaya dalam hidup.
10. Dia jengkel melihat kelakuan gadis itu.

Exercise 3

1. Dia mengaku mencuri wang lelaki itu.
2. Dia belajar menyanyi.
3. Dia setuju menolong kita.
4. Dia berjanji datang ke rumah saya.
5. Dia menolak jemputan untuk menghadiri pertemuan itu.
6. Dia mencuba menangkap bola itu.
7. Dia gemar membaca buku di perpustakaan.
8. Dia hendak membayar hutang.
9. Dia masih ingat mengunci pintu itu.
10. Dia ingin bertemu dengan pengarang itu.

Exercise 4

1. Mereka pergi menonton wayang gambar sesudah makan.
2. Sudah enam bulan dia belajar menyanyi.
3. Dia akan pulang untuk makan tengah hari sekejap lagi.
4. Dia datang meminjam wang dua minggu yang lalu.
5. Sejak kematian suaminya perempuan itu hidup menderita.
6. Dia mengancam membunuh lawannya minggu lepas.
7. Dia masuk kerja pada pukul delapan pagi.
8. Dia keluar makan pada pukul satu tengah hari.
9. Dia lari menyelamatkan diri tatkala bangungan itu roboh.
10. Dia bangun menyambut para tamu pada pukul tujuh pagi.

Exercise 5

1. Aminah cantik tetapi sombong.
2. Aminah atau Fatimah mesti pergi ke pasar.
3. Tuan pengerusi bangun lalu bercakap.
4. Badannya belum sihat tetapi dia pergi juga.
5. Dia membaca hingga kepalanya sakit.
6. Dia kaya tetapi tidak sombong.
7. Semua orang pergi kecuali saya seorang tidak pergi.
8. Pemuda itu berjalan sambil menyanyi.
9. Kami minum kopi sambil berbual.
10. Saya tidak akan ke majlis itu kalau saya tidak diundang.

Exercise 6

1. Saya akan pergi besok. Saya akan pergi lusa.
2. Dia selalu makan di rumah saya. Dia selalu minum di rumah saya.
3. Dia belajar. Dia bekerja.
4. Fatimah bercakap. Fatimah tersenyum.
5. Ahmad membeli sepasang kasut. Ahmad keluar dari kedai itu.
6. Budak lelaki itu pandai. Budak lelaki itu malas.
7. Dia tidak datang. Dia dijemput.
8. Saudara boleh datang tiap-tiap hari. Saudara tidak boleh datang pada hari Jumaat.
9. Saya akan naik bas. Saya akan naik keretapi.
10. Rumahnya sendiri ada. Dia menumpang di rumah orang.

LESSON 20

Exercise 1

1. Lelaki itu nampaknya ramah.
2. Lelaki itu nampaknya bengis.
3. Lelaki itu nampaknya gelisah.
4. Lelaki itu nampaknya bingung.
5. Lelaki itu rupanya bingung.
6. Lelaki itu rupanya bahagia.
7. Lelaki itu rupanya kaget.
8. Lelaki itu rupanya sakit.
9. Lelaki itu rupanya cekap.
10. Lelaki itu rupanya sombong.

Exercise 2

1. Ramai petani naik haji tahun ini.
2. Hasil tanaman turun harga.
3. Pensyarah itu sudah habis modal.
4. Ramai penumpang hilang nyawa.
5. Ushawan muda itu jatuh miskin.
6. Senjata dapat melukai orang.
7. Perkara itu tidak masuk akal.
8. Budak itu tidak tahu bahasa.
9. Pemuda itu putus harapan.
10. Wangnya tinggal sedikit.

Exercise 3

1. Dia merasa lega sekarang.
2. Makanan itu terasa manis.
3. Dia merasa sedih sekarang.
4. Makanan itu terasa pedas.
5. Dia masih merasa takut sekarang.
6. Badannya merasa sakit sekarang.
7. Dia merasa tenteram sekarang.
8. Kakinya merasa kebas sekarang.
9. Dia merasa selamat sekarang.
10. Dia berasa lapar sekarang.

Exercise 4

1. Lelaki itu menjadi buta.
2. Penjudi itu menjadi gila.
3. Mimpinya menjadi kenyataan.
4. Penulis itu menjadi terkenal.
5. Makanan itu menjadi basi.
6. Bandar itu menjadi lengang.
7. Suasana pertemuan itu menjadi tegang.
8. Ahmad menjadi pengerusi jawatankuasa.
9. Budak miskin itu menjadi kaya raya.
10. Gadis itu menjadi ratu kebaya.

Exercise 5

1. apa
2. Mengapa
3. Berapa
4. Siapa
5. siapa
6. di mana
7. Bagaimana
8. Mengapa
9. Bila
10. Bila

Exercise 6

1 (a) Dari mana lelaki itu datang?
  (b) Siapa datang dari Malaysia?

2 (a) Murid itu suka menulis

dengan apa?

(b) Siapa suka menulis dengan dakwat merah?

3 (a) Aminah pergi ke pasar dengan siapa?

(b) Siapa pergi ke pasar dengan ibunya?

4 (a) Di mana Cikgu Ali tinggal?

(b) Siapa tinggal di Bedok?

5 (a) Bila adik selalu membaca buku?

(b) Siapa selalu membaca buku pada waktu malam?

6 (a) Di mana dia hendak melanjutkan pelajarannya?

(b) Siapa hendak melanjutkan pelajarannya di luar negeri?

7 (a) Rumah saudara jauh dari mana?

(b) Rumah siapa jauh dari bandar?

8 (a) Minggu lepas kamu berkelah di mana?

(b) Bila kamu berkelah di tepi laut?

9 (a) Siapa suka makan durian?

(b) Lelaki tua itu suka makan apa?

10 (a) Kamu kenal siapa?

(b) Siapa kenal lelaki itu?

PART II

LESSON 1 - (B)

(*a*) Lebih separuh daripada rakyat Singapura yang tinggal di rumah pangsa.

(*b*) Kemudahan-kemudahan yang disediakan untuk penghuni rumah pangsa ialah tempat untuk majlis perkahwinan, tempat beribadat, padang permainan, tempat riadah, kompleks sukan dan kompleks renang.

(*c*) Masalah baru yang dihadapi oleh penghuni rumah pangsa ialah kejadian jenayah seperti rompakan, merosakkan harta benda, masalah kemasyarakatan seperti orang kurang bertimbang rasa sesama jiran.

(*d*) Kita menghendaki sebuah masyarakat yang bersatu-padu dan rukun damai.

LESSON 2 - (B)

(*a*) Mas atau Muhammad Arif Ahmad ialah pengarang Sarah Pengarang Kecil.

(*b*) Cita-cita Sarah ialah ingin menjadi seorang pengarang besar supaya dapat memimpin manusia melalui karangan-karangannya.

(*c*) Cita-citanya itu dikatakan setinggi langit kerana di dalam darjah bukan Sarah murid yang paling pandai. Tidak mungkin Sarah boleh menjadi seorang pengarang.

(*d*) Darjah itu menjadi riuh-rendah kerana ada murid-murid yang mengejek mentertawakan Sarah; tetapi ada juga yang memuja-mujanya.

LESSON 3 - (B)

(*a*) Keluarga Encik Murad tinggal di sebuah rumah banglo di kawasan kediaman swasta di Katong.

(*b*) Sebagai ketua keluarga Encik Murad mencari nafkah untuk keluarganya. Dia juga melapangkan masa untuk berbual-bual dengan ahli keluarganya, mengawasi kemajuan pelajaran anak-anaknya dan memberi didikan agama yang cukup kepada anak-anaknya.

(*c*) Tanggungjawab suri rumahtangga seperti Siti Aisyah, ialah menguruskan rumahtangganya dengan baik supaya rumahnya sentiasa bersih dan kemas.

(*d*) Anak-anak Encik Murad mempunyai cita-cita mereka yang tersendiri. Yazid, anak yang sulung, bercita-cita menjadi seorang jurutera. Siti Fatimah, anak yang kedua, bercita-cita menjadi seorang guru bahasa Inggeris di sekolah menengah. Siti Khadijah, anak yang bongsu, bercita-cita menjadi seorang doktor.

LESSON 4 - (B)

(*a*) Sang Nila Utama adalah cucu Raja Suran. Baginda membuangkan mahkotanya ke dalam laut kerana perahunya dimasuki air dan hampir tenggelam.

(*b*) Tujuan Sang Nila Utama datang ke Temasek ialah untuk membuat negeri di situ.

(*c*) Sang Nila Utama telah terlihat seekor binatang yang tangkas dan berani iaitu singa.

(*d*) Mengikut ahli sejarah peristiwa Temasek dibuka menjadi Singapura oleh Sang Nila Utama tentu tidak mungkin terjadi sebelum kurun yang ke-13.

LESSON 5

(*a*) Taraf didikan Harun Aminurrashid boleh dikatakan tinggi pada waktu itu kerana dia mendapat didikan dari Maktab Perguruan Sultan Idris, Tanjung Malim. Pekerjaannya yang pertama ialah menjadi guru.

(*b*) Setelah meninggalkan Maktab Perguruan di Semenanjung Malaysia, ia pergi ke Brunei untuk menjadi Penguasa Pelajaran Melayu.

(*c*) Nama novel Harun yang pertama ialah Melur Kuala Lumpur. Novel ini diterbitkan pada tahun 1930 dan isinya mengenai percintaan yang suci antara dua remaja iaitu Sulaiman dan Norissa dalam masyarakat yang masih diselubungi adat dan susila tradisi.

(*d*) Setelah kembali ke Singapura, dia mengundurkan diri menjadi guru dan berkecimpung sepenuh masa dalam bidang penerbitan dan kesusasteraan.

LESSON 6

(*a*) Rumah panjang yang dilawati oleh rombongan Singapura itu letaknya di Kampung Mongkos, Serian, kira-kira 100 km dari bandar Kuching.

(*b*) Seorang pelawat yang memasuki rumah panjang itu mesti mencecahkan kaki di dulang yang berisi air.

(*c*) Ketua agama mengelilingkan ayam putih di kalangan para pelawat untuk mendoakan 'selamat' kepada mereka.

(*d*) Setiap pelawat mesti mencecahkan kaki di dulang yang berisi air, minum air tuak yang telah disediakan dan bersalaman dengan semua penghuni rumah itu. Sebelum bersalaman dengan mereka, ketua agama akan mengelilingkan ayam putih pada para pelawat. Beginilah caranya 'selamatan' diadakan.

(*e*) Kehidupan di rumah panjang sentiasa tenang kerana mereka mempunyai ketua agama yang menjaga ketenteraman di situ dan mereka masih lagi mengikut tradisi lama mereka.

LESSON 7

(*a*) Perbualan di atas berlaku di perkarangan sebuah perpustakaan pada pagi Sabtu, jam 8.15 pagi.

(*b*) Mereka berbual tentang isi buku yang sudah dibaca.

(*c*) Nama buku yang dikatakan membosankan oleh Jamilah itu ialah Sejarah Melayu.

(*d*) Anita berpendapat buku itu sangat berguna kerana dari buku itu kita dapat mengetahui asal usul dan keagungan bangsa Melayu pada masa dahulu.

(*e*) Iskandar Zulkarnain ialah seorang penakluk dunia zaman dahulu. Orang Islam percaya bahawa dialah yang menyebarkan agama Islam. Orang Melayu percaya dia adalah nenek moyang raja-raja Melayu.

LESSON 8

(*a*) Setelah Halimah mengikuti kursus di Kuala Lumpur, dia telah cuba meniru kehidupan orang di bandar.

(*b*) Tetamu-tetamu Halimah datang dari bandar. Mereka berpakat membelikan dapur oven minyak tanah untuk Halimah.

(*c*) Tujuan kunjungan tetamu-tetamu Halimah ialah untuk menyiasat aduan Halimah tentang suaminya.

(*d*) Agus mengatakan bahawa rakan-rakan Halimah bukan memimpin melainkan meruntuhkan kerana wanita-wanita dari rumah-rumah miskin akan meniru cara hidup mereka sedangkan wanita-wanita miskin tidak mempunyai kemampuan untuk berbuat demikian.

(*e*) Setelah Agus bertengkar dengan rakan-rakan Halimah, Halimah merasa malu dan masuk ke dalam meninggalkan tetamu-tetamunya sementara tetamu-tetamu itu pulang tanpa meminta diri lagi.

LESSON 9

(*a*) Ekonomi Asean tidak terlepas daripada masalah kerana kemelesetan ekonomi dunia dan inflasi yang terburuk dalam masa tiga dasawarsa.
(*b*) Usaha-usaha yang ditumpukan oleh negara-negara Asean ialah membaiki mutu persaingan untuk membolehkan jentera ekonomi bergerak sesuai dengan pertumbuhan ekonomi dunia dan meluaskan eksport hasil pengilangan.
(*c*) Pada pendapat Bank Dunia, eksport barangan mentah yang tidak akan bertambah baik.
(*d*) Negara-negara anggota Asean mengharapkan kerjasama yang berterusan antara sektor swasta dengan pemerintah dan kerajaan Asean.
(*e*) Faedah yang didapati oleh negara-negera Asean daripada usaha China untuk memodenkan ekonominya ialah negara-negara Asean boleh membekalkan bahan-bahan mentahnya kepada China dan dengan itu perdagangan Asean akan bertambah baik.

LESSON 10

(*a*) Asal bahasa Indonesia ialah dari bahasa Melayu.
(*b*) Erti lingua franca ialah bahasa perantaraan di antara orang yang berlainan bahasanya. Bahasa yang dijadikan lingua franca di kepulauan Nusantara pada zaman dahulu ialah bahasa Melayu.
(*c*) Pemimpin Indonesia memilih bahasa Melayu sebagai bahasa persatuan kerana bahasa ini adalah bahasa perantaraan bagi berbilang kaum di Indonesia. Bahasa Jawa atau Sunda tidak dipilih kerana kedua bahasa tidak digunakan oleh suku lain dan sangat sukar untuk dikuasai.
(*d*) Bahasa Melayu dan bahasa Indonesia berbeza kerana perkembangan sejarah yang berlainan. Bahasa Indonesia dipengaruhi oleh bahasa Belanda kerana Indonesia dijajahi oleh Belanda. Sementara Bahasa Melayu pula dipengaruhi oleh bahasa Inggeris kerana Malaysia dijajahi oleh Inggeris.
(*e*) Di bawah ini diberi lima contoh perbezaan antara perkataan Melayu dan bahasa Indonesia.

INDONESIA	MELAYU
senduk	sudu
mobil	kereta
sambut	jemput
polisi	polis
sukar	sulit

About the Author

Dr. Liaw Yock Fang acquired his B.A. and M.A. in Indonesian Language and Literature from the University of Indonesia in Jakarta, Indonesia. He also holds a Drs. and Dr. of Literature degrees in Indonesian Language and Literature from the University of Leiden, Leiden, the Netherlands.

His main publications include *Sejarah Kesusastraan Melayu Klasik* (History of Classical Malay Literature) (1975) – a new version of the book, now in two volumes, has recently been published in Jakarta; *Undang-Undang Melaka* (The Laws of Malacca) (1976); *Pelajaran Bahasa Melayu 1A – 6B* (co-author, 1982) – a series of textbooks approved by the Ministry of Education for primary schools in Singapore; *Kursus Bahasa Nasional I – IV* (1984) – also an approved series for secondary schools in Singapore; and *Nahu Melayu Moden* (Modern Malay Grammar) (1985) – a new version of the book, with the co-operation of Prof. Abdullah Hassan, from Universiti Sains Malaysia, has recently been re-issued under the same title in Kuala Lumpur.

Dr. Liaw has been teaching Malay/Indonesian languge and literature since 1966. He has for a number of years served as an Examiner in Malay in the former Malaysian Certificate of Education (MCE) Examination and the present Singapore Cambridge GCE 'O' and 'A' Level Examinations. He is also a member of the Malay Language Council (Majlis Bahasa Melayu) in Singapore.

Dr. Liaw is now an Associate Professor with the Department of Malay Studies, National University of Singapore.